The Breaking Point

José Robles Pazos in 1918.

The Breaking Point

❧

Hemingway, Dos Passos, and
the Murder of José Robles

STEPHEN KOCH

COUNTERPOINT
A Member of the Perseus Books Group
New York

Frontispiece photo of José Robles Pazos courtesy of Dolores B. de Robles

Published by Counterpoint,
A Member of the Perseus Books Group

Counterpoint books are available at special discounts for bulk purchases in the
United States by corporations, institutions, and other organizations. For more
information, please contact the Special Markets Department at the Perseus Books
Group, 11 Cambridge Center, Cambridge MA 02142; or call (617) 252-5298 or
(800) 255-1514; or e-mail special.markets@perseusbooks.com.

Designed by Brent Wilcox

Library of Congress Cataloging-in-Publication Data
Koch, Stephen.
    The breaking point : Hemingway, Dos Passos, and the murder of José Robles /
Stephen Koch.
        p.   cm.
    Includes bibliographical references.
    ISBN 1-58243-280-5 (hardcover : alk. paper)
    1. Hemingway, Ernest, 1899–1961—Homes and haunts—Spain.
2. Dos Passos, John, 1896–1970—Homes and haunts—Spain.   3. Hemingway,
Ernest, 1899–1961—Friends and associates.   4. Dos Passos, John, 1896–1970—
Friends and associates.   5. Spain—History—Civil War, 1936–1939—Biography.
6. Authors, American—20th century—Biography   7. Authors, American—
Homes and haunts—Spain.   8. Americans—Spain—History—20th century.
9. Robles Pazos, Jose—Friends and associates.   10. Murder—Spain—History—
20th century.   11. Robles Pazos, José—Death and burial.   I. Title.

PS3515.E37Z6728   2005
813'.52—dc22

                                                                2005001087

05 06 07 / 10 9 8 7 6 5 4 3 2 1

For Susan Sontag
Long friendship

Contents

Acknowledgments

I owe special thanks to Señora Dolores Benitade de Robles, the widow of Francisco ("Coco") Robles Villegas, who both gave me an indispensable interview and supplied the photograph of her father-in-law that serves as the frontispiece of this book. Part of *The Breaking Point* emerged from research I did originally for my book *Double Lives: Stalin, Willi Münzenberg and the Seduction of the Intellectuals*. It was while I was preparing to write *Double Lives* that the late Margaret Regler, the widow of Gustav Regler, pointed out to me the Comintern's passionate preoccupation in securing Ernest Hemingway as a spokesman for the Popular Front. Mrs. Regler also gave me a typescript of her husband's battlefield notes from Spain, which has proved useful in establishing a precise chronology for many events. Not long after I interviewed Mrs. Regler, I also interviewed Joris Ivens in Paris. During that interview, Ivens quite gratuitously brought up the issue of the "fascist spy" who was a "friend of John Dos Passos." It was in those very early days of discovery that I first began, in some confusion, to sense the stirrings of this story.

My thanks go to Lucy Dos Passos Coggin for her cordial support. She has incidentally saved me from a number of blunders about her father's habits and personality. Antonio Muñoz-Molina read the entire manuscript and saved me from more errors over Spanish matters than I care to contemplate. It was the indefatigable Stephen Schwartz who first directed me to the late Victor Alba. Victor Alba, in turn, put me in touch with Dr. Josefina Cuesta, Professor of Modern History at the University of Salamanca, whose assistance in the archives of the Spanish Republic was essential. To my friend P. Adams Sitney I owe a lucid view of Joris Iven's place in the cinematic vanguard. To Amanda Vaill I owe refinements and details about the Murphys. I am indebted to Elinor Langer, Josephine Herbst's biographer, and Hilton Kramer, Herbst's literary executor, for their thoughts about Josie's role in the story. I am likewise indebted to the distinguished Spanish writer Sr. Francisco Ayala, for his memories of José Robles. I am grateful to Mr. Sandy Gellhorn for a delightful interview about Martha Gellhorn, in which he helped me focus on his mother's truly remarkable qualities as a letter writer: I predict that it will be for her letters that Gellhorn will be most remembered. I owe thanks to Mr. Gellhorn for a photocopy of Hemingway's beautiful, previously unpublished, letter to Martha, written early in their romance and cited in Chapter 4. It was a gift to him from his mother.

The Breaking Point could not have been written without the assistance of librarians in the special collections of the Firestone Library, Princeton University (for its archives of both Hemingway and Carlos Baker); the Beinecke Library at Yale (the repository of Josephine Herbst's papers); and the University of Virginia in Charlottesville (the prime repository of the John Dos Passos archives). I am particularly grateful to Ms. Vesta Gordon, of Charlottesville, for her help in the Dos Passos Archive, and to Mr. Jesse Rossa in the Special Collections of the University of Delaware Libraries, for procuring a copy of Hemingway's elusive but essential piece for *Ken*, "Treachery in Aragon," found at long last in the Louis Henry and Marguerite Cohn Hemingway Collection there. Unfortunately, Martha Gellhorn's papers, in the Boston University Library, will (at her insistence) remain closed to scholars for twenty-five years following her death. Luckily, Caroline Moorehead was made an exception to the rule, and her valuable biography of Gellhorn frequently quotes essential material that remains unavailable to others.

Closer to home, I am grateful to Chris Carduff and Michelle Tessler, both of whom were key to the acquisition of *The Breaking Point* for Counterpoint. And more thanks are due to my editor at Counterpoint, the so young and yet so smart David Shoemaker.

And, though I've said it before, I'll say it again: thanks to my agent, Michael Carlisle, at Inkwell Management, Inc. He is still the bright voice of sanity and cheer.

Finally, to Angelica and Franny, who were there at the dinner table each evening as I surfaced from my day's deep dive into 1937. I could love you two better, but not more.

S.K.

PART I

THE GOOD TIMES

chapter 1

WHEN A MAN
MAKES FRIENDS

John Dos Passos met José Robles Pazos for the first time in 1916.[1] It was on a night train from Toledo to Madrid, and the hour was late; both were very young men; and the First World War was at its height. In 1916, a third-class ticket on the dilapidated old clunker that ran from Toledo to Madrid must have cost next to nothing, and the ride would have been jolting and slow. It probably took the train hours to crawl the fifty miles that lie between Spain's ancient royal stronghold and its modern capital: long enough for strangers in a compartment to get to know each other, especially since both of these strangers were just out of college, were studying at the same *instituto*, and both were at the age when making friends comes easy.

The gangling myopic American kid who would one day write *Manhattan Transfer* and *U.S.A.* had just spent the day in the ancient fortress town, flying high on every work of art he saw and every human situation he ran across. After eating a late-night Spanish dinner on some *terraza* in Toledo, and washing it down with a carafe or two of wine, young Dos—everyone called him "Dos"—was heading back to Madrid and his graduate student's *pensión*. The Toledo he was leaving rose up behind him, magnificent on its mountain. In 1916 the citadel must have still looked very much as it did when El Greco had painted it three hundred years before: an imperious bulwark perched on a rock, shimmering in obsolete majesty, menaced and menacing, a fortification against time, lit against the Spanish darkness by moonlight so bright that it made the buildings give off a white, almost ghastly, glow. The twenty-one-year-old Dos was high on everything he saw in the ancient stronghold: high on the great Cathedral with its Grecos, high on the Toledo *carnaval*, with its people, masked and drunken, dancing the *jota* in ancient streets. But how could Dos fail to be intoxicated with Toledo? He was intoxicated with all of Spain, with Spanish capes and gates and mules and mountains; with the Spanish light and the Spanish night, with Spanish women, with Spanish everything. Even the Spanish *dust* moved Dos to ecstasies. The foot-caressing dust of the Spanish road! That powdered velvet of peasant feet!

The tall young American took up lots of space, and even when fully sober, he swayed a bit when he walked. Then—and always—Dos Passos dressed like a gentleman, but his arms dangled, and his legs were long, and he had a swanlike neck on which was perched an unprepossessing head with a receding chin. Even at 21, his hairline was creeping back noticeably, and he squinted at the world through blinking, intensely interested, but very myopic eyes. The kid sank down onto his hard third-class seat with a tired happy groan.

The compartment was a blur. Dos fumbled in a jacket pocket for his indispensable glasses—they were pince-nez—and clipped them to his nose. Everything came clear. Someone sitting across the way was looking at him.

The man staring back at Dos seemed to be just his age, and he was every bit as tall. Spanish, for sure. A thoroughly Spanish Spaniard, with a face like an eagle's, very brainy-looking. The hair he wore slicked back from his clear, hard face was black as a crow's wing, so black it was almost blue. Glowing with Iberian pride, this stranger was as elegant and self-possessed as Dos was rangy and excitable, and he assessed Dos Passos through shrewd eyes that did not need glasses. The train began to lurch out of the station. The Spaniard's smile was a little mocking, but not unfriendly. Dos Passos's smile was big and broad.

"*Hola,*" Dos said through that Harvard accent of his.

It was soon clear that José Robles and John Dos Passos had plenty to say to one another, and by the time the bleary train finally crept into Madrid, they were friends for life. That can happen, as the seventy-year-old Dos Passos would sigh, when you're twenty-one.

John Roderigo Dos Passos was in Spain studying art and architecture at the Centro de Estúdios Históricos because in 1916 Spain was a neutral country and therefore pretty much the only place in Europe that Dos's father, John Randolph Dos Passos, the flamboyant lion of Wall Street known as the Commodore, would pay for his son to be. In 1916, one of John Randolph's leading goals in life was to keep his son from getting himself killed in this horrendous insensate European war that was ripping civilization to shreds and slaughtering people by the millions. John Randolph fully approved of his son's love of art and architecture; what scared him was Dos's youthful impulse to head for where the action was. In 1916, the "action" was in a French and Belgian landscape of shattered leafless trees, torched villages, reeking rat-infested trenches, and desolate fields strewn with the mangled corpses of young men exactly his son's age. The Commodore was going to pay for *that* in a pig's eye.

It was Spain or nothing.

"Pepe" Robles and Dos—during their twenty-year friendship, Dos Passos invariably referred to Robles as "Pepe"—had more in common than their shared fascination with art and language. In those days, Pepe was much further to the left than Dos, but both of them saw themselves as radicals, and both were radicals carrying a heavy load of excess bourgeois baggage. Both came from "important" families. The Robles clan was monarchical, aristocratic, and very well connected. José's conservative brother was an army officer who was, or soon would be, in the personal entourage of the King. Dos Passos's father was a rich, influential, even famous corporate lawyer and Wall Street Republican who in his American way was every bit as well connected as the Robles family. Not long before, Dos had been forced to get all gussied up in a wing collar and dress suit for dinner at the American embassy in Madrid, because his father just happened to be a great friend of the ambassador. Of *course*.

There was, however, a hair on the soup of Dos Passos's heritage. John Roderigo Dos Passos was, as his biographers delicately put it, the "natural" son of John Randolph. He was "illegitimate." He had already reached the age of fourteen before his father at last married his mother in 1910. During the fourteen years of wandering before that wedding, John Randolph had been unwilling or unable to divorce his legal wife, though it is clear he ardently wished he could. The first Mrs. Dos Passos was psychologically unstable; John Randolph had long since ceased to love her. Even so, he did not see his way clear to divorce and remarriage.

While waiting out her anguished years of her genteel disgrace, Lucy Sprigg Madison had traveled around Europe guarding her secret and raising her son, who was discreetly known as "Jack Madison." They were two upper-crust waifs straight out of some unwritten tale by Henry James. Lucy kept little Jack Madison moving from fancy spa to high-toned school to tactful resort, lavishly but quietly financed by the guilty, grieving Commodore. It was a kind of odyssey-in-reverse: Telemachus wandered with Penelope while Odysseus tended the home fires. When John Randolph's legal wife died at last in 1910, the senior Dos Passos instantly made Lucy into an "honest woman." Their son, who by now had assumed the name John Roderigo Dos Passos, had been sent to Choate, where at first the guys made fun of him because he spoke English with a strong foreign accent. His first language had been French.

In Madrid, Dos Passos swiftly discovered that his sharp-featured new friend had an even sharper tongue. Pepe Robles was filled with tart cynical stories about the wicked Spanish world and the revolution it so richly deserved. Pepe laughed a lot; all his radical talk glinted with mockery, some of it aimed at his new friend's soft-headed, liberal "do-goodism." So *American*.

They got along beautifully. Pepe Robles was going to show Dos Passos the *real* Spain. Instructed by Pepe, Dos would see the great, true art of the great, true Spain. Pepe would teach Dos Passos that Don Quixote and Sancho Panza were not mere characters in a novel, but the country's spiritual soul. Robles would show Dos a suffering Spain that was "all that society and respectability reject."[2] They soon had many friends in common, and in no time this clique of smart Spaniards and their American sidekick were spending weekends crossing the country together, hiking the mountains together, looking at art together, and seeing the people together. They all argued constantly—about poetry, about progress, about primitivism, about Spain's entry into the modern world. Robles took Dos Passos to Toledo to see El Greco's hierarchical, mystical, architecturally sublime painting *The Burial of the Conde de Orgaz* in the *capilla* of the Iglesia of San Tomé—a massive image of death and redemption, surging up in the small chapel space, showing the body of a pious count being laid into the dank pit of his tomb while the spectator strains back to see his soul's upward flight into a shining heaven. Dos stood beside Pepe, staring up at it, overwhelmed, moved especially by "the infinite gentleness of the saints lowering the Conde de Orgaz into the grave." Among Dos's friends, El Greco's great painting was a symbol, because their generation was "working to bury with infinite tenderness the gorgeously dressed corpse of the old Spain."[3]

There was more. Pepe Robles introduced Dos to bullfighting—the running with the bulls, the mystery of blood and death, and the moment of truth—and for good measure got him into flamenco too. Dos's Harvard friends despised bullfighting. Bullfighting was primitive, brutal. Sport? It was maybe two steps up from cockfighting. Robles listened with a scornful smile: typical *norteamericano* liberalism. He and his friends would teach Dos about life as a Spaniard lived it. "Our life," they told him, "is one vast ritual. Our religion is part of it, that is all. And so are the bullfights that so shock the English and Americans,—are they any more brutal, though, than fox-hunting and prize-fights? And how full of tradition are they, our *fiestas de toros*: their ceremony reaches to the hecatombs of the Homeric heroes, to the bull worship of the Cretans and of so many of the Mediterranean cults, to the Roman games. Can a civilization go farther than to ritualize death as we have done?"

Yet beautiful though all this might be, it had to change.

"Our culture is too perfect, too stable. Life is choked by it," his friends would say. Revolution had to come, even if "the new Spain" was "a prophecy, rather than a fact. Old Spain is still all-powerful."[4]

Insights like these left Dos fascinated, enchanted. The Spain he saw through Pepe's eyes touched him more deeply than capes and painting, and in a way that did indeed challenge America with its love of energy and optimism. Here was a great nation that seemed to understand instinctively the bond between human nobility and death. Here was a people that possessed that genuine tragic sense of life that until now had been hidden from Dos's callow American eyes. Dos discovered Unamuno *and* Cervantes. He discovered Jorge Manrique, whose long poem on the death of his father is the most famous elegy in Spanish.

Nuestras vidas son los rios
Que van a dar en la mar,
Que es el morir. . . .
Our lives are rivers
. . . on their way to the sea
that is death.

In his brilliant early book on Spain, *Rosinate to the Road Again*—naming himself Telemachus—Dos Passos describes drinking with Harvard friends, trying to get them to "come to grips with old lady adventure—sort of a search for the Holy Grail." The young firebrand wanted to show his Cambridge pals the vibrancy and power of tragic ritual. After beer and roast pigeons in the Café del Oro de Rhin in the Plaza Santa Ana, Dos chanted Manrique for them, swaying with "the rhythms of death sweeping around the world," and then he led them all through the dark stony maze of streets to a huddled little theater for some flamenco: they were going to see the greatest dancer in the world—*the* greatest—a gypsy named Pastora Imperio, performing what she called a "dance of death." Pastora Imperio would hit these guys where they lived. She *was* Spain! Pastora was intensely sexy. She was sex itself. But she brought to the Eros of the dance that true Spanish tragic sense. Watch her and you could see what Manrique was saying. It was right there in her dazzling footwork, caught in the flash of her snapping fingers. "She is right at the footlights; her face, brows drawn together into a frown, has gone into shadow; the shawl flames, the maroon flower over her breast glows like a coal . . . she draws herself up with a deep breath, the muscles of her body go taut under the tight silk wrinkles of the shawl, and she is off again, light, joyful."[5]

That would teach them adventure![6]

When the performance was over, "Telemachus" and one Harvard pal set out, drunk, to walk to Toledo. *Rosinante to the Road Again* tells the story of their walk into a dawn that rose "merry with the jingling of huge two-wheeled carts, each drawn by three or four or sometimes five hulking mules. Always in the lead was a little donkey trotting along with mincing steps." This was *Cervantes'* road. Dos was a tourist no more. He had heard the rhythms of death pounding in his soul, and he was truly alive at last. . . .[7]

But Death still had a thing or two left to teach its initiate.

In January 1917, back in the States, without any warning, the Commodore suddenly collapsed and was gone. And this death was real.

After he married her, Lucy Madison subsided into her recovered respectability. She became hypochondriac, then withdrawn, then really ill, dying before her time. Meanwhile John Randolph became more and more present in his son's life. Father and son were in constant communication. The archives bulge with their letters, almost all in French, on every possible subject, not least the politics over which they so sharply disagreed. Theirs was maybe a compensatory closeness, but it continued right until the January morning in 1917 when the Commodore was found on the bathroom floor of his house in Washington, dead of galloping pneumonia.

Now twenty-two, Dos stood stricken in a telegraph office in Madrid, staring at the yellow cable from his half-brother, bearing its news. Home. He had to go home. Spain was over.

All through his grieving—and it was hard, heavy grieving—one image kept coming back to Dos Passos. He kept seeing his father on the beach near his house in Sandy Point, Virginia. For some reason crows, lots of crows, used to cluster in swarming flocks on the sand dunes there. They were nasty and loud and ominous and deathly black. John Randolph used to scare them off by "calling back" at them. He would shout into the swarm, imitating their cry, not with the classic "caw! caw!"—but something that had sounded to Dos more like some kind of laughter.

"Ha!"

The Commodore shouted it at them at the top of his voice, a sort of barking, laughing sound. It made the birds fly up as if he had pelted the swarm with a rock. "Ha!" It seemed really to work. They were scattering and scared. Then the Commodore would move in on them, closer and closer, laughing louder and louder.

"Ha!" The Commodore didn't stop, and now that he was gone, Dos kept seeing the image of it: his father advancing on the black birds that flew up and away before the onslaught of his shouting laughter.

"Ha-ha! *Ha-Ha!* HA-HA!"

John Dos Passos did not inherit much in 1917. Though John Randolph had made a great deal of money in his life, he had spent a great deal more. His estate was seriously encumbered, and in any case young Dos had no head either for business or for defending his own interests. Rather than follow his father into law and power, the puzzled scion decided to follow Pepe Robles deeper into radicalism. The war and its horrors obsessed him. "Every day," wrote this grieving son of a Republican, "I become more red." He was absolutely determined to go to this great war he so detested, and see it up close. Now there was no more Commodore around to stop him. Dos was soon in a uniform as an ambulance driver, and back in Europe, "taking . . . loads of pulverized people about."[8]

He saw combat at Verdun; he saw troops gassed in Belgium. And somewhere in Italy, near the end of the war, he met another young American ambulance driver named Ernest Hemingway.

Years later, historians would try to reconstruct the exact details of that first meeting. "All I remember," the seventy-four-year-old Dos would admit, "is talking to a very good-looking young man at the Section 4 mess."[9] But clearly the meeting took place in a little town called Schio, sometime in May 1918. Both Hemingway and Dos Passos were there, evacuating the same "pulverized people" from the same field hospital.

Their friendship had to be. The next time Hem and Dos met, they met in postwar Paris, on the sunlit boulevards and in the fluttering cafés. It was expatriate time. Their generation had found Europe and was now getting lost in it. It was 1922: Picasso and Stravinsky were the great names. Gertrude Stein and Ezra Pound and the Ballets Russes were items in the moveable feast. In that year of modernist grace James Joyce's *Ulysses* was published and every young American had to "make the pilgrimage" and buy a copy.

And quite suddenly John Dos Passos had turned into a sort of somebody. Right after the armistice, Dos had written a novel about the war called *Three Soldiers*. Then he'd gone off to Persia for a year, returning to find the book in every bookstore window. Dos Passos was almost famous.

Right around the time he bought his own copy of *Ulysses*, Dos Passos found himself having dinner with the still very young Ernest Hemingway and Hem's very new bride, the round-faced, laughing Hadley Richardson Hemingway. Dos had become a real writer, and if Hem was still a mere journalist, he was obsessed with his apprenticeship, struggling to write what he later called just "one true sentence." Dos impressed Hem. Hem impressed Dos. They dined at the famous Brasserie Lipp, which sparkled with mirrors and burnished art nouveau, and everything that went down during that first good time was typical. In his typical way, Hemingway held forth, glowing with his soon-to-be-famous charm. In her typical way, Hadley listened and laughed and made everything easy for everybody. In his typical way, Dos soaked it all up.

Hem was "talking beautifully about some international conference he'd recently attended. His knowledge of prizefighting and the policeblotter lingo picked up in Kansas City and Toronto have him a direct vocabulary that pinned his stories down. Everything was in sharp focus. I found his acid estimates of Clemenceau and Lloyd George and Litvinov thoroughly invigorating." Litvinov, the Soviet emissary, Hem said, "had a face like a ham." The Bulgarian prime minister Stamboliyski looked "like a ripe blackberry in a bunch of daisies." Whatever wisecrack Hem made about Clemenceau has been lost, though Clemenceau did look much like a very weary walrus. Meanwhile, Hemingway had just met some genuine literary leftists: first there had been Max Eastman and Lincoln Steffens. And now there was Dos. "We agreed," Dos wrote, "on a restrained heroworship of Liebknecht and Rosa Luxembourg."[10]

Two years later the friendship just took off. By then the Hemingways' son Jack—"Bumby"—had been born, Hemingway had found his way to "one true sentence," and evenings, Dos would come round to the Hemingways' apartment on the rue Notre-Dame-des-Champs, to help give the baby his bath. "Bumby was a large, healthy, sociable infant and enjoyed the whole business. He would be tucked into bed and, when a pleasant buxom French peasant woman who took care of him arrived, we would go out to dinner."

Dos was twenty-eight; Hemingway all of twenty-five. They were going to teach each other to write. Hem had decided they should hone their prose by reading aloud from the King James Version of the Old Testament. "We read to each other," Dos Passos recalled. "Choice passages. The Song of Deborah and Chronicles and Kings were our favorites."[11]

From the very start, each friend felt—foresaw—the other's genius. Dos was sure of it: "Hem would become the first great American stylist." What impressed Dos about Hem's style was the startling purity of the *light* it cast on everything; the crystalline deliberateness of its action; the way it made every word sound new. "Hem," Dos wrote, "had uncommonly good eyesight. The hunter's cold acuity. In those days he seemed to me to see things and people uncolored by sentiment or theory. Everything was in a cool clear white light, the light which pervades his best short stories, 'A Clean Well Lighted Place,' for example."[12] Hem for his part saw Dos as a truth teller. Burning with his own lean, hard acuity, he was excited by the *abundance* of Dos's prose, by its panoramic breadth. Dos with that ear of his heard it all, and he was going to say it all; he was going to be the first twentieth-century writer to show the real world the *real* U.S.A.[13]

Meanwhile, the war was over. It had left behind ten million dead and the Russian Revolution—which would leave behind tens of millions more. The twentieth century was turning into a century of survivors, and each in his different way, Hem and Dos would give those survivors some sort of an American voice. Hemingway shrugged off not just radical politics, but all politics. That sort of crap bored him. Dos Passos on the other hand felt the Old World—old Europe and old America, too—shaking on its corrupt foundations. He just couldn't stop thinking about radical change, and justice, justice, justice.

Meanwhile, José Robles, by now a young husband and father, had been inspired by Soviet events to go ever deeper into radicalism, to true communism. His brother opposed him. His family opposed him. The arguments were terrible. At last Robles decided to put an ocean between himself and all this reproach and reaction. He followed his increasingly well-known friend Dos—he was a writer now, and a famous writer, to boot—to America. Arriving with his wife and young family, he got a job teaching Spanish at Johns Hopkins University, and waited for the Spanish revolution to come.

Hemingway's rise through apprenticeship into celebrity was swift. He was possibly the most dedicated writing student of all time, and certainly the most successful. Looking for mentors, he went straight to the top, seeking out, and winning over, first Sherwood Anderson, then Gertrude Stein, then Ezra Pound, and at last the Parisian demi-god himself, James Joyce. By 1926, Hem was, Dos wrote, "a figure in the top literary Valhalla of Paris."

As such, Dos had to introduce Hem to his friends Gerald and Sara Murphy, the prime American arbiters of taste in Paris. Many years later, after he turned against the Murphys—and Hem's tricky suspicious streak made him turn against many friends—Hemingway blamed Dos for luring them into his life. ("Yes, by God Hem"—Hemingway mimicked Dos's voice—"I do like them. I see what you mean but I do like them truly and there's something damn fine about her.")[14]

Hemingway was a blamer. In his last years this character fault became psychosis: he became clinically paranoid. But even in the early days, whenever things went badly he needed to find somebody—other than himself—to take the fall. People, he was convinced, were out to get him. An odd spin-off of this conviction was a tendency to idealize people he'd rejected *after* he'd rejected them. It was his way of keeping the blame machine running indefinitely. If a rejected person was, in retrospect, actually wonderful, then Hem could heap new blame on whoever made him kick the paragon out of his life. Thus, once he'd jilted Hadley, Hemingway began to see her as the ideal companion and mate. Life with Hadley had been pure, lovely, and perfect. Somebody had wrecked their beautiful scene together. Who could that somebody be? The alleged perpetrators changed over time, but years later Hemingway settled on "the rich"—that is, on the Murphys. Though he'd continued to love Sara Murphy especially through the twenties and most of the thirties, he later decided to blame them for wrecking his Parisian idyll. *They* had dogged his success. *They* had been envious of his happiness with Hadley. *They* had sabotaged it all.

"Right from the beginning," Dos Passos would write, "Hem was hard on his women."[15] This puts it politely. By the end of the twentieth century, the image of Hemingway as the great American misogynist had become a leading cliché of his legend. Sadly, though it *is* a cliché, the biography offers plenty to make it credible.

At his best, Hemingway always remained capable of great charm and real love. He could and did admire women for their achievement and on their merits. He *did*, after all, sit at the feet of Gertrude Stein. He *did* tell the Nobel committee that Isak Dinesen deserved their prize more than he did. That said, a wide sadistic streak ran through all his relationships, and his intimacy with women could—and invariably did—kindle that sadism to high levels of abuse and beyond.

The rack upon which Hemingway tortured his relations with women was the triangle. All through his life, his favorite moral morass consisted in loving two women at once. At the end of *A Moveable Feast*, he reduced his classic m.o. to a formula. "An unmarried young woman becomes the temporary best friend of another young woman who is married, goes to live with the husband and wife and then unknowingly, innocently and unrelentingly sets out to marry the husband . . . and if [the husband] has bad luck, he gets to love them both. First it is stimulating and fun and it goes on that way for a while. All things truly wicked start from an innocence."[16]

Of course the real motive behind Hemingway's triangles was never "bad luck." The repetitious drama of "loving two women" was, at root, a ritual in his lifelong struggle for self-renewal, and it came into play whenever Hemingway grew restive, yearning for a new start. A new life meant a new woman. But if that new life with its new relationship was going to be born, the old one had to die. The agonies of rebirth *meant* the agonies of a death. From this fusion of end and beginning, death and birth, Hemingway extracted the creative renewal he was sure was unavailable in any other way.

Hemingway was famous as a connoisseur of the "good life." It was not so good that he loved it. In reality, that "good life" was always contaminated by the sadistic self-loathing that lurked coiled inside his psyche lifelong. When its emotions gnawed at him hard enough, not even a whole lot of alcohol could make them stop, and no matter how good his "good life" might seem to be from the outside, Hemingway wanted out.

When Hem grew restive in his marriage to Hadley, the first candidate to be the "second woman" in this triangle was a beautiful, hard-drinking, promiscuous Englishwoman named Duff Twysden. Duff was not born to the aristocracy, but her early marriage to an alcoholic baronet had turned her into "Lady Duff." Hadley later claimed that Lady Duff lived by a code: she adamantly refused to sleep with a married man. Maybe. In any case, Duff does not seem to have slept with Hemingway, even though he was consumed by a hot infatuation with her that churned into jealousy when Duff did indeed go to bed with Hem's unmarried friend Harold Loeb. Right around this time, Hem and Hadley, Duff, and a Scots paramour of Duff's went with Loeb for the Pamplona *feria* of 1925, and it was this group of people Hem used as the dramatis personae for his first novel, *The Sun Also Rises*, building the story around his jealous rage and turning Duff into Lady Brett Ashley.

Though Duff Twysden reached Hemingway emotionally, she could never have been a successful candidate for the other woman in the Hemingway triangle.

Not like Pauline.

Pauline Pfeiffer, whom Hemingway met just a little after the Duff melodrama, was absolutely perfect as the renewing woman. She was a rich young American living in Paris, working at *Vogue*. She was different in every way from Duff Twysden. Duff was unerringly charming but often impossible. Pauline was unerringly charming but always thoroughly agreeable. Her specialty was *handling* impossible people. She was smart, well connected, socially skilled, and happened to be—no minor detail—an exceptionally gifted editor. Right to the end, Hemingway viewed Pauline's literary judgment as second only to that of his Scribner's editor, the great Maxwell Perkins. He showed Pauline every page he wrote. When she thought something was wrong, he fixed it. And when Pauline was impressed, Hem stopped worrying. Though no great beauty—Martha Gellhorn was the sole conventional beauty among Hemingway's four wives—Pauline had a lovely presence and was sexually just Hemingway's speed. Best of all, Pauline had a real gift for intimacy. Whenever the emotional weather darkened, Pauline grew better, kinder, and stronger. She bore with Hemingway's fears; she listened to his night thoughts; she could look straight into his very dark dark side, always staying steady with tact and love. In his early love letters to Pauline, written once the Hadley-Pauline-Hemingway triangle was in place and torturing each of them nonstop, we first glimpse the treacherous depression and self-loathing that drove and terrified Hemingway all though his life and that ultimately took his life. They are love letters, but they are strange. His thoughts, he tells her, are "everything contemptible." He is afraid of madness: "you lie all night half funny in the head and pray and pray and pray and pray you won't go crazy." Suicide is never off his mind. "I think all the time I want to die."[17]

Thus Pauline became the woman in Hemingway's rebirth-through-death triangle, and it was inspired by his love for her that he wrote *A Farewell to Arms*, which ends, let's recall, in a death through childbirth. Causing agony, the man lived in agony. Lord Lazarus did his comeback really well. He did it, as Sylvia Plath put it, so it felt like hell.

"You lie," he wrote, "and you hate it and it destroys you and every day is more dangerous, but you live day to day as in a war."

"As in a war." Funny way to put it.

The "war" of the Hem's birth-in-death triangle—between Hadley and Pauline—took place in 1926, beginning that snowy winter in the Swiss ski resort of Schruns. Dos was there. Hadley and Bumby were there. And somehow or other, properly invited of course—her manners were impeccable—Pauline Pfeiffer also showed up on the slopes. Dos Passos would remember Schruns as one of "the best times." "Mealtimes we could hardly eat for laughing. Everybody kidded everybody during that week at Schruns. We ate vast quantities of trout, and drank the wines and beers and slept like dormice under the great featherbeds. We were all brothers and sisters when we parted company. It was a real shock to learn a few months later that Ernest was walking out on Hadley."

Hemingway's new life with Pauline coincided with his public success, and it was mainly lived in Key West. In 1924, Dos the wanderer "discovered" Key West, then a ramshackle little wreck of a town, a forgotten last clod of America dropped as an afterthought into the tropical sea. Dos loved every dusty street and fluttering palm. It was almost Spain in America. "In the little Spanish-speaking cigar factories that dotted the town," he wrote, "the cigarmakers had a habit of hiring somebody to read to them at each long table while they worked. They listened with avidity not only to the socialist newspapers, but to the nineteenth century Spanish novelists and to translations of Dostoyevski and Tolstoi."[18] Dos instantly saw that Key West "suited Hem to a T." He wrote to Hemingway in Paris, announcing that Key West was *the* American place to be: Provincetown, but warm in the winter.[19]

In April 1928, Hemingway and Pauline, who was now pregnant with their first son, Patrick, arrived. The old expatriate life was over. With *The Sun Also Rises*, Hemingway had gone from being chic to being genuinely famous. With *A Farewell to Arms*, finished (though not begun) in Key West, he would clinch his grip on that fame forever. Dos meanwhile had turned out his first masterpiece: the dazzling *Manhattan Transfer*. While conservative critics raged—one called it "an explosion in a cesspool"—the best writers on the scene were properly rapturous. "A spiritual Baedeker to New York," Hem called it. Sinclair Lewis told the world that it was "a novel of the very first importance. . . . The dawn of a whole new school of writing." D. H. Lawrence thought it the best book about New York that he'd ever read: "an endless series of glimpses of people in the vast shuffle of Manhattan Island . . . a very complete film of the vast loose gang of strivers and winners and losers." Among those blown away was Scott Fitzgerald, who had just published *The Great Gatsby*. He wrote to Perkins: "Wasn't Dos Passos's book astonishingly good?"[20] Dos proceeded next to *The 42nd Parallel*, the first novel in his great trilogy, *U.S.A.* Hemingway loved it all: "Trilogies are undoubtedly the thing," he wrote to Dos. "Look at the Father Son and Holy Ghost. Nothing's gone much bigger than that."[21] And he added: "you can write so damned well it spooks me that something might happen to you— wash and peel all the fruit you eat."[22]

Both men were now famous. Yet they reached fame by different routes and lived with fame in different ways. There is such a thing as a gift for being famous. It is an attribute of star quality, and it may or may not accompany a related, but quite separate, gift for making art. It is quite possible to be a genius and not have it at all, as was close to being the case with Dos Passos. Hemingway, on the other hand, was endowed with the talent for fame to a spectacular, world-class degree. Hemingway's presence in any room would be remembered for a lifetime. People barely noticed Dos. Hem was a glossy media celebrity; Dos was quietly admired by highbrows. Hemingway was a legend from the start. Everything he touched served that legend, and decades after his death the process was still churning on. Dos Passos's image was swallowed up in a kind of anti-charisma.

There were other differences. They were famous for different views of life. Hemingway was "apolitical." As a modernist, he was seen as an heir to Stein, Pound, and Joyce, admired for the technique of living, an adept of the good life. Few writers have more effectively turned a sense of how to live—the *technique* of living well—into a credible image of heroism. The "Hemingway hero" became a crucial twentieth-century figure.

Dos Passos, on the other hand, was known as a *radical*. Nobody cared how he lived or what wine he drank. When people thought about him, they thought about politics and revolution. His name evoked Eisenstein, *Ten Days That Shook the World*. He was bound to a radical art and vision that might or might not change the world. His novels had no heroes at all. On the contrary. They showed nothing but human shoddiness, outlined in a kind of incandescent moral murk. How to live? These books were about how *not* to live. Most of Dos's characters were defeated by life or snared in its meretriciousness and lies. They were, one and all, losers in a lost world.

So Hem, in his genius (and that genius was real), offered his readers a new heroism and a look at the "good life" as it might be lived. Dos, with his no less real genius, showed the world the bewildered masses in visions of degradation. One—surprise!—was more popular than the other. And though both were famous, Hem was, and would remain, more famous than Dos.

Way more famous.

Hem also suffered in ways Dos did not.

On December 6, 1928, in Oak Park, Illinois, Hemingway's father, Dr. Clarence Hemingway, rose early as usual. It was probably just after first graying winter light. Keeping as quiet as possible, the doctor went down into the basement where, since it was December, the furnace was roaring at full power. Dr. Hemingway pulled open the iron door of the firebox, and gingerly pushed some papers—most biographies designate them as "personal papers"—into the little boxed inferno. Then the doctor latched the door again, and still very quiet, climbed back up to his bedroom on the second floor, closing the door behind him. Clarence Hemingway kept a Smith and Wesson .32 revolver in his room. It was an old weapon, quite worn, which *his* father,

Anson Hemingway, had acquired when Anson was fighting as a Union soldier in the Civil War more than sixty years before. But it still worked perfectly. And it was loaded.

The time had come.

Doctor Hemingway ground its muzzle behind his right ear and fired.

The pistol's one loud *crack* snatched his thirteen-year-old son, Leicester, at home with the flu, out of the book he was reading. The shot, ringing through the house, made the boy jump from the bed. Leicester stood straining, listening for something more. But there was nothing more. Just silence. Just lots and lots of silence.[23]

During the first year of grieving over his father's suicide, Hemingway decided that Dos needed a wife. In 1929 Dos was living in Greenwich Village, mired in running a revolutionary theater with his friend John Howard Lawson, who in decades to come would go on to an illustrious career that included being a leading communist cultural apparatchik in Hollywood.

Hem's first idea was to introduce Dos to his sister Madeline. After their father's suicide, Madeline had come to Key West to type the manuscript of *A Farewell to Arms* and help take care of baby Patrick. Hem saw an opportunity. So far as Hem was concerned, Dos and Madeline both suffered from the same main problem. He was going to fix it. John Dos Passos as his brother-in-law. Hem liked the sound of it.

It turned out to be the reverse of love at first sight. When Dos showed up in Key West, Madeline took one look at her prize, and that was that. "I was shocked to see a bald man with nervous, jumpy movements. Ernie had neglected to give me a physical picture of his friend. . . ."

Hem fumed, but Dos didn't care, because there was another Hemingway woman visiting Whitehead Street; *she* saw a husky highbrow who'd followed caravans through Persia, and she seemed to like him fine. Her name was Katy Smith, and Katy was *almost* Hem's sister. She had been his high school girlfriend; her brother Bill was Hem's oldest best friend, and she had known everybody in Hem's life from way, way back: Hadley, Pauline, Hem's mother the imperious Grace, the suicided Clarence, Madeline, everybody. Katy "called Hem 'Wemmage' and treated him affectionately condescendingly as a girl does her younger brother." "They were all very thick," Dos wrote. "From the first moment," Dos wrote, "I couldn't think of anything but her green eyes." It was a lasting love match.

The first days of this romance were marked by one strange moment. As Dos and Katy were falling in love, a crate from Hem's mother in Oak Park arrived at Hemingway's house at Whitehead Street. It was a biggish box, nailed shut. For some reason Hemingway didn't want to open the crate. He kept putting it off. Katy couldn't understand why Wemmage was so *nervous* about opening a *box*. Come on, *open* the damn thing.

Not now, Hem said, a little jumpy. Later. I'm busy now.

At last Pauline lost patience and took a hammer to it herself, clawed off the top, and started pulling stuff out. The first items out were several of Grace's paintings—Grace was something slightly more than a Sunday painter. They must have been put in clean and carefully rolled, but they came out badly smeared by the remains of a large chocolate cake, also in the box, which shipment had left mashed and moldy, a crushed mass of chocolate gunk. It was only after the gunk was scooped out that Pauline spotted one last item in the bottom of the box.

It was the .32 that Clarence had used to kill himself.

The room was still. People stood speechless.

"Hem's mother," Dos would write, "was a very odd woman. Ernest was terribly upset."

Grace's gift of the fatal weapon to her son soon became a prime item in the long bill of particulars Hemingway spent his life assembling against the woman he was sure would have "destroyed" him if she got the chance, just as she had (so he insisted) "destroyed" Clarence Hemingway before him. And that .32 in the crate did strike Katy and Dos as pretty spooky. They never knew the decisive detail, never mentioned in all of Hem's tirades against Grace. At his father's funeral, Hemingway had asked—*insisted*—that his mother send him the fatal weapon. Grace had been reluctant. Now at last she was only doing what her son had asked.

"Ernest was the only man I have ever known," Dos Passos mused, "who *really* hated his mother."[24]

But Hem was thrilled when Katy and Dos were married in the fall of 1929. "Damned glad you men are married," he wrote, "I'm happy as hell about it." Dos now had something more than a brilliant talent. Dos had a wife and a life. When the thirties came, no year was complete without Katy and Dos coming down from Cape Cod at least a couple of times to see Hem and Pauline.

They were such wonderful times that Dos later had trouble putting his finger on why, or even when, things became complicated. "Pauline was as much fun as ever, Gigi and the Mexican Mouse"—the Hemingway sons, Gregory and Patrick—"were as cute as you'd want, but things got rocky between Ernest and me more often than they used to."

Spain was somehow part of it. In 1933, Hem and Dos once again crossed paths in Spain. It was just at the time that the Spanish Republic had been declared, and liberal, reformist hopes were high. Dos recalled the two of them getting drunk at lunch with the American ambassador, a historian-turned-diplomat named Claude Bowers, who loved the idea that two of America's

most impressive young writers were both staunch His-
panophiles. Spain was being transformed. In 1931, the monar-
chy and the dictatorship it supported had been overthrown and
replaced by a progressive republic. Dos the radical was of course
thrilled, while Hem watched from his usual apolitical distance.
Republics were fine with him so long as they didn't mess with
the *feria*. "Hem had no stake in any of it," Dos would write.
"His partisanship was in various toreros." "Those lunches," he
wrote, "were the last time Hem and I were able to talk about
things Spanish without losing our tempers."[25]

For Dos, the wind of a Spanish revolution was stirring at last.
When Pepe Robles brought his family up to Provincetown for the
summer, he and Dos conferred endlessly. The rumor was that
Robles had been offered a very big job back home—perhaps the
governorship of a province—which he had turned down because
he was sure that Spanish politics were heading for a more radical turn, and he did not want to end up on the wrong side of the
revolution he'd been waiting all his life to join. Dos himself went
to Spain, wrote glowing articles, joined committees, signed petitions, and even tried calling up what was left of his deceased father's pull in the American establishment.

And Robles turned out to be dead right. That liberal Spanish
Republic was being stretched to the breaking point, and in 1936
the Civil War that Robles had foreseen did come. Robles, who
with his wife and children was on vacation in Spain when the
war broke out, immediately decided not to return to Hopkins,
but turned himself over, body and soul, to the *causa* he had been
waiting for, ever since the days of his radical youth, when he'd
met the young Dos on that night train from Toledo. Pepe was instantly made a lieutenant colonel in the Republican army.
Within weeks Robles was near the secret heart of really heavy-
duty politics in Spain.

At the same time, things were changing in the friendship of America's two most promising young writers. Without knowing quite how, they too were moving toward some sort of breaking point. When it came at last, it wasn't exactly over career. And it wasn't exactly over politics. And it wasn't exactly over sex, either. Yet come it did, and when it did it was somehow about every one of those things, each merging into the other.

The breaking point between Hem and Dos came one day in the early spring of 1937, when a group of armed men, not fascists and not outlaws, not the enemy and not police and not men from the Republican army either, came knocking at the door of Pepe Robles's modest apartment in Valencia. They were secret policemen of some sort, and though they refused to identify themselves, they seemed somehow connected to the government. They entered the apartment without a warrant, and without offering any explanation, they ransacked the place. They were looking for something: a notebook in which Robles had been jotting down his impressions of the war. After they had found that notebook, they slapped handcuffs on Robles, and, while his wife Márgara watched helplessly, they took him away. There was no talk, no discussion. They left no record of any arrest. There is no record of any charge. There was just that knock on the door—just *the* knock on the door. After Robles was taken away, they—whoever "they" were—held him briefly in Valencia.

And then, for reasons that even now remain totally obscure, and always working in complete secrecy, this squad without a name took José Robles Pazos to some unknown place, where, acting without any inquiry or any trial or any legal proceeding whatsoever, they blew out his brains.

chapter 2

THE LAST GOOD TIME

Six or eight months before Robles was shot, during the summer of 1936, John Dos Passos's reputation crested in one of the greatest public triumphs of his career.[1] He had completed *The Big Money*, the torrential culminating third novel in his great trilogy, *U.S.A. The Big Money* is a brilliant book, a superb conclusion to one of the most masterful American literary achievements of the era. It rightly lifted Dos into an entirely new realm of recognition. John Dos Passos's work was no longer a rarefied highbrow taste. That summer, his face was on the cover of *Time*.

And assessing Dos's achievement, *Time* pulled out all the stops. It placed Dos Passos among the supreme figures in the history of American literature. It calmly compared him to Tolstoy and James Joyce. In one magical stroke of the media wand, *Time* transformed, overnight, a little-read, much-admired writer of dazzling but taxing, heroless, and almost plotless novels into the most famous left-wing writer in the English-speaking world, a genius and visionary who, as the caption beneath the cover picture of deceptively rugged-looking and forceful Dos proclaimed, *"Writes to be damned, not saved."*

Judged strictly in terms of career, that summer of 1936 was the perfect moment to be on the left. In 1936, the dominant force sweeping through all the democracies was an essentially leftist wave of political opinion known as the Popular Front. And in the summer of 1936, the Popular Front itself reached a kind of climax. Virtually the same week that Dos was on *Time's* cover, civil war broke out in Spain, galvanizing enlightened opinion worldwide and pulling it even further leftward. The editors of *Time* were on to the pulse of opinion. In the same issue of *Time*, there appeared the first reports of new military action amid the violence and confusion of Spain—something edging toward Civil War. Pepe Robles was there, on summer vacation from Hopkins, deep in it all.

But that was the late summer of 1936. Earlier, the return of spring had meant for Dos Passos not war but a trip south to Hem. In April of that year, three months before the publication of *The Big Money* and the almost simultaneous outbreak of war in Spain, John and Katy Dos Passos had decided to accept Hem's invitation to come south again. Dos thought he was done with the book. So, why not?

"We missed you both like hell all winter," Hem wrote in a long letter filled with wit and wicked wisdom. Pauline was taking the boys for a visit to their grandparents; while they were away, Hem was going to take his beloved boat, the *Pilar*, across the Straits of Florida to Havana. So—since *The Big Money* was done—"if you are ready to tropic up a little why not join me at Havana?"

The *Pilar* was Hem's obsession and his delight. It was thirty-eight feet long, slept eight, and had been named as a tribute to Pauline. "Pilar" was one of Hem's secret love names for Pauline, borrowed from a basilica devoted to the "Virgin del Pilar" in Sarogossa. Hem used the *Pilar* mainly for marlin fishing, a sport to which he had become boisterously addicted in 1932, and which he found not only utterly satisfying as a sport, and as an escape from his demons, but also—like bullfighting—as an aesthetic spectacle, a ballet, danced, as Hem liked things to be danced, to the death.

He especially loved taking the *Pilar* on what he called "the trip across"—the passage across the Straits of Florida between Key West and Havana. The glittering plunging beauty of the boat cutting through mounting brilliant purple and blue seas, the movement between two nations and two worlds, the arching battling fish—it all intoxicated him. And that spring he wrote to Dos that he was going to make "the trip across" in May. The *Pilar* would be piloted by his fishing pal Joe—"Josie"—Russell, and it would carry a passenger: an almost too-perfect blond beauty with an aristocratic *Town and Country* look named Jane Mason. Hem slyly confided: "Mrs. Mason is almost as apt at going places without her husband as Josie is without his wife."[2] Sly Hem did not add that he and Mrs. Mason were at the end of what most biographers agree was a pretty torrid sexual relationship, and were now in the process of turning away from one another. Jane lived in Havana; her husband Grant was director of Pan Am's Cuban operations. By crossing the straits with Hem, Jane Mason was rather more returning to her husband than straying from him.

It was soon agreed Sara Murphy ought to come south, too. Sara was grieving. That winter, her son Boath, a perfectly healthy sixteen-year-old boy, had been struck down with spinal meningitis, a complication of measles. Unlike the toddler variety of measles, measles in an adult or near adult is a virulent, life-threatening respiratory disease. Even in the early twenty-first century, surviving its onset is anything but assured. In 1936, Gerald and Sara knelt helpless at their gasping son's bedside, Sara clutching his hand, saying, "Breathe, Boath, *breathe*." The boy struggled. "*Breathe*," she kept repeating. "*Breathe*." It took all he had. She kept on calling to him: "*Breathe*." She kept on calling out the word even after Boath had stopped.[3]

In 1936, Hemingway still genuinely loved Sara Murphy. He had not yet demonized the pair. He really did want to help her grief with whatever happiness and consolation a friend could hope to give. Sara had always loved the Hemingways' hospitality in Key West. Pauline was a great hostess, and Hem was a splurging host, the greatest companion in the world. Sara had gone down regularly before Boath's death, when Hemingway "still looked like the Ernest of Pamplona and Schruns, a little burlier perhaps, and needing to wear his glasses more often; but full of fun, always ready to sweep up Pauline or Sara in his arms and swing them around to 'You're the Top,' or the new Fats Waller records Gerald had sent. . . . He and Pauline . . . took [the *Pilar*] out almost daily. And the Hemingway's new house, a big Victorian stucco affair, was grand, with a peacock strutting on the lawn and palm trees all around."[4]

So why not "tropic up" with Hem in Havana? There would be fishing, and though Hem the intrepid sportsman was a performance that could easily wear thin, the fishing could be pretty exciting too. The spring before, the Dosses had gone sailing with Hemingway off Bimini, and had witnessed an epic battle. Far out from shore, a huge tuna—something between 800 and 1,000 pounds—struck Hem's line. The battle with this leviathan turned out to be far beyond "sport." It lasted eight hours, a long, violent, primeval struggle. As Dos and Katy hovered near Hem, the battle felt like something from the days when there were giants in the earth. The huge fish fought, cresting and arching, thrashing against the pull of the surging boat, imperial in its power. Hemingway fought back, single-minded—he would not lose the thing. It was frightening and dazzling at once, and it went on and on. Sunset reddened the sky, and still the fight didn't stop. Night fell, and the battle continued in darkness. Suddenly a squall rose up, and the seas joined in the violence. The air shrieked around the *Pilar;* they were lashed with rain. They struggled through the storm until calm returned, and brought what seemed like victory. The huge exhausted fish lay heaving in the black water alongside the *Pilar.* Next they had to get the monster gaffed to the side and brought into Bimini harbor. While they were tying the fish alongside, Dos peered into the black water around them, suddenly aware of streaking unseen forms moving around the boat. Sharks, as ravenous as they were silent, had been drawn to the blood. Hemingway headed the *Pilar* toward the harbor, trying to outrun the scavengers' feast. When it pulled into the marina they were greeted by crisscrossed beams from fishermen's lights and searchlights on the pier that showed, lasted to the side of the *Pilar,* a skeleton, nothing but the tuna's head, backbone, and tail.

It was *The Old Man and the Sea.* The novel was conceived that night.

The thirty-eight-year-old Hemingway, however, was not the old man, Santiago, proud but resigned. On the contrary. Hemingway promptly mounted a machine-gun on the deck of the *Pilar.* Sharks? He'd fix *them.*[5]

"It's terrific to see the bullets ripping into them," Katy wrote to Gerald Murphy, "the sharks thrashing in blood and foam— the white bellies and fearful jaws—the pale cold eyes. I was aghast but it's very exciting."[6]

Dos sometimes wondered if maybe the trouble with Hem started back then, in 1935. Take, for instance, the bust. That spring, some sculptor had done a bust of Hemingway, and Hemingway had mounted it in the entryway on Whitehead Street. When Dos walked in and saw it there, he had burst out laughing.

Big mistake. Hem stood listening to Dos laugh, and didn't crack a smile. Dos kept compounding the mistake. Each time he came though the door, he'd tossed his hat onto the bronze head. Hem still didn't smile.

The idea in May 1936 was for Dos and Katy to pick up Sara in New York, then drive to Miami and board the brand-new wonder of the Caribbean world, Pan American Airlines "flying boat," a seaplane that left Miami from a dazzling new terminal on Dinner Key, and fly in record time to Hem in Havana. They would stay as always in Hem's favorite Havana watering hole, the Ambos Mundos Hotel, a shambling five-story structure of flesh-colored stucco, with lots of little non-working balconies and high stately French windows opening out onto the brilliant harbor. Nearby was a fine marina for the *Pilar*. Downstairs was a café they all liked. And around them, the great green and blue Caribbean.

The trip should have been perfect. But it wasn't perfect. It wasn't even all that good.

Dos was a big part of the problem. By rights, he shouldn't have been taking a vacation at all. He wasn't really done with *The Big Money*. He'd arrived with not one but *two* sets of galley proofs—the American *and* the British—and spent his time in paradise correcting the typesetters' errors in hundreds and hundreds and hundreds of pages. Dos was buried in his galleys in the Ambos Mundos. He was buried in his galleys on the *Pilar*. He was buried in galleys at breakfast. He was buried in galleys before bed. Every time Hem looked, Dos's myopic face was still buried in galleys. Hemingway seethed.

At least Hem could comfort Sara. He worked hard at showing Katy and Sara a good time. One day he piloted the *Pilar* to a superb isolated cove on the Cuban coast, took them all ashore to an untouched, unseen beach that looked as pristine as it might have been the day Columbus landed, and laid out a picnic for them all. At night, he took them all to the Ambos Mundos café, where they sang and danced. Three Latin musicians in straw hats sang songs and shook out rumbas: "There's a Small Hotel" and "No Habo Barrera in El Mundo." Hem danced with Sara, sang to her, and now and then a real smile surfaced on her face. Sara's biographer toys—uncertainly—with the possibility that Hemingway made some sexual move toward Sara during this visit. If so, it's clear she said no. Her letter to Hem after the visit does raise one's suspicions: "You don't REALLY think I am being snooty with you, do you? Please don't. It isn't snooty to choose."[7]

The climactic event of the week was a fancy-dress dinner party at the home of Jane and Grant Mason. This was the kind of social event that a high-powered *Social Registrant* like Sara could master in a glance—and that the secretly snobbish Hemingway liked rather more than he was quite ready for the world to know.

Who knows what Hem's guests guessed about the sexual drama behind the Masons' party? Jane Mason and Hem, after their "secret" affair, were now going their separate ways. Jane was a hard-drinking, unstable, decidedly upper-class woman—a lesser Duff Twysden, not sexier but more conventionally beautiful, more American, duller, and much more ominously disturbed than the model for Lady Brett. Like Duff, Jane was promiscuous enough to drive Hemingway crazy with other men. She was also (like him) a chronic depressive, and a grim enough case to scare him. If Jane Mason was auditioning for a part in Hemingway's triangle of renewal, she didn't get the part. Once he saw that Jane was not going to be a bearer of new life, Hemingway turned her into a killer, portraying her as the "accidental" murderess at the center of his short story "The Short Happy Life of

Francis Macomber," a disturbing and only half-successful work that could serve as a textbook outline of Hemingway's misogynistic pathology.

When it was all over, Hem's guests took Pan Am's flying boat back to Miami, and headed home. Something had gone wrong, and Dos knew it. Back in Provincetown, he sent Hemingway a case of champagne and a kind of apology. At Pan Am's Miami terminal, they crossed paths with Pauline, on *her* way home. She looked, Sara thought, "like a delicious and rather wicked little piece of brown toast." But Sara was worried about Pauline, and there's a throb of anxiety in her thank-you note to Hemingway: "Oh Ernest, what wonderful places you live in and what a good life you have made for yourself and Pauline."[8]

"Good life"?

It was far from good. In May 1936, the insidious acids of depression and self-contempt were once again corroding Hemingway's being, soaking into every permeable part of his existence, seeping through every hairline crack in his sense of himself. And there were many more hairline cracks than any outsider would ever have guessed. His marriage: only one year before he had portrayed Pauline, not unlovingly, as "P.O.M," or "Poor Old Mama," in the *Green Hills of Africa*. Now Pauline was beginning to be seen in a harsher light, closer to the rich, shallow, "social" consort of Harry, the writer-hero of "The Snows of Kilimanjaro," the great short story that is the successful twin of the pathological "Macomber."

The hero of "The Snows of Kilimanjaro," Harry is another avatar of Ernest *agonistes*: yet another famous-writer-hero, suffering this time on African safari. Harry is dying. He has developed gangrene in his leg, and the rot—his rot in his *being*—is poisoning him inch by inch. Unless he gets help, the toxins will soon finish him off. As he dies, the safari sits marooned on the Serengeti, waiting for a rescue plane that may or may not arrive in time to save him. Hyenas, alerted by the smell of death, have begun to circle the camp, inching in closer. Harry spends his time bickering with his wife, a woman much like Pauline, whose shallow love cannot touch, much less assuage, the sadistic self-loathing mobilized by his collapse.

"The Snows of Kilimanjaro" is a brilliant, repellent, thoroughly disturbing masterpiece, one of Hemingway's greatest achievements. Its medium is bickering. It is defined by the yammering of sadistic self-contempt running in a squirrel cage of self-pity. Though Hemingway was all of thirty-six when he wrote it, Harry is a has-been as a writer. He is riddled with regrets as he lies dying in a ghastly African twilight. His wife, modeled on Pauline, is called "this rich bitch, this kindly caretaker and destroyer of his talent." But no: Harry interrupts this silent tirade. Is the Pauline-character really the "destroyer of his talent"? "Nonsense. He had destroyed his talent by himself. Why should he blame this woman because she kept him well? He had destroyed his talent by not using it, by betrayals of himself and what he believed in, by drinking so much that it blunted the edge of his perceptions, by laziness, by sloth, by snobbery, by pride and prejudice, by hook and by crook."

Every word in "The Snows of Kilimanjaro" is defined by a husky, helpless, deep-throated dalliance with self-destruction, with disease, with moral collapse. If anyone wants a close look at what was eating at Hemingway's soul in early 1936, one careful reading of this appalling and perennially compelling tour de force is all that's needed.

"I am crazy as a coot," the dying Harry says to his wife. "And I am being as cruel to you as I can be."

Well, *was* Hemingway really Harry the has-been? By 1936, Hemingway's talent and career were both in trouble. He had spent much of his time since *Green Hills* trying to write a new novel, a book to be called *To Have and Have Not*. It was going to be about have-nots oppressed, Hemingway style, by haves. With this theme Hem hoped to win back the leftist critics who kept yammering about how he'd not fulfilled his talent, how the lost generation was history, how he'd turned into his own cliché. Exactly the goddamned New York leftists who were so enchanted with Dos. He'd show *them*.

Except that *To Have and Have Not* was not going well. By the May visit, Hem was running scared. As often happens when writers try to force a phony idea into existence, Hem couldn't make the damn thing hold together. The book kept breaking apart into set pieces and unrelated short stories. Since it did not have an authentic unifying idea, it just would not cohere. Edmund Wilson would shrewdly shrug off the finished product as "Hemingway in pieces."

Loss of his talent was, after madness and suicide, Hemingway's worst fear. He had not lost his talent: he had written "The Snows of Kilimanjaro" in the midst of this morass. Yet there was plenty wrong, and the trouble went deeper than problems with critics. The hyenas of a pathological depression that Hem did not understand and from which he could not defend himself were circling his camp. They were getting bolder, coming closer. In the silence and the dark, he could hear them muzzling around the flap of his tent.

It had moved up on him now, but it had no shape any more. It simply occupied space.

"Tell it to go away."

It did not go away but moved a little closer.

"You've got a hell of a breath," he told it. "You stinking bastard."⁹

Hemingway was going to die unless . . . something changed. He needed a new grip on his talent. He needed a new grip on his sanity. He needed a new war. He needed a new woman. He needed a new life.

And then came the convulsion in Spain.

The terrible upheaval—the revolution—that Pepe Robles had so prophetically foreseen broke out in Spain two months after Dos and Katy got back home from Havana, just as *The Big Money* was being published. By 1936, liberalism in Spain had been pushed to the breaking point, just as Robles had predicted. The elected Spanish government was veering to the radical left. In response, the radical right, led by a shrewd right-wing young general with fascistic leanings, Francisco Franco, organized a rebellion of the Spanish army's officer corps and set out to march on Madrid and "save the country." It was civil war, breaking out just as Dos made the cover of *Time*.

For Pepe Robles the coming of the Civil War announced his destiny; it was the substance of all things hoped for, the great transforming convulsion he had been waiting for all his life. He now wholeheartedly attached himself to the government he had declined to join in 1933 and was soon swept to the top because of his forceful bearing and native intelligence, his grounding in revolutionary thinking, his broad knowledge of radical politics in Spain, and—above all—because of his knowledge of Russian. The Republic did indeed have some important, albeit secret, work for him to do.

The Spanish Civil War was *the* war of the Popular Front, and it can't be understood without understanding the essentially fraudulent role played by the Front in Stalin's foreign policy. The Popular Front itself was a Soviet-sponsored propaganda campaign. It was instituted and run by the Comintern, or Communist

International, that is, the mainly covertly controlled foreign arm of the Soviet government, used to manage communist parties outside Russia and to promote Stalinism in the democracies. The Popular Front propaganda campaign was designed to pull the democracies leftward by affiliating democratic liberals with the Soviets against fascism. It was the single most successful propaganda campaign ever mounted by the Soviet state. It worked by co-opting the spontaneous and fully justified fears of the Nazi threat then running through all the democracies. It argued that the democracies should join with the Soviets in opposing Hitler but insisted that as the Hitler menace grew, the "capitalists" in the democracies were not *really* resisting fascism. They were appeasing Hitler. Behind their "democratic" masks, many were little more than fellow-fascists. Only through a decisive turn away from the near-fascism of "late capitalism" toward the "genuine antifascism" of the Soviets could the world's antifascists hope to stop the Nazis.

Such was the propaganda logic in 1936. It was very persuasive. A great many very smart people in Europe and America believed it.

They were wrong. Behind the façade of the Front, Stalin didn't have the faintest intention of joining the democracies, then or ever, in any *real* showdown with Hitler. Stalin's true, albeit secret, strategy was to avoid war with Germany at all costs, ideally by fomenting a war between the Nazis and the democracies in the West, thus diverting the threat to the Soviet border. After 1934, Stalin was not seeking confrontation with Hitler: on the contrary, throughout the length of the Popular Front, he was, in deepest secrecy, seeking an *alliance* with Hitler, offering Hitler immunity from Soviet attack in the East if and when the Nazis attacked the democracies in the West. The Popular Front was *never* intended to "stop Hitler." At most, Stalin used it as a tactic to pressure Hitler into coming to terms. The idea was to encourage Hitler to attack the West, while using the Front as a cover for Stalin's search for a deal with the Reich.

With the outbreak of Spanish Civil War, everyone froze. Was this the start of *the* war? Travelers froze: Genteel American girls making their premarital tour of Europe received terse parental cables summoning them back: COME HOME NOW. Governments froze. From Washington to Paris, chancelleries proclaimed, through assorted mixtures of hypocrisy and urgency, their "nonalignment." Most were none too fond of either revolution *or* fascism; all feared entanglement in a web of alliances like the net that in 1914 had dropped over Europe and dragged country after country into the horror of general war. Whole populations froze. Far from Spain, the Poles, who seemed to know instinctively that they were on the front line of the nightmare to come, put Warsaw under blackout: the grander hotels covered every window and unscrewed every light in their marquees. Their guests were told: "The Luftwaffe"—the German air force—"could be over Warsaw in half an hour."

War was coming, and the smart money saw it as a struggle to the death between the radical right and the radical left. The democracies would *have* to choose between the two, and for decent, enlightened people, the choice was clear. It had to be the *antifascist* choice.

Opposing Hitler *meant*—it was so *obvious*—a turn toward Stalin.

Max Perkins "was desperate for a novel,"[10] and after he returned to Key West from Cuba, Hemingway resolved to give him one, no matter what. He *had* to solve his problems with *To Have and Have Not* over the summer in Wyoming. Hemingway's favorite spa in the northern part of America was a dude ranch on the border between Wyoming and Montana, near a Montana town called Cooke City. It was known as the Bar-L-T, or the Nordquist Ranch, and there Hemingway and Pauline had been escaping the suffocating Florida August for the past six years. The Nordquist Ranch stood in true high country. To get there you had to cross a handmade bridge made of rattling planks over a tributary of the Yellowstone River, a crashing torrent that went careening through the property. The cabins, surrounded by pines, were made of chinked logs and their doors had leather hinges, and it was all in the shadow of two Rocky Mountain peaks, Pilot and Index, rising 5,000 feet above the floor of the valley, 12,000 feet above sea level. In 1936, the family moved into one of the larger cabins, perched on a little hill above the river, with a huge flagstone fireplace, and an extra room in which Hemingway could write.

The Hemingways left for Wyoming in mid-July—exactly when Franco's rebellion broke out in Spain, and maybe ten days before Dos's *Time* cover hit the stands. In Wyoming, Hemingway followed the papers, tempted—not compelled, but tempted—to go to Spain and see what was happening for himself. In contrast to Dos, Hem was not a full partisan of the Republican cause. Not yet. He certainly tilted toward the Republic, but he did not yet see the war as a black and white choice between fascism and liberty. In any case, war interested him apart from its politics, and his mind was roiling with thoughts of death, just as it had been when he wrote "Snows." "Lately," he wrote to the novelist Marjorie Kinnan Rawlings, "I have felt I was going to die in a short time. Hope that is nuts." A month later, he was joking with Archibald MacLeish about that favorite fantasy, suicide: "It will be a big disgust when I have to shoot myself." Maybe "will arrange to be shot in order not to have bad effect on the kids."[11]

When not fishing or shooting grizzlies or entertaining guests—for Hemingway was a host even in the high country—he was closeted in a spare room of the family cabin, pounding out *To Have and Have Not.*

The book's unfixable fragmentation was driving him crazy. "I find," he wrote to the editor of *Esquire*, "that despite the noble example of Dos when I write a novel it has to go from one thing to another."[12] This one didn't. But he imagined he had found his glue: Rage. Fury. Vengeance. Hem would break himself in pieces and spread his self-contempt over all the sinister phonies—"haves," the whole damn pack of them—who were threatening him, *using* him, "destroying his talent," as the putrefying Harry puts it.

That rich bitch Jane Mason, for example. He'd fix her. He would transform her into a bored, slinking, smug, man-collecting slut named Helene Bradley, limned in a portrayal so scurrilous that it makes "The Short Happy Life of Francis Macomber" look like a feminist tract. The novel also attacks Pauline, but shrewdly turns her into Katy, so that the husband attacking her would be not himself but Dos. Hemingway's neurotic response to Pauline's need to avoid further pregnancy is finessed into a situation in which a character based on Katy speaks as if she were Pauline, attacking her writer-husband with a concentrated, venomous hatred that was remote from anything typical of the real Pauline even if the marital loathing she expresses produces the best (Joyce-inflected) pages of a bad novel: "Love is what we had that no one else had or could ever have. And you were a genius and I was your whole life. I was your partner and your little black flower. Slop. Love is just another dirty lie. . . . Love is that dirty aborting horror that you took me to. . . . I'm through with you and I'm through with love. Your kind of picknose love. You writer." Dos and Katy are slandered in other ways. Katy is made a kleptomaniac ("she likes to steal as much as a monkey does"), while the Dos character is presented as an (of course) unmanly blowhard, a political and artistic poseur, a cuckold, a masochist, and a deadbeat. The book sneers at Dos Passos's method as shallow and artistically trivial: when the Dos character—his name is Richard Gordon—glimpses the have-not wife of the novel's have-not hero (later played by Humphrey Bogart in the movie), Gordon goes into ecstasies over the brilliant portrait he will make of her, spun out of thin air. Like many of Hemingway's insults, there was an edge of truth in this. Even at their most impressive, Dos Passos's soaring images of squalor are sometimes marked by a certain shallowness. Hem's implication was nasty but shrewd: that Dos Passos was sometimes a kind of tourist in his own vision.

All of this is held together (or rather, not held together) by an incredible and incoherent plot. The key to the novel's dominant bitterness is of course Hemingway's own self-contempt. The original manuscript, now on deposit in the JFK Library in Boston, includes several ruthlessly ugly self-portraits: pictures of Key West's washed-up star writer, a drunken "slob," shambling alone through the streets, hung-over, corrupt, despised. It is invariably Richard Gordon who glimpses Hem passing by in these Hitchcock appearances and who invariably looks down on his rival's wretchedness with contempt. It is Richard Gordon who calls the meandering has-been a "slob." In other words, in *To Have and Have Not*, Dos Passos is made into the vehicle of Hemingway's own self-loathing. Hem had figured it out. It wasn't *Hem* who despised the man he'd become.

It was *Dos* who despised him.

Right?

For the rest of the summer and early fall, Hemingway surged forward with this meretricious enterprise, piling up pages. Free! He was free! What better way to break a block than with rage? Hemingway was filled with excitement about what he was doing—so much so that he uncharacteristically showed the holograph manuscript to a visiting sportsman friend, a man good at shooting grizzlies, but not blessed with any special literary judgment. Tom Shevlin didn't like what he read. He thought the pages were "lousy." Too intimidated to say so outright, Shevlin merely hinted, indirectly, at his reservations. Hemingway's rage was immediate, blazing, and very loud. Shouting imprecations, he flung the manuscript out a window into a bank of September snow and subjected the cowering Shevlin, though a guest, to the silent treatment—not one single word—for three full days.

Writing in the high country, Hemingway kept his eye on the headlines. By September 26, he wrote to Maxwell Perkins that he wanted to get over there as soon as he was done in Wyoming. "I hate to have missed the Spanish thing worse than anything in the world but have to have this book finished first."[13] He would go, if the "show" in Spain wasn't all over by the time his book was done.

But by the end of October, the show in Spain was far from over. Franco's November siege of the Spanish capital was about to begin. But his book, he felt, was done. He was going to put it in a vault for Max. He was free to go to Spain. He had loaded the gun of *To Have and Have Not* with all his hatred. It was the weapon with which he proposed to blow away what was left of his old life.

chapter 3

THE APPARATCHIK
APPEARS

Like smoke without fire, Joris Ivens materialized in the life of John Dos Passos about two months before Dos and Katy drove south with Sara for their Havana visit to Hem.[1]

Sometime that March of 1936, Joris and his Dutch girlfriend, Helene von Dongen, appeared out of thin air. It's easy to argue now that Dos should have been on his guard against this smiling Dutchman—but then again, why? Joris Ivens seemed smart, fun, and very talented, a charmer with a deep rolling laugh, who despite his thirty-eight years looked, as Dos would recall, innocent as a kid, "a high school boy playing hookey."[2] Besides, Dos wasn't the suspicious type. Suddenly Joris and Helene were at every party, every opening, and every screening in left-wing Greenwich Village, the prettiest new couple around. Joris had a knockout smile and dark blue eyes, wavy black hair, and virile jaw perfected by dimples. Women adored him. The tempting Helene was always at his side, sizing up the social scene with large languid eyes, sharp with scorn. Helene didn't smile half as much as Joris, but she was just as smart and just as chic—a tricky mix of innocence and experience, small breasted, supple, and so sexy it was a little scary.

If Joris and Helene *looked* perfect, their socialist credentials proved they *were* perfect. They had come straight from Moscow, that citadel of the future, and though neither was Russian, both had been real players in the Soviet Union's cinematic avant-garde. In the Greenwich Village of 1936, that fact alone placed them near the top of the human pinnacle. Soviet-style filmmaking was not to be confused with mere crass moviemaking, Hollywood-style. Film-makers like Ivens despised Hollywood. Filmmaking was high art, not low pandering. Filmmaking was socialism, not capitalism. Filmmaking was documentary—visionary, yet real—and not mere vulgar storytelling, the drug of the masses. If Communism was the politics of the future, the cinematic avant-garde was its art.

And Joris and Helene embodied it. Ivens's avant-garde films *Borinage* and *The New Earth* were viewed (and still are viewed by some film historians) as major documentary filmmaking. Back in Moscow, Ivens had kept company with the grandest fig-ures in the Soviet avant-garde: Pudovkin, Meyerhold, Vertov, and even *the* great director Sergei Eisenstein himself, the magus under whose wand the masterpieces of the future were being shaped. That made the Dutchman an angel from the world to come, a shining creature who (for some perplexing reason) had decided to leave the paradise of the new and bless the Americans with his presence, "the best new documentarist since Eisenstein."

He came knocking at the door of Dos's life almost as soon as he arrived in New York, and it's clear that Dos opened the door wide, and with a welcoming smile. By April the two of them were toying with collaborating on a film—a big attack on Hollywood—and Dos was cheerfully doing Joris career favors: helping publicize the New York premiere of *The New Earth*, and introducing the Dutchman to his famous friends, like the poet and editor Archibald MacLeish. In the New York of 1936,

MacLeish mattered to downtown because he embodied uptown. MacLeish was that rare thing, a working artist with real power in the media. He was one of Henry Luce's favorite intellectuals, a senior editor at *Fortune*, impressively—even luminously—connected in Washington. He was a leftish New Dealer under the spell of the Popular Front and the Soviet vanguard. Like Dos, "Archie" soon found himself basking in the Ivens glow. "Ivens was the great camera man of his time," he would recall, "an absolutely fearless man, a passionate and convinced Communist, who was as mild as your grandmother, really quite a lovely guy."[3]

It seemed natural that Ivens would seek out Dos. Dos Passos was the most eminent "experimental" leftist writer in English. In ways that were typical of the Soviet vanguard, the Dos Passos novels of the late twenties and early thirties were viewed as "documentary," transcending mere bourgeois fiction. They were surrounded by the halo of revolution. And they were modernist. They were *new*. *Manhattan Transfer, The 42nd Parallel, 1919,* despite their bitter tone and plotless fragmentation, seemed to flow as one new, compelling, singular vision. They had no heroes; everyone in them was trapped, confused, at a dead end. Yet they seemed to sing out like a kind of Walt Whitman in prose, not the euphoric Whitman of *Leaves of Grass* to be sure, but a dysphoric twentieth-century variant, singing the big song in a minor key, yet irresistibly. Dos heard America singing, but the song, coming from Dos, was a discordant rapture of distress. Dos Passos turned Whitman's ecstatic optimism inside out. His novels opened a shattered yet panoramic view of America as a vast, heaving human ruin, figured in an unstopping torrent of unsequential but genuinely dazzling prose.

"You can write so damned well it spooks me," Hem had exulted in a letter to Dos after reading *1919*, and it was true: paragraph by paragraph, Dos Passos wrote as well as or better than anybody of his era. The great passages admittedly tend to come in set pieces that are stronger than the completed work seen as a whole. But that's true of Whitman, too—and the set pieces are often magnificent, in a class by themselves. Parts of the trilogy are not only better than most of Hemingway, they are also better than most of Virginia Woolf, and better even than most of the "Parisian demi-god," James Joyce. Their radicalism and modernism are at once political and artistic, and their prose surges forward powered by the same gusting wind that carried Picasso, Stravinsky, and, yes, Eisenstein. The great Dos Passos novels are not very novelistic; their narrative makes a rather feeble frame for their wild music, but even so they are wonderful. When they appeared, they seemed part of a new world view, one that offered a uniquely honest view of a squalid, ignored, hurt America without heroes or hope. That such a dark vision could shine so brilliantly seemed to give irony itself a new look.

In the realms of advanced cultural taste, all this linked Dos to Russia and made him seem part of the same great vanguard that included Soviets like Eisenstein, Pudovkin, and Meyerhold. And if they were his inspiration, he was also theirs. The most advanced new writers in the USSR—one thinks of Boris Pil'nyack and Victor Serge—had embraced Dos Passos as a pioneer and a culture hero whose work burned with the glow of everything revolutionary and new.

Except that all that was about to change. The Soviet regime was having second thoughts about modernism. And it was having second thoughts about Dos.

And Ivens was lying. He was not an "independent radical." He had not sought out Dos Passos because of admiration for his art. He was a political propaganda agent on a mission. And his mission was not benign.

To the end of his long life (he outlived Dos, Hem, MacLeish, all three), Ivens would deny—and deny and deny—any connection to the Soviet government. He was an "independent" socialist filmmaker who now and then happened to be led by his dewy convictions to make a movie with Soviet help. His time in the Soviet Union? The pilgrimage of an idealist. A lifetime of uncritical service to Soviet propaganda? Nothing but the happy, happy coincidence of his own high ideals and a great nation's power and promise. His communism? It was unforced. It was pure. It was above all *independent*.

All these denials were false. Joris Ivens did not come to America in 1936 as an "independent" artist. The Comintern sent him. He *was* a filmmaker, of course, and his achievement was real. He really *did* make impressive films. He really *did* know Meyerhold, Vertov, and Eisenstein. (Whether he was their "friend," once they got into trouble with the regime, is a different matter.) But first, last, and always Ivens was in the Stalinist propaganda *apparat*, an apparatchik in the worldwide network of artists and agents under the sway of the Comintern's propaganda czar, Willi Münzenberg. Münzenberg was, in turn, a protégé and ally of Karl Radek, Stalin's prime adviser on both Germany and culture. Ivens's career as a filmmaker, however impressive, was purchased by strict obedience to the political dictates of the Soviet regime.[4]

Which had sent him to New York. As soon as Ivens arrived, he contacted Gerhart Eisler, who was then serving (covertly, of course) as the Comintern's chief of undercover operations in the United States. The two men would remain in steady contact until the end of 1936, when both left the United States, both dispatched on new missions in Spain.[5] Ivens also filed regular reports with Mezhrabpohm Films, the Comintern film company in Moscow, founded by Willi Münzenberg. He was also in regular contact with a Soviet agent in place in New York.

In New York, Ivens was instantly made a leading mentor to a film collective for talented young communist artists known as Nykino. The young people in Nykino worshipped the Soviet avant-garde, and Dos Passos was one of Nykino's celebrity sponsors. Nykino was, in turn, a subsidiary of an umbrella organization serving Soviet cinema in America known as Amkino. (One of Ivens's secret service contacts held a cover job at Amkino.) Meanwhile, all of Ivens's screenings and lectures were handled by Amkino's booking agency, The New Film Alliance.

Incredibly, in 1936, though Dos Passos was involved in all these organizations, he does not seem to have grasped that they were all interlocking Comintern fronts. Nor did he grasp that Joris Ivens was a Comintern agent. He bought the routine denials and cover stories without a blink. He really believed that Joris was an idealistic independent artist who just happened to love the Soviet avant-garde, a nice, Dutch Catholic boy.[6]

In the mid-1930s, the Soviet regime, after years of courting him, decided it had had enough of John Dos Passos.

While he was in Wyoming, attacking Dos in the first version of *To Have and Have Not*, Ernest Hemingway cannot have had the faintest inkling that the Comintern was simultaneously preparing an equally venomous political attack on his old friend. Had he known, he would surely have been incredulous, outraged. And he would have scoffed at the idea that he himself might be used as the instrument of that attack. And yet that was exactly the event taking shape.

By 1933, Stalin had come to the conclusion that the modernist avant-garde, which had played such a luminous role in the early cultural history of the USSR, had served its propaganda purpose, and he was preparing to liquidate it. In a move that coincided with the establishment of the Popular Front and the initiation of the Great Terror, the old avant-garde or modernist ideas of the Soviet vanguard were to be replaced by a new, explicitly anti-modernist artistic ideology: socialist realism. The new doctrine was not optional. It came straight from the top, launched by Karl Radek in a speech delivered at a huge writers' congress called the First All-Union Congress of Soviet Writers held in August 1934, in front of a large audience that included many distinguished foreigners, such as André Malraux and Klaus Mann.

In his speech, Radek confronted Soviet artists, and revolutionary artists everywhere, with a plea to re-examine their art. Were they really doing enough to serve the needs of the people? Radek thought not. Too many Soviet artists, he felt, had failed to rise to the challenge of *truly* revolutionary art. They had been seduced, sad to say, by the snares and delusions of bourgeois modernism and its fake avant-garde. This false vanguard believed that mere form alone, provided it sported some sort of revolutionary look, could generate revolutionary art. Enchanted by the obscurities of Western-style, bourgeois—no, petit-bourgeois—modernism, some Soviet artists had sunk into the practice of empty formalism. The result? An art of fragmentation and chaos. It might have a revolutionary façade, but it was nothing but a mask for petit-bourgeois values.

It was time to change paths. A new, *genuinely* revolutionary art—the art of socialist realism—must now be embraced. Artists should stop baffling the people with the hocus-pocus of empty fractured esthetics. Writers and filmmakers should uplift the people with clear realistic stories about the triumphs of socialist goodness over bourgeois evil. Socialist painters should drop their abstract, modernist nonsense and paint images of socialist heroism. Socialist music should sing Soviet triumphs with singable songs. Like all bourgeois things, the modernist avant-garde was corrupt and corrupting. It should be shunned. It should be rooted out. It should be liquidated.

Radek did not hesitate to identify the offending artists. True revolutionaries looking for examples of all that was wrong with the arts today need look no further than two decadent westerners. One was James Joyce. The other was John Dos Passos.

By the time Radek finished his speech, the Soviet modernist vanguard was as good as gone. Within four years, Meyerhold would be shot. Pil'nyack would perish in the Terror. Victor Serge would be sent to the gulag. Dziga Vertov would be marginalized. Eisenstein would be demoted and humiliated. While this was going on, Popular Front propagandists would continue to talk up the Soviet vanguard. They knew its appeal to the young in the West. But a grave had been dug. And on that grave, the executioner had planted its death's heads: the faces of Joyce and Dos.[7]

Radek's 1934 speech had no more enthusiastic an admirer than Joris Ivens. Ivens immediately wrote an essay applauding and echoing all the sentiments of the new Kremlin line, and shortly afterward gave a speech in Moscow doing the same. Ivens immediately turned against his old friends in that vanguard. He obediently deprecated his own avant-garde work, including *Borinage* and *The New Earth*. "Socialist realism," Ivens announced, would rescue revolutionary art from the "sterile impasse of empty esthetics" in which the old vanguard was trapped. For this to happen, "documentarist theories of film"—the very ideas Ivens had once adopted from Eisenstein and Vertov—had to be "defeated." The "fact fetishists in literature"—those still under the spell of Joyce and Dos Passos—had failed to convey socialist realism's life-giving "simple line." They refused to produce an "exciting story about people." Joyce? Dos Passos? Ivens attacked both Joyce and Dos Passos by name. They made "mangled art." "Reality as chaos."[8]

Such were the real ideas Joris Ivens brought with him when he arrived in New York. Like the Popular Front itself, Ivens's mission was essentially duplicitous. Publicly, he seemed to be a shining embodiment of the Soviet vanguard—the better to please naïve Eisenstein-struck American radicals like Dos Passos. Covertly, he was part of the regime's determination to undermine and destroy precisely that vanguard, a Comintern agent explicitly linked to Radek's targeting of Dos Passos as an influence to be liquidated, a source of corruption, a maker of "mangled art." Under cover of this duplicity, Ivens ingratiated himself with a delighted Dos Passos, involving Dos in his plans, winning his trust, and making himself look like what he was not: a friend.

And then, suddenly, the Spanish Civil War broke out. Was this . . . "It"? Everybody froze. Even Stalin briefly held his breath.

The course of the Spanish Civil War coincides almost exactly with the course of the Great Terror of 1936–1938. Virtually the same week that Dos's face was on the cover of *Time* and the Civil War ripped Spain in half, the first of the great Soviet purge trials opened for business. On August 14, 1936, the first defendants, all senior Bolsheviks, Lenin's lieutenants, climbed up into the dock in the Great Hall of the People in Moscow. Gripping the rail of the prisoners' dock, they gaped out through conquered, fear-blasted eyes at the prosecutor Andrei Vyshynsky, and certain death. The charges were read; orchestrated hysteria over their imaginary conspiracies immediately filled every communist-controlled medium of expression in the world. Once-proud Bolsheviks groveled. The revolutionaries sobbed. In their "confessions," invariably extracted under torture or the threat of it, October's heroes smeared each other and themselves with claims of treason. They confessed to unspeakable crimes. They could barely stop confessing. Death, they said, was too good for mad dogs like themselves.

Meanwhile denunciations, witch hunts, and arrests swept through Soviet society en masse, indiscriminate and uncountable. The gulag swelled. The basement executioners could barely keep their sizzling pistols loaded. Millions would die.

And Stalin's propagandists worried. Seen from the European perspective, the purges didn't . . . well, they didn't inspire *confidence*. Stalin brushed their handwringing aside, and was mainly right to do so. "Europe," he snorted, "will swallow it all!"[9] And mainly, Europe did. The list of distinguished people in the democracies who accepted and endorsed the purge trials makes shocking reading today. The trials seem, now, so obviously rigged. How could *any* intelligent observer have failed to see that? It was one function of the Popular Front to blind those people by making Stalin, in his "antifascism," seem indispensable to the struggle against Hitler.

The Spanish War came as a lucky break for this strategy of illusion. The Popular Front needed an antifascist cause, something that would serve Stalin without creating any serious inconvenience to Hitler. Spain was that cause.

Stalin's response was at first cautious, as usual. His prime goal was to avoid war with Germany. His secret negotiations with Hitler had been rocky, but Stalin was sure they would bear fruit. Stalin was rightly convinced that when Hitler was ready really to begin his war against the democracies, the German dictator would *have* to come to terms with him. He was sure that Hitler could not—and therefore would not—fight a two-front war, sure that Hitler could not—and therefore would not—simultaneously attack the democracies in the West *and* the USSR in the East. To make war against one meant coming to terms with the other. Stalin's goal therefore was to induce Hitler to attack the democracies first. If Spain served that goal—fomenting war in the West—then it might be all to the good.

Yet Stalin did not want to entangle himself if Franco was going to win easily or soon. If on the other hand the war dragged on, he had no objection to Western leftists pouring heart and soul into a Spanish bloodbath—so long as it did not cost him much, or interfere with his *real* goals: reaching a solid deal with the Nazi Reich, and transforming the USSR into an *absolutely* totalitarian state.

As time went by, Spain looked better and better to Stalin. Franco did not win quickly, and even though Spain did not spark a general war, it was a useful propaganda sideshow. The Popular Front could use it to pitch its prime propaganda claim: that the democracies must "stop Hitler."

In New York, Joris and Helene were ordered to start turning out just that kind of propaganda, and they were soon at work on two films about Spain—a country about which, incidentally, neither of them knew much of anything at all. At this stage, nobody dreamt of actually *going* to Spain. Both films were to be cheap and made without undue effort, compiled from existing footage. One was called *Spain and the Fight for Freedom*. It focused on the social revolution going on in Spain. In September 1936, Dos Passos and MacLeish were enlisted to write its voice-over narration. Simultaneously, Joris and Helene were putting together a second film called *Spain in Flames*. This was to be a simple piece of good-guys/bad-guys battlefront propaganda.

Ivens was perfectly prepared to keep exploiting Dos. True, Dos Passos had been officially attacked in the USSR, but what did these Americans know about that? The cultural line within the Soviet Union was rarely exactly the line used by the Popular Front. Münzenberg's men had no problem with exploiting artists proscribed in the USSR, if the artists were exploitable. Dos was still exploitable. Dos was famous. Dos looked independent. Dos brought in people like MacLeish. And by using Dos and

MacLeish together, the Comintern thought it just might hit the jackpot.

Hemingway.

Dos threw himself into *Spain and the Fight for Freedom*. It is a shame that the entire film—which I gather was later amalgamated into *Spain in Flames*—seems to have been lost. It was apparently quite well done. After seeing it in February 1937, Edmund Wilson wrote to Dos, "I saw your Spanish film and thought it was awfully good—the best put-together picture I think I ever saw."[10] But it has vanished.

Meanwhile, the Comintern was preparing for deeper Soviet involvement. Early in the fall of 1936, Stalin ordered it to begin recruiting volunteers for a set of International Brigades, irregular foreign legions recruited mainly from various national communist parties and shaped into a Popular Front army that could be shipped to Spain under covert Soviet command.

Shortly before, Stalin dispatched two important Red Army generals, Generals Ian K. Berzin and Vladimir Gorev, and their staffs as "advisers." The presence of both generals was to be kept secret. Both were remarkable men, though Gorev was the more skilled tactician, a shrewd, urbane, multilingual, and decidedly ruthless figure, filled with concealed contempt for the Spanish left and the Republic he had been sent to advise. Gorev had his orders. From the moment he arrived, his job was to assert Soviet interests in the war, and prepare for a Soviet takeover of the Spanish government.

He had a code name, Sancho, and Sancho would clearly need to have a high-level Spanish adjutant, a liaison to the Republic. This liaison would have to be a well-connected and politically sophisticated Spaniard, very intelligent, and a Russian speaker. The job was about as sensitive as you could get, and the man the Spanish Republic chose for it seemed perfect.

They chose José Robles.

They made Robles a colonel, just so he could fill it.

With the generals came the chief propagandist, Mikhail Koltsov—a patron and friend of Joris Ivens back in Moscow. Koltsov was perhaps the ultimate Popular Front intellectual. A man of dazzling brilliance and urbanity, he was famous in the propaganda apparatus for his skill in manipulating the egos and opinions of cultural celebrities in the West like André Malraux, André Gide, and Louis Aragon. For all his cynicism, Koltsov was on the surface all charm, all wit, and all seeming depth within depth. Koltsov captivated Hemingway exactly as he had earlier entranced Malraux, Gide, and Aragon. Hemingway thought him "the most intelligent man I have ever met" and turned him into Karkov in *For Whom the Bell Tolls*, the sole Russian in Hem's gallery of heroes.

While he was in Spain, Koltsov directed the war's propaganda. He was also seen and feared by insiders as Stalin's eyes and ears on the scene. It was said that no secret agent in the country had more power. It was reported that Koltsov spoke at length to the dictator himself, on a secure line, every day. He would also make it a priority to ingratiate himself to Hemingway and shape the way he saw the war.

Then in November 1936 one big event tipped the scales toward even deeper Soviet involvement. By the end of October, Franco had four columns moving in on Madrid. They reached the outskirts of the city. It was three-quarters surrounded. Everyone despaired.

Especially the government. As Franco approached, Berzin and Gorev insisted that the city could and should be held. On the night of November 6, 1936, disregarding this advice, the government turned tail and decamped. A long frightened column of black limousines and trucks piled with officials and files went streaming out of the city under cover of night. That afternoon, the Republic's chief press officer, a man named Rubio Hidalgo, had summoned Arturo Barea, then a young censor, press officer, and crypto-communist in his department, to his office in the Foreign Ministry.

> "Shut the door, Barea, and sit down. You know, the whole thing is lost. . . ."
>
> He wiped his gleaming pate with a silk handkerchief, passed his dark pointed tongue over his lips, and said slowly:
>
> "Tonight, the Government is transferring to Valencia. Tomorrow, Franco will enter Madrid."
>
> He made a pause.
>
> "I'm sorry, my friend. There's nothing we can do. Madrid will fall tomorrow."[11]

Rubio Hidalgo was wrong.

As Franco's columns tore into the northern and western suburbs of Madrid, the aroused *madrileños* fought like demons. Though their government had run, their Soviet "advisers" had not. Seeing his chance, Sancho wasted no time filling the void with Soviet power. He ordered 2,000 Comintern volunteers, members of the International Brigades stationed in Albacete, to enter Madrid. Marching from the east into the center of the city, these soldiers—few could speak even elementary Spanish—were nominally under the command of an elderly Spanish general, José Miaja, whom the fleeing government had left behind to preside over Madrid's surrender. They were really under de facto Soviet command, and every honest witness knew it. Even the people in the streets called the Internationals "the Russians."[12]

On the morning of November 7, the International Brigades came streaming into Madrid, flying their flags and singing their songs, the cavalry, so to speak, galloping to the rescue. The effect was electrifying. The city suddenly rose up in defiance, and Gorev, not the government, was in charge, directing the defense from his headquarters in the Ministry of War.

It must have been something like the supreme moment in José Robles's life. All through the three weeks of this great and desperate battle—Franco finally gave up and ended his assault around November 27—the man beside Gorev was Pepe Robles. Robles was with Gorev in the ministry, with Gorev in the bunkers, with Gorev at the battlefronts, interpreting, translating, advising, seconding, serving as the Russian's Spanish right hand. We catch a glimpse of him in an account provided by the Popular Front journalist Louis Fischer:

> On November 15, I was in Madrid. I went to the War Office to see General Goriev [sic] who had taken command of the military situation. I asked an attendant where I could find General Goriev. He beckoned me to follow him and walked through long corridors calling out to everyone he met, "Have you seen the Russian general, have you seen the Russian general?" Goriev's presence there was a secret, but Spaniards hate secrets.
>
> As I sat in Goriev's office, his Spanish interpreter and aide, Professor Robles of Johns Hopkins University, came in to tell him that Colonel Fuqua, the American military attaché, was outside and wanted to get the latest information. With the directness of an old army man, Fuqua had applied to the source. Goriev instructed Robles to talk to him.[13]

The November defense of Madrid changed the moral face of the Spanish War. The victory may not have changed the ultimate military odds, but for much of the world it did clarify who were the good guys. An embattled citizenry had risen up and rescued their city. They had fought the fascists in the streets, fought them in the back alleys, fought them in the squares and parks and from the trees and rooftops, and in the end, if they had not exactly won, they had held their ground. They had confounded the beast. Their slogan—*¡No pasarán! They won't get through!*—rang around the world. Even though their own political leaders had seemed to abandon them, they had turned themselves into a citizen army—a resistance—so strong that by the end of November, a frustrated Franco called off the assault, leaving Madrid for later—for the very last day of the war, as it turned out—still partly surrounded, under siege, but still in the Republic's hands. So it would stay for fifteen more months. The *madrileños'* struggle had been wonderful, and everyone knew it. They had defended their city in the first of a sequence of citizen battles in modern urban warfare that in the face of terror, from London in 1940 to Stalingrad in 1942 to Sarajevo in 1998, would lift very large numbers of seemingly unimpressive people into a kind of ordinary magnificence that stirs and sears the soul.

And at the center of it all stood José Robles. The battler was at long last in his battle. Pepe had been waiting for some moment like this one all his life. November brought it with unexpected grandeur. Those three weeks must have been among the great weeks of José Robles's life. Even now they seem to shine.

November made the Comintern change its propaganda tack. Joris and Helene could no longer settle for two forgettable little pictures about nasty fascists and heroic revolutionaries in Spain. Now they needed a movie that could make a real splash.

The film would have to *look* independent and noncommunist. For this Ivens was ideal: his work was always marked by what one film scholar recently called "the rhetoric of independence."[14] The picture would have to be made in Spain, and as quickly as possible. And it would need a *big* name. A *real* star.

Hemingway's biographers invariably claim that in January 1937 Hemingway "worked" on finishing *Spain in Flames*, which Helene was then rushing to completion. That claim may be literally true, but it is a little misleading. There were maybe three or four days in January 1937 that Hemingway can possibly have devoted to real work on this film. He did *something*, and he was clearly shown a rough cut. He doubtless spent time in the editing room, and may have done some last-minute tinkering with the voice-over. But Hem had no decisive role shaping the film. Nor, when the film was released, was the celebrity name above the title Ernest Hemingway's.

The name on the credit crawl was John Dos Passos.

But the focus now was on a "big" Spanish film. To this end, Ivens started by creating a classic Comintern front, a group of malleable celebrities used to sponsor and legitimize the project, help raise money for it, and conceal Soviet control. Ivens named his group Contemporary Historians. He ran it, under orders from the regime. As Ivens's biographer notes, "Ivens maintained tight control over Contemporary Historians and worked in close consultation with party and Comintern functionaries."[15] Ivens would have consulted Gerhart Eisler and probably Münzenberg's lieutenant Otto Katz, who had been involved with Ivens on many projects and happens to have been in New York at the time.

Contemporary Historians consisted of uninquisitive left-wing celebrities from the worlds of film and theater, most of whom—like Dorothy Parker, Dashiell Hammett, Lillian Hellman, and Clifford Odets—were covert party members or, like the Broadway producer Herman Shumlin, Stalinist fellow travelers. The Committee's duties were light. Dos Passos remembered their "working meetings" as lavishly lubricated gossip sessions during interminable lunches at the fashionable Manhattan restaurant 21.

Since they were not communists, Dos and MacLeish were useful front men, and for the moment, they really believed they were in charge. Self-delusion works wonders. Dos thought Joris was independent. And since he himself and Archie were also independent, surely their committee was independent, too. Right? *The Spanish Earth* was going to be their film. Wasn't it? MacLeish, probably with Dos, worked with Lillian Hellman on the scenario. MacLeish had even suggested a title: *The Spanish Earth*.

So, *The Spanish Earth* was surely "theirs."

Wasn't it?

The last celebrity lured into Contemporary Historians was Hemingway. Ivens reeled him in with the utmost care. Around Thanksgiving—just as Franco was giving up on the November assault—the papers reported that Hemingway had made a deal with the North American Newspaper Alliance, or NANA, for a series of reports from the front in Spain, compensated at astronomical fees, far beyond the dreams of even celebrity reporters. So by late fall, Ivens was aware that by early spring Hem was sure to be in Madrid.

Ivens acted on these facts quickly. Still concealing the Comintern's ideological hostility to Dos, he gave Archie and Dos leading, if illusory, roles in Contemporary Historians and urged them to press Hemingway into joining them on Hem's January visit to New York.

Then Ivens left New York. Better for him to be away. He sailed for Europe around Christmas, leaving Helene to supervise the details in New York.

In Paris, Ivens consulted with Münzenberg, Vladimir Pozner, and other Comintern superiors, picked up his highly skilled long-term cameraman, another Comintern apparatchik named John Fernhout, and proceeded directly to Spain. There he did not so much as glance at the scenario Hellman and MacLeish had written. Instead he consulted with the people who *really* mattered—above all, Koltsov. Then he began shooting the *real* film, working quickly and effectively. By the time any one of the Contemporary Historians actually got to Spain—in fact, by the time they'd downed their last drink at 21—*The Spanish Earth* was mainly shot.

Hemingway is sometimes cited as having "made" *The Spanish Earth*. This too is misleading. It never occurred to Ivens that this film would belong to anyone but himself and the regime. The first time that Joris Ivens ever laid eyes on Ernest Hemingway was in the Deux Magots Café in Paris late in February 1937. Hemingway was on his way to Spain for the first time in the war. Ivens had just returned from Spain to Paris, where he would show many of the already completed rushes of *The Spanish Earth* to his Comintern superiors. This he did in a private screening attended by a number of the most important Soviet propagandists in Europe.

Hemingway, the *auteur* of *The Spanish Earth*? He was not invited to attend the screening. Nobody even troubled to tell him it was taking place.

chapter 4

DEPARTURE

It was early afternoon a little before Christmas 1936. Back in Key West, Ernest Hemingway stood at the bend in the bar of Sloppy Joe's Saloon, surveying its beer-drenched tropical dimness.[1] Beyond the windows, glaring sunlight was scattering against the slats. This place—already the most famous saloon in Key West— was *his*. Hem had made it; he had given the joint its very name, after its floor, sloppy from water seeping from the barrels of iced fish that the owner, Josie Russell, kept in the kitchen. Now Hem held his commanding position beside "Big Jimmy" Skinner, the saloon's 300-pound African American barkeep, celebrating a good morning's work revising the seething manuscript of *To Have and Have Not*, drinking a Hemingway special—probably a potent *mojito*—dressed in his standard Key West attire: a none-too-fresh T-shirt, rope-soled shoes, and Basque shorts held up, just barely, by a ragged piece of rope. He was the duke in his domain.

Presently the door of Sloppy Joe's swung open, and as three strangers came strolling in, Hemingway saw what he had been waiting for: the woman who was going to save his life.

It wasn't every afternoon that a woman like Martha Gellhorn walked into Sloppy Joe's: a woman that young, that beautiful, that . . . *grand*. At twenty-eight, Martha Gellhorn was radiant with self-possession and her own excellence, quite tall, walking with a striking, swaying (some thought practiced) stride. She wore a black dress that worked wonderfully on a perfect figure about which Gellhorn would remain vain to the end of her days. Her strawberry blond hair—it was practically orange—spread across her shoulders in tumbling profusion. This very special woman was about to meet the man whose mere name, in bitter later years, she would later spit out like profanity—her son called it "the H-word." And Hemingway was gazing delighted at the woman he would later call "my biggest mistake."

But that was at the end. The beginning was enchantment and romance. Martha Gellhorn walked into Sloppy Joe's accompanied by an older woman and a man more or less her own age. Sizing up this trio over the rim of his drink, Hemingway quickly concocted a story. First of all, these people were rich. Hem decided they had just come off a yacht—a splendid yacht—moored in the marina. (In fact, they'd come to Key West on the Miami bus.) The Older Woman? The Girl's Mother. Had to be. (Right: she was Martha's forever-best-beloved mother, Edna Gellhorn.) And the Guy? Glaring, Hem decided he must be the Girl's Husband. (Wrong. He was Martha's younger brother, Alfred, on winter break from his first year in the med school that would launch him on his career as a distinguished physician.) Sizing up his rival through slits of jealousy, Hemingway figured it would take him maybe a week tops to turn *him* into history.[2]

The Girl seemed totally unaware that Ernest Hemingway was looking at her. She focused on talking to her companions. Hemingway strained to catch the conversation, but he was stuck at just that maddening distance at which you can catch a voice but not its words. The Girl had a strong rolling voice, ringing almost, with a decidedly patrician "Bryn Mawr accent."

The three must have ordered something. When they finished, they left. Martha was still talking when the saloon doors closed behind them, and she hadn't tossed even one wandering glance at the celebrity at the bar. She hadn't noticed him. It seemed.

*Hadn't **noticed** him?*

In December 1936, Martha Gellhorn was an intensely ambitious young writer, and Ernest Hemingway was her intellectual and artistic hero. She had just published—to warm acclaim—her second book, a collection of New Deal reportage called *The Trouble I've Seen*. Her first book had been fiction: a collection of stories with an epigram from *A Farewell to Arms*: the (dubious) claim that "nothing ever happens to the brave." She was on the rebound from a powerful love affair with a smart, socially prominent, young Frenchman, Bertrand de Jouvenel, who was the son of an aristocratic French publisher as well as stepson to the great Colette. Bertrand had left his young wife for Martha, but Bertrand had just become history. Throughout her years at Bryn Mawr—it *was* Bryn Mawr—Martha Gellhorn kept Hemingway's picture prominently pinned on her dormitory room wall. Now Martha was free, and Hemingway was on her mind.

*Hadn't **noticed**?*

Hemingway definitely noticed.

The next day, after his morning work was done, Hemingway was back at Sloppy Joe's, same place, same time, and he did not have to wait long. At almost the same minute as yesterday, the saloon doors swung open and Martha Gellhorn returned, still with her mother and "husband," and still talking. She was back in the black dress, and it still did wonderful things when she walked to their table. Big Jimmy had poured the man who liked to be called "Papa" his drink, and was wiping the bar when Hem picked up his glass and strolled to the Gellhorns' table. Skinner watched. The great man introduced himself. Then Martha Gellhorn stopped talking. She gave Hemingway her hand, bathing him in her most radiant smile.

Beauty, Skinner thought, *and the Beast*.

The three Gellhorns and Hem in Sloppy Joe's talked the afternoon away, right up to the December dusk, exchanging charm for charm.

Back at the Hemingways' house on Whitehead Street, Pauline was offering drinks to the evening's dinner guests. Four places had been set at the grand Spanish table of antique walnut. The cook, Miriam Williams, had made a fine fish dinner. At the same moment, Hemingway was urging all three Gellhorns to join *him* for dinner at a nearby restaurant—Penna's Garden of Roses— where he promised the food would be a big improvement over Sloppy Joe's. When Pauline felt she couldn't shrug off Ernest's absence any longer, she asked if one of the guests would mind swinging round to Sloppy Joe's—it *had* to be Sloppy Joe's—and see what the problem might be.

Hemingway greeted Pauline's messenger without a blink and introduced him to Miss Gellhorn and her family. Miss Gellhorn was a wonderful young writer with a new book just out, and her lovely face had just been on the cover of the *Saturday Review*.

Dinner? Well, something had come up. Tell Pauline to go ahead without him. Or maybe everybody would like to come round to Penna's later for dessert? Because that's where Ernest would be. At Penna's. With the Gellhorns.

It had begun.

People who knew Hem well were perplexed by the infidelity. Despite a lot of macho boasting about his conquests, his passion for Pauline had always been overwhelming. "I have never understood," Archibald MacLeish would say, "how he broke through so strong a feeling, although I watched Miss Gellhorn conduct her amazing and quite shameless attack on that marriage."³

Shameless attack?

Not according to Martha Gellhorn.

Martha Gellhorn always insisted upon the absolute innocence of her time in Key West. Seduction? What happened in Key West that Christmas was the meeting of a young writer with an older writer. Period. Going to Key West was entirely Alfred's idea. Before that very day, Martha had never *heard* of the town Hemingway made famous. Still less had she heard of some low bar called Sloppy Joe's. Running into Hemingway there was sheer chance. Her entire exchange with Hemingway in Key West had been strictly literary. There was no romance, no flirtation. Nothing like that even flickered through her mind.

The Whitehead Street house? She'd insisted she had been inside it exactly once—though the archives contain a letter in Martha's hand thanking Pauline for her hospitality and speaking of having been there so often that she *had* become a "fixture" there, "like a kudu head."⁴ Pauline? Well, Pauline had been a little cross with her when they first met. Martha couldn't imagine why—though Pauline's friends were immediately aware of something going on, and sensed Pauline responding by battening down against it, with studied silence and arch irony. Romance? Martha claimed never to have been with Hemingway after dark—though we know she and her family were with Hemingway after dark the first night. Besides, she claimed the whole visit was chaperoned by her mother and brother—though we know most of her stay happened after Edna and Alfred left Key West, and left her behind. She was with Hemingway constantly. "Where is Ernest?" Pauline would ask, looking around an empty room. Then, pause. Then, a lifted eyebrow. "Oh, I suppose he is busy again, helping Miss Gellhorn with her writing."⁵

Could Martha Gellhorn really not have noticed Hemingway's sexual interest in her? We *know* he started churning out hot fantasies about her from minute one. People who were there didn't think Martha *seemed* unaware of it. "There was no question about it," said the Hemingway's friend Lorine Thompson. "You could see she was making a play for him. Pauline tried to ignore it. What she felt underneath nobody knew."[6] Glancing out her kitchen window one evening, Miriam Williams was not surprised to see Hem and Martha out back, "kissing and carrying on."[7]

Lies, Martha snapped back. Nothing but Hemingway lies.

The two *did* talk. As 1936 turned into 1937, they were rapt in the ecstatic talkfest of smart people falling in love. They talked and talked and talked. And it turned out—a coincidence!—that both were going to be in Spain that spring. One of their prime topics was Spain and its war.

Their views on Spain were not yet identical. Though instinctively pro-Republic—"Franco," Hem wrote in November, "is a son-of-a-bitch of the first water"—the author of *A Farewell to Arms* was not yet an unequivocal partisan of the Spanish Republic. Gellhorn was. She bought whole the Popular Front line on the subject and reacted with spitting contempt against doubters. Her devotion to the platitudes of the Front remained steadfast until the day she died. Socially, she moved in the upper levels of Popular Front chic. It was during a weekend at the Connecticut home of the rich American Stalinist Frederick Vanderbilt Field, for example, that the communist film director Joseph Losey sat by the fireplace listening to his fellow guest Martha Gellhorn hold forth on how much Hemingway was in love with her and expanding on his manly chest and his prowess as a lover.[8]

Hem's chest aside, Martha silently condescended to her lover's grasp of politics. This was typical. So would Ivens and other Comintern types, who viewed Hem as a political simpleton whose "undeveloped" heart was in more or less the right place. So long as *they* guided it.

In those days, Hemingway's problem with the Spanish *causa* was simple: he didn't trust causes. He was the magus of the "separate peace"; he was the man who had helped lead his generation—the generation of the First World War—into the apolitical Bohemia of the twenties with its rejection of the rhetoric of war. Martha, on the other hand, belonged to a new generation of the thirties. Martha believed in "commitment."

With this difference came a divergence in their view of war. For the old apolitical Hemingway, war was horror; hateful, organized mass murder; a curse brought down on humanity by corrupt old men. Yet it was also incomparably compelling and interesting; the fullest and most important experience any human being—certainly any writer—could have. It was the evil that defined human destiny. And what were evil and destiny but *the* subjects of a serious mind? In war, life is lived with an intensity impossible in any other terms, precisely because war is tragic and vile, debasing and exalting at once. One lived most intensely nearest to death.

Hem's view of war, in short, was the reverse of simple.

The Popular Front, on the other hand, disdained such apolitical complexity. In Popular Front ideology, the moral business of war was naming the good guys and the bad guys, the better to help the former defeat the latter. Anything in between looked a little like treason. There was tragedy when, and only when, the good guys lost. Then and later, *the* issue for Martha Gellhorn in any war was simple: right and wrong. Wars—to which Gellhorn was drawn lifelong—were intense because war offered the most significant possible experience of this great watershed between right and wrong, which was invariably political. And so the proper response in war was simple: uphold the right and attack the wrong. Failure to do so was the result of stupidity, cow-ardice, or corruption.

That's not how the pre–Popular Front Hem saw it. He looked for humanity on both sides of the trenches, and the notion that "commitment" to a state—or a state's cause—could trump that perception of a common humanity still made his lip curl in dis-gust. Commitment? Until Martha, Hem had believed that "com-mitment" lied. "Commitment" killed. "Commitment" was the enemy of art. The role of the artist was to forge a separate peace. Art *was* the separate peace. "Commitment" was chickenshit.

Yet in 1936 Hem's views were becoming hopelessly unfash-ionable. His separate peace was on its way out, and he knew it. A new generation had discovered a new ethical chic, and the liv-ing, breathing, beautiful, perfect embodiment of it was Martha Gellhorn.

One thing united them. Both believed in the prime virtue of courage. In Hem, courage amounted to a counter-phobic obses-sion: he monitored his fear the way hypochondriacs take their temperatures. In Martha, he found a fellow traveler in his fight for bravery. They talked and talked about war and Spain and mastering fear. As they did, Spain and its war began to look like their never-never land, their romance.

Right after Christmas 1936, Hemingway offered Gellhorn the privilege of reading the entire manuscript of *To Have and Have Not* in all its libelous irresponsibility. On or very near the same day, Hem sent a telegram to Perkins announcing that his novel was done. Instantly grasping that it was a *roman à clef*, Martha lav-ished flattery on its author, feeling almost childish delight in how smart she was about its *clef*. Reading this ruthless study in dying friendships and ruined marriages, Martha did not miss a trick.[9]

At exactly this moment, Hemingway, who had been troubled by an ominous libel suit pending against Scribner's and Thomas

Wolfe, summoned his lawyer Maurice Speiser and Arnold Gingrich, his editor at *Esquire*, to Key West. The idea was for them to examine the manuscript of *To Have and Have Not* before Max Perkins saw it and give their opinion on some of the more delicate issues involved. Gingrich and Speiser read the book. They were not as enthusiastic as Martha. Gingrich sat down and told Hem straight out that the book was clearly—transparently—libelous and, at least in its current state, unpublishable. This was not the answer Hemingway was fishing for. The meeting ended in a chill, and Hemingway immediately started cooking up ingenious but legally meaningless reasons why Gingrich had to be wrong.[10]

Then on January 9, 1937, Martha Gellhorn suddenly left Key West, heading home to Saint Louis. Her departure seems to have hit Hemingway as a shock. At the crack of dawn the next morning, very agitated, he slapped his gear into a suitcase and went tearing off after her, using as his pretext a long-planned business meeting in New York. He *had* been planning a trip—settling details of his Spanish trip—but even so, this departure was frantic and unprepared. Hem was determined to catch up to Martha Gellhorn before she got out of Florida.

Facing the obvious, Pauline kept her cool. Just as Hem went tearing off, Arnold Gingrich wired Whitehead Street from Chicago, concerned about a rumor that Hemingway was ill. Pauline replied with this telegram: SECOND HAND REPORT ABSOLUTELY BASELESS. ERNEST IN MIAMI EN ROUTE TO NEW YORK IN SHALL WE SAY PERFECT HEALTH?[11]

Hem caught up with Martha in Miami. They were together and alone on the night of January 10. The next day, they took a train to Jacksonville, where Hem changed for New York, and Martha for Saint Louis. According to Gellhorn, it was during this train ride that Hemingway left her absolutely *astonished*—just *speechless*—with a declaration of love.

What followed was a long-distance *folie à deux*. The new couple—and "couple" was now the word—stayed in constant contact, exchanging letters and telephone calls daily, sometimes hourly. Back home in Saint Louis, Martha pretended to write. In New York, Hem installed himself in his customary squalid splendor in one of the grand hotels of which he was a lifelong connoisseur. This one was the Barclay. Around him was an array of expensive junk, boxed and unboxed, from the New York stores. The floor and wastebaskets were littered with empty Jack Daniel's bottles. Reeking empty glasses were perched on every piece of furniture. Books and newspapers were everywhere. He was busy every minute, negotiating with NANA, talking with Max Perkins, and dealing with the ever-clamorous press. In public, flashbulbs flared around him at the Stork Club and 21. In private, there were calls to Martha "every five minutes," especially when he was feeling "a little lonely and very excited."[12]

Martha got over her astonishment quickly. She was now fully receptive to Hem's long-distance romancing, returning his countless calls and letters with countless calls and letters of her own. By now both were explicit about the need for secrecy. Hem opened a separate bank account to finance the affair, knowing that Pauline—who managed their money and accounts, and was a stickler for every penny—would spot any new large category of expenditure that might be labeled "Martha." They began to banter about making their relationship permanent. Writing from the Barclay, not long after the ride to Jacksonville, Hem wrote to Martha saying, "if you get fond of people and get over it for Christ sake get over it now before I start thinking of you as something permanent like the horses in the fountain of the Place de l'Observatoire or the Lion de Belfort that Bumby saw, out of a dead sleep, coming back from Austria one time in a taxi from the gare and I said 'What's that, Bum?' and he said 'Le Lion de Belfort, a good friend and an old friend.'"[13] They loved the "conspiracy" of their coming rendezvous in Spain. Martha wrote to Hem: "have gotten myself a beard and a pair of dark glasses."[14]

Martha soon joined him in New York. There they were together and in love. It's fair to wonder—given the venomous hatred it became—whether the feeling between them was "true love." If it wasn't, it was a mighty persuasive look-alike. Each of them was a charmer, and each charmed the other silly. But there was much more. Each offered the other a life with new meaning. Martha offered Hemingway renewal, the restoration of his creative energy, and rescue from himself. Hemingway offered Martha courage, a world-class career mentor, and a future. It's possible to vulgarize such motives. True enough, Hemingway was looking for an out, and Martha was looking for a star. But what passed between them was surely better than that. Hemingway's responses to Martha during this period are those of a man whose imagination has come alive at her touch. The few Gellhorn letters to Hemingway that can be read—in transcripts now in the Princeton University Library—are passionate and amazingly articulate love letters. They are alive with intimacy, sensibility, and—there is just no other word—love. They are wonderful. It's through her letters—not her fiction, not even her journalism—that the talent of Martha Gellhorn still shines in a new age. Gellhorn's adopted son Sandy once remarked, "my mother was one of the great letter writers of the twentieth century." This is not mere filial devotion. It may be a simple literary fact.

It surely passed through Hem's mind that Martha would be thrilled to see him allied with a Popular Front project like *The Spanish Earth*. These winter weeks were when, as Helene courted him, Ivens's carefully set celebrity trap snapped shut.[15]

Martha was with him when Dos and Archie signed Hemingway on as a member of Contemporary Historians. Dos fictionalized the scene in *Century's Ebb*.

> George Elbert [Hem] was sober but he was in a nasty temper. Walking as he often did with a slight limp, he hauled his big bulk across the room until his chin almost touched Jay's [Dos's]. "What about this Dutch bloke?"
>
> "Everybody says Dirk de Jager [Ivens] is the best documentary film man since Eisenstein."[16]

And of course Hem met repeatedly with Max Perkins about *To Have and Have Not*. Simultaneously, Hem put the screws on *Scribner's* magazine to run a short story by Martha—Hem's first but by no means last career favor for Martha. Within a month she was pushing him to get her next book in front of Perkins.[17]

Then came a call from the past, a bell from his Paris life, tolling. Ten months before, Gerald and Sara Murphy's son Boath had died at the peak of adolescent good health. The irony was that it had always been Boath's brother Patrick who was the sick one: tubercular, in various sanatoriums for years. And now, just after Christmas, the long-feared end was coming for Patrick, too. Three days after arriving in New York, Hemingway left the city with Pauline's sister Jinny and Sidney Franklin—the "Brooklyn bullfighter" whom Hemingway was using as his yes-man and fac-totum—for a drive to the sanatorium at Saranac Lake where Patrick lay dying, watched over by his parents. It was time to say goodbye.

Patrick was keeping a diary. "Ernest came to see me for a few minutes before I went to bed. He is giving me a bearskin for Christmas, but it isn't ready yet."

There wasn't a whole lot of time left to get the bearskin ready. Patrick's sister Honoria, the only Murphy child to survive to adulthood, reported that Hemingway emerged from the boy's sickroom shaken. Once the bedroom door had been firmly closed, he burst into tears. "He looks so *sick*," Hemingway sobbed. "I can't stand seeing that boy so *sick*."[18]

Patrick died two weeks later, slipping into a coma. Once again, his parents knelt by a bedside. "You're just fine, Patrick," they kept saying. "We're here with you."

Scott Fitzgerald, who two years earlier had both offended and immortalized the Murphys with *Tender Is the Night*, was among the first to respond. In the old days, the rich and glamorous Murphys had left a more callow Fitzgerald merely dazzled. That was then. Fitzgerald's letter consoling Gerald and Sara over Patrick's death is a heartbreaking document.

When Hemingway got home to Key West, Pauline, alert to danger, made her countermove. If Ernest absolutely *had* to go to Spain, Pauline would go with him. Hemingway gaped. Go *with* him? Had Pauline gone crazy? That was out of the question. Spain was no place for a *woman*. Spain was *dangerous*. It was impossible, *impossible*.

They argued. The argument grew heated, then fierce, and in the end it was decided that Pauline would not go to Spain. She was mollified a little to hear that Hemingway would be taking Sidney Franklin with him. Pauline liked Sidney. So good with the boys. A little uncomplicated, maybe, but loyal. Pauline liked loyalty.

Cold comfort. Pauline had lost round one.

Sidney Franklin was the only American matador alive, and Hemingway had clinched Sidney's little career by incessantly publicizing that fact. Sidney responded—Pauline was right—

with loyalty. Sidney believed in being good to people who were good to him. That meant being good to Hem. And Pauline.

Sidney also knew Spain like a second home, and knew it in a more get-down real-life way than did fancy literary types. He spoke Spanish as well as Dos and a lot better than Hemingway. Hem, meanwhile, would need a right hand in Spain, and he did not hesitate to turn Sidney Franklin into his valet. Once Hem and his retinue hit the Hotel Florida in Madrid, Sidney was the man who made his life as master of revels workable.

Whom Hem disliked, Sid disliked. So it was a bad sign when Sid didn't like Dos. Meeting Sid at the Barclay, Dos found the Brooklyn matador "perched on the back of a sofa with a glass in his hand." When Dos said hello "a reptile glaze came over his eyes. His only mark of recognition was a stifled belch."[19]

According to *Century's Ebb*, Hem tried to cover Sidney's [in the novel, Cookie's] hostility.

> "Cookie's a wonderful guy," George Elbert spluttered in Jay's ear as they waited for the elevator. "Don't you go making hasty judgments about him. The only Brooklyn boy who ever made a name as a bullfighter. He's not at his best today. . . . Bad luck at Hialeah. . . . It's not the money. But it hurts him to play the wrong horse. You damn commies look down your nose at everybody.". . .

Martha detested Sidney from minute one. She saw this simpleton as a hostile witness, loyal to Pauline. After Hemingway's death, when Franklin had the temerity to question some of her claims about events in Spain, she instantly labeled him a liar.

It was almost time to depart. Though Gellhorn would always insist that Hemingway left for Spain without seeing her after Jacksonville, and had earlier feared that Hem might leave for Spain without finalizing a rendezvous in Madrid, we now know that, contrary to her claims, she was with him in New York until the day he sailed.

The scene around them in New York was hectic, loud, hard-drinking, and conducted in the blaze of the flashbulbs. He met with Dos, with Archie, with Max . . . and with Martha, who was with Hem most nights at his raucous round table in the Stork Club, though it's clear that she detested the scene surrounding him in New York. "They were in a crowd," writes Caroline Moorehead, Gellhorn's most recent biographer, "everyone drinking, rushing in and out, answering the telephone, going to the Stork Club and Twenty-One."

"Oh, it was very dashing," Martha wrote to a friend years later. "And vulgar."[20]

With Dos Passos, Martha was downright rude. Having read *To Have and Have Not*, Martha fully understood that there was no need to be polite to Dos Passos. And she was not. From the first handshake, she radiated contempt, "frozen-faced and icy."

Hem's hostility was more subtle, a shiver of nastiness in the air. He was querulous, inattentive, as in this moment from *Century's Ebb*: "George Elbert wasn't listening. He complained of a sore throat and kept poking his neck with his finger to see if it was swollen. Then he started humming. The most aggravating thing about George Elbert was a way he had of humming while you were trying to talk to him."

While Hem was making the gossip columns, Dos was making news in the trenches of left-wing intellectual life in New York— the branch of the literary world that Hem despised above all others. At just this time, a little band of intellectuals, standing almost alone in the worldwide left, was raising a protest against the Soviet Terror. Trotsky had moved from exile in Norway to

Mexico, and just as Hemingway was arriving in New York for his first visit, the "Great Exile" had demanded an impartial public hearing of Stalin's charges against him. In mid-January 1937, an organization called the American Committee for Leon Trotsky announced that it was organizing the independent commission Trotsky had asked for, chaired by the Columbia University philosopher John Dewey, and holding hearings in the Coyoacán neighborhood of Mexico City, from April 10 to 17—exactly when Dos and Hem were expected to be in Spain. The man behind the American Committee was a thirty-three-year-old novelist and Trotskyist firebrand James T. Farrell, author of ambitious and now classic novels of the Chicago Irish-American underclass, the *Studs Lonigan* trilogy. Farrell was himself a little unscrupulous. For one thing, he packed the roster of his committee with names he was using without permission.

In one of her most elegant essays—an account of her break with Stalinist opinion called "My Confession"—Mary McCarthy describes the sleight of hand Farrell used to pilfer her "signature" even though she had not expressed the faintest interest in joining his committee. At first, McCarthy was outraged when she discovered Farrell's ruse—but its consequences set her on a lifelong course of opposition to the Stalinist juggernaut in cultural politics. She was not the only writer whose signature Farrell lifted. Another was Edmund Wilson, who later became McCarthy's husband. And another was John Dos Passos.

A member of Contemporary Historians a self-proclaimed Trotskyite? It must have made the Comintern agents' blood freeze.

Dos tried to clear up the confusion—he was no Trotskyite—by going to the press with a straightforward denial. He was not a communist of any kind. Yet he did say he *was* awfully *interested* in the Trotskyist defense. Dos told reporters that he would love to be in Mexico for the show.

This was fatal talk. In the Soviet Union itself, anyone even re-motely connected to Trotsky was in mortal danger. Outside Russia? It is difficult today to recapture the language of loathing, the hate-your-guts invective, that Stalinist and Popular Front propa-gandists shot against anyone even marginally connected to Trot-sky's detested name. The counterattacks on Farrell's committee were hysterical. Lillian Hellman and the other Stalinists among the Contemporary Historians helped lead the pack with pre-cisely the invective that got Mary McCarthy's back up. She now signed on to the Trotsky committee for real, gladly, and with a will. And though in the end Dos Passos went to Spain rather than Mexico, he had been tarred with the Trotskyite brush, too.

On February 27, 1937, tearing himself away from Martha Gell-horn, Hemingway sailed for Europe on a sterling new French Line ship, the *Paris*, in a blaze of flashbulbs. Max Perkins came to see him off and wrote a cheery letter to Pauline about how fine it all looked. With Hemingway was Sidney and a hanger-on named Evan Shipman, a compulsive gambler who, though he called himself a poet, was more notable for the time he spent at the racetrack than writing poems, a man with enough money to support his habit and be full-time Hemingway flunky. He was going to Spain, too, where he would volunteer as a driver for the International Brigades.

To sidestep suspicion, Martha probably did not see Hem off that day. Instead she followed on another ship, perhaps a week or two later.

A couple of days after Hemingway sailed, just before Dos and Katy likewise left, Dos found himself summoned to dinner at an Italian restaurant in Greenwich Village by Carlo Tresca.

Carlo Tresca was a wise man in the *real* non-communist left worldwide, the doyen of Italian anarchism in the United States—

with his goatee, his expansive warmth, his glower of Mediterranean outrage, and his leftist battle passion. Tresca was in New
York as an exile from Europe's ideological inferno. Somehow or
other, he mingled the hopeless romanticism of the anarchist
dream with a relentless, quite clear-eyed *realpolitik*. Since the
days of Sacco and Vanzetti, Tresca had been Dos Passos's friend
and, despite Dos's "American naiveté," his political confidant.
Tresca was a totally undeceived anti-Stalinist, one of the first and
best in the senior ranks of the American left. He was about to
serve as one of the "commissioners" in Dewey's forthcoming tribunal over Trotsky in Coyoacán.

But tonight, Carlo was settling in for a little hard, straight,
get-down talk with his good but naïve friend Dos.

First they did some business. Dos wanted to interview some
anarchists in Spain, the leaders in Northern Spain and Catalonia. Carlos Tresca was giving Dos the letters he needed to make
those contacts. And there was another man Dos should meet: a
charismatic young Marxist named Andrés Nin. He'd once been
one of Trotsky's private secretaries—that's right, the old man
himself. He ran an anti-Stalinist cadre in Barcelona known as
the POUM.

Carlos handed Dos the letter that would get him in to see Nin.

Then there were the political realities of the war. Over their
fettuccini, Tresca wanted to instruct his friend on the new realities in Spain. First of all, understand that this was not a simple
war between the left and fascism. The Spanish Civil War was not
a two-way war. Spain was a *three*-way war. There was of course
the primary battle between the fascists, backed by Hitler and
Mussolini, against the Republic, which was made up of a loose
coalition of liberals and the radical left. But tragically, this coalition was also at war with itself, and in ways that the stupid outside world had not even guessed, let alone grasped. On one side

was the current prime minister, Francisco Largo Caballero, backed by the anarchists, by Spain's traditional working-class parties, and by the syndicalists. On the other side were the Soviets and the factions within the Republic serving the Soviets. The Stalinists, both Soviet and Spanish, detested Largo's coalition. They were preparing to destroy it, take over the Valencia government, and set up a regime that would serve Stalin's interests more forthrightly. That three-way split, Tresca proclaimed with uplifted finger, was *the* truth about Spain, without which, at this moment, nothing could be understood with clarity.

Dos balked. Oh no. No. For once Carlo was wrong. Dos knew the Republicans. His friend Pepe knew all the prime actors well, and Pepe had guided Dos through the whole scene. Communists? There were next to no communists in the Spanish government. They were in a minuscule minority.

Tresca waved aside this little protest. When had Dos been there?

Two years ago.

Two years was a very long time in politics. Carlo's information came from the best sources there were. Here's the fact: the Soviets were planning to take control in Valencia. Maybe they had been nowhere two years ago. Today they were on the verge of running the government, and running it Stalin's way. Spain had become dangerous, and not just because of the damned *fascisti*. People would be killed. Katy must not go with him.

Dos was incredulous. Tresca wearily waved his incredulity aside.

The next subject was this damn movie Dos had gotten himself mixed up in making and that Tresca's own companion, Margaret DeSilver, a rich woman, had been foolish enough to help fund. Dos beamed: yes, yes, his movie, *The Spanish Earth.*

Stalinist propaganda, Tresca snapped. He spoke "with the self-possession of a croupier at Monte Carlo."

Dos drew himself up, shocked. Oh, no, no, no. He and Hem had been firmly, repeatedly assured that they would be completely in charge of shooting *The Spanish Earth*.

Tresca laughed in his friend's face. "Completely in *charge*?" Would Dos perhaps be interested in knowing that his "cameraman" was a crypto-communist apparatchik?

Dos stared back. This was too much. "I've known hundreds of Party members," he protested to Carlo, "and I don't think this boy fits the specifications. His people are Dutch Catholics."

Tresca may have laughed again, but the conversation was becoming unfunny. He asked Dos to listen carefully. Carlo's sources, he once again made clear, were not wrong. Dos's director was a Stalinist operative. Dos would have no control over a single frame of *The Spanish Earth*. Moreover, Dos did not understand what he was about to confront in Spain. When he got there, party members would supervise him everywhere he went. Not just Ivens. The party would choose everybody he saw.

Oh no, no. no. Dos knew Spain, knew politics, knew Ivens. Knew them well.

"John," Tresca said at last, quietly and firmly. "They are going to make a monkey out of you . . . a *beeeg* monkey."

Dos blinked back, hurt and unbelieving. Tresca would not relent. John Dos Passos was going to a country he no longer knew. He had no idea what he was going to face in Madrid.

"Listen to me, John," Tresca said, leveling his gaze. "If the communists don't like a man in Spain, right away, they shoot him."

PART II

THE THEATER
OF WAR

chapter 5

THE CAPITAL OF
THE WORLD

José Robles was probably murdered right around the time Hemingway reached Spain.[1]

The *Paris* docked in Le Havre on March 6; Hemingway reached Valencia ten days later, on March 16. The precise date of Robles's arrest is unknown: Dos Passos eventually concluded that his friend had been shot in mid-March, but only after Robles had been held for an indeterminate time between being seized and being put to death.

It was night when an anonymous arrest squad arrived at the Robles's cramped quarters in a side street in Valencia. They demanded entry. They were "extralegal police," and when they came bursting in, they presented no identification. They held no warrant. They did not mention any charge. They wanted Robles, but they also wanted something that belonged to Robles, and they ransacked the place, searching for it: a notebook in which Robles had been making jottings about his war experience, observations for what he had been guileless enough to tell people he might turn into a book when the war was over. The secret policemen were determined to get that notebook.

Once they had it, they slapped handcuffs on their man, and while Márgara watched, dazed with incomprehension and fear, they took him away.

Robles was held prisoner under "conditions of great secrecy," for . . . a certain period of time. How long? Long enough for his killers deliberately to weigh the exact timing and purpose of his death. It was probably during his imprisonment that Hemingway and Dos left for Europe, and Hemingway made his much-publicized entry into the theater of war. It is quite possible that Robles was still alive—though where? in what condition?—when Hemingway arrived in Madrid. Only one date is certain: by the 26 of March, ten days after Hemingway got to Madrid, and about a week before Dos Passos reached Spain, José Robles had been put to death.

Through all the decades left to him—John Dos Passos died in 1970—Dos would be haunted by the imagined image of Robles's last hours and minutes. Knowing nothing of the factual details, the clichés of execution crowded his mind. He'd picture his tall, proud friend, imprisoned, accused, standing before his killers. He'd see the trigger pulled, see the human flinch of agony before the bullet, and imagine the light of consciousness shattered. But what did he—and what do we—really know about what happened? Almost nothing. After his arrest, and after one (perhaps two) visits from Márgara, José Robles vanished without a trace. Was Robles interrogated? By whom? About what? Was he tortured? How? And why? What did they—whoever "they" were—want? A great many other victims would be tortured and interrogated around this same time, the most famous of whom is probably Andrés Nin, the man Tresca wanted Dos to see in Barcelona, and whom Dos would indeed interview just before Nin was seized and taken away in May. After decades of official and quasi-official lies, the archives have disclosed many of the concrete details about Nin's arrest, interrogation, torture, and eventual murder. We know who took him and who tortured him, and when and where. We know who gave the order to kill him and just where they dug his shallow grave.

But Robles?

Even during the sixties, at Spence's Point, Virginia, long after he had learned the few facts he knew, Dos Passos was still seeing Robles being shot, seeing bullets ripping into him, the crumpling corpse oozing blood, the face of a twenty-year friendship stilled, the dead eyes open. Sometimes he imagined Pepe waiting for the end in a squalid cell with straw on the floor; sometimes he imagined some rotting food in a pan at his feet, anonymous prisoners huddled in the cell with him. Sometimes he would picture the chief of some sort of drumhead tribunal strutting into the stinking space and reading out some sort of "verdict." He would see Robles yanked away; the image of the cell would give way to the scene of a firing squad. He pictured how Pepe might stand, his friend's familiar posture, waiting for death.

("Right away they shoot him.")

Dos would imagine the row of rifles lifting for the aim.

("The infinite gentleness of the saints lowering the Conde de Orgaz into the grave.")

Most likely, there probably wasn't any drumhead trial, any court-martial, verdict, or firing squad. The most notable fact about Robles's killing is the total absence of any paper trail, at least in Spain, indicating what happened. The squad that arrested Robles was anonymous. It was not from either the Spanish police or the army. One might protest that in this terrible war thousands of Spaniards died undocumented. True enough, but those thousands of anonymous dead were not senior figures in the Republican establishment, placed in highly sensitive positions, with influential connections, people whose disappearance and death could become a matter of international controversy. And the most important people in the Republican government were not elaborately covering up their deaths.

Robles was no mere incidental casualty of war. He was killed for some reason that mattered to his killers. And it also mattered to them that he vanish without a trace.

In the full glare of publicity, the *Paris* landed in Le Havre on March 6, and after ten days of doing business in Paris, Hem and his new pal Ivens boarded an Air France puddle-jumper in Toulouse and flew into the war-ravaged land to the south. Five days after Hem got to Spain, Martha Gellhorn joined him, making the rendezvous they'd been planning since Key West. Two weeks after Martha's arrival, a talkative, likable, hard-drinking French communist truck driver named Marcel got Dos into Spain, crossing the border at Perpignan and proceeding to Valencia, where after an ambivalent official greeting, Dos was confronted, for the first time, with the mystery of Robles's disappearance.

The theatrics surrounding Hemingway's arrival in France in the chilly springtime do not play well in retrospect.

The man who stepped before a phalanx of cameras and flash-bulbs at the pier in Le Havre was Hem the macho kick-ass, weighing in for his next bout. He stood posing for his publicity, peering through steel-rimmed glasses, answering the hollering reporters' questions with his dukes up, striking pugilistic postures, drawling answers with a country-boy "yop" and "nope," all the while keeping his chest "bulging out of his coat like a parapet." He was thirty-eight years old. The cameras loved him. He seemed to surge with energy, flushed with color against his still very black hair. He was going to Spain to check out the "toys" that the "boys" were playing with. He was going to see how the "little people" were dealing with this great big war.

Yop.

The publicity frenzy continued in Paris, where Hem spent a crowded ten days getting his papers in order and tending to his fame. He installed himself in the very grand Hotel Dinard; Sidney Franklin was put up in a lesser establishment nearby.

Hemingway soon went to the Deux Magots on the Boulevard Saint-Germain to meet Ivens, who had returned from Madrid to show his Comintern bosses—but not Hem—the nearly completed rushes of *The Spanish Earth*. Their rendezvous at the Deux Magots was a boisterous get-acquainted session spiked with contempt. The two men drank and backslapped; Hemingway talked about what a great time they would have: "My beautiful girlfriend is coming. She has legs that begin at her shoulders."[2] Sizing up his man, Hem intuited Ivens might be brave. In this at least he was right. "He was absolutely fearless," MacLeish remembered.

But when they talked about the disasters of war, Ivens silently separated himself from Hem. Bourgeois sentimentalism, Ivens thought. Revolutionaries did not wring their hands over the human cost of history's march. "Anyone who worries about the finer shades is a bad propagandist," Ivens thought. "The Nazis tell lies and the Russians tell the truth. That is what the message has got to be."[3] After their meeting, Ivens would quite falsely tell his Comintern contacts that Hem had come to Spain without even knowing which side he was on.

Not long after Hem left New York, Dos had made the transatlantic crossing with Katy on the old three-funnel Cunarder *Berengaria*. A cold, wet sky had clamped down hard around the white-capped vastness of the North Atlantic as the ship made its way to England. The cutting briny chill on deck never let up. On board, Dos mixed and mingled with various grandees of the New Deal. Bernard Baruch was on board, and so was Joseph Kennedy, who was crossing with his sons. Seizing the opportunity, Dos Passos set out to promote American aid for Republican Spain among these Important People. Listening to him while surrounded by girls young enough to be his great-granddaughters, the noncommittal Baruch leaned on his cane, smiled, and asked Dos to join him on a constitutional around the first-class deck. Kennedy condescended, brushing off Dos's little speech with the remark that Dos and his friends had got themselves some top-notch publicity in Hemingway. "My boys read everything he writes."

Once in Paris, Dos spent ten days or so doing interviews for *Fortune*, which in 1937, with MacLeish as an editor, had a surprisingly leftish tilt, at least among its staff. The interviews were about the French Popular Front, including one with the French premier, Léon Blum.

Getting into Spain in those days was not easy—not unless, as Hemingway bitterly complained, you were one of the 12,000 Italian fascists being brought in to fight for Franco. *They* swept in without a hitch. Though Hemingway's papers were validated quite quickly, Sid's were not. In the end, Hemingway went ahead with Joris, leaving Sid to untangle the mess on his own, which he did two weeks later, so that he left Paris at the same time Martha Gellhorn did.

Even Hem had some trouble crossing the border. Two tries by car failed. Things worked only when Hem and Ivens got onto an Air France flight first to Barcelona, and then to Alicante, a town on Spain's southern Mediterranean coasts.

In Alicante, Hem and Ivens deplaned into a victory fiesta. Hem was enchanted. There were few things in life that he loved more than a Spanish fiesta, and this fiesta was celebrating a victory, one of the Republic's few: its recent triumph in the battle of Guadala-jara. Alicante was intoxicated with the win; people spilled out onto the sidewalks with accordions and guitars, making the music that got the people dancing. Under the flowering trees, lovers were locked in kisses, and out on the sparkling jewel blue of the Mediterranean waves, even the pleasure boats seemed to be danc-ing for joy. Suddenly, and for a change, people were tasting not tragic defeat but good simple victory. Hemingway joined them, singing and dancing and drinking from their wineskins until he and Ivens piled into the car sent by the Ministry of Information for the drive north to the capital in Valencia. The road between the towns snaked through coastal orange groves. Ivens drove and Hem rolled down all the windows, so the smell of orange blos-soms filled the car. Their colors went rivering by them on both sides. Hemingway's eyelids sank; he dozed and dreamed; then snapped awake, only to doze again, dreaming about orange blos-soms, about weddings, about flowers, about brides.

There were precious few orange blossoms in the assaulted city of Madrid. "The first thing you remember," Hem wrote about the city when he arrived in mid-March, "is how cold it was." After a pompous official welcome and lavish lunch in Valencia, Hem was supplied for the duration with not just safe-conduct papers and Valencia's fulsome official blessing but every possible privilege the regime could bestow on a correspondent, beginning with not one but two cars, complete with chauffeurs. The drive from the Mediterranean Valencia to the embattled, bloody, besieged gran-ite cold on the heights of Madrid took seven hours. In that third week of March, you could still see your breath while walking through the smashed streets. At night, snow swirled in a darkness deepened by blackout. In one sense, Madrid was abandoned; the government had fled. But the city was also filled with people, and not just Spaniards. Everywhere you looked, you saw journalists, those tourists in desolation. There were a few Russians; there were many International Brigadiers of many nationalities, men whom the *madrileños* had started out by calling "Russians" before switching to call them—as a joke—"Mexicans." Though Franco and his senior general, Emilio Mola, had relented in the November assault, Madrid remained under light siege. The dust from shattered buildings, a bitter mix of granite and plaster. The dust got onto your tongue and into your nose and eyes and you couldn't spit it away. In the streets, bomb craters were pockmarks on a miniature moon. Everywhere the façades of buildings had been sheered away, leaving honeycombs of rooms sagging in the open air. Dos Passos called it the "dollhouse effect." On the sidewalks, you could see spoors of human blood, ribbons left by the running wounded, their blood's crimson turned black or a rusty brown.

As Hem and Ivens first approached Madrid from Valencia, their chauffeur—his name was Tomás—was overwhelmed with emotion. Tomás was short—around four feet—and his Spanish lisp was rendered a little comic by toothlessness. Like anyone spending time with Hemingway, Tomás had of course been pulling steadily at Hem's constantly passed silver whisky flask as he drove. When the driver saw the outline of Madrid rising in the road before him, it was almost more than Tomás could bear.

"Ah!" he called out, "Madrid! The capital of my heart!"

Hemingway stared. What had Tomás just said? This was just too damn perfect. The year before Hem had written a short story—it is a great short story—about the death of a very young man who has come in from the country to work in the big city as a waiter, only to be accidentally killed while playing around as a *torero* with his fellow waiters, after hours. The story is called "The Capital of the World."

"The capital of my heart!" Tomás said.

"And the capital of my soul," Hem murmured, as if answering a priestly invocation.

Everybody who was anybody was at the Hotel Florida.

The Hotel Florida stood on the Plaza de Callao on the Gran Vía until it was razed in 1960; in 1937 it was where the Ministry of Information put up reporters known to be partial to the cause of the Republic. Life in the Florida during the siege has been the subject of many a memoir. The place sounds like a cross between a celebrity cruise, a brothel, and the loony bin. Life there could be rough, and a little scary, but fun. Before the war, the Florida had been a medium-sized gem of Mediterranean art nouveau, with its atrium soaring up through all ten of its stories. Even in 1937, hunkered down against the siege, the place did have a certain chic. The cluster of famous faces gathered in the atrium of the Florida in those days was like some sort of Hirschfeld cartoon of journalistic celebrity.

Early in the war, André Malraux had stayed in the Florida. By March another French writer-aviator, Antoine de Saint-Exupéry, the author of *The Little Prince*, was in residence, as was the dashing Hollywood star Errol Flynn, the stately Duchess of Atholl, the rich, smart Virginia Cowles, the chattering English journalist Claud Cockburn, and now Ernest Hemingway, soon to be followed by John Dos Passos. Since the end of Franco's assault, Madrid was living with danger in a new way. Shells were still flying into the city, and they were still killing people. Some of those shells of course managed to paste into the Hotel Florida, and when they did, there could be pandemonium among the celebrities. But the Florida was a sturdy structure and the shells were not very big. It was still war, but in a mildly desperate way, Madrid was a comparatively safe place. Between real safety and real risk, there was room for a kind of apocalyptic tourism. The Florida was a Mecca for movie stars and Broadway divas who wanted to spend a week or so seeing, and being seen, as they played with the fire of real war.

Yet the Florida didn't offer much in the way of *luxe, calme*, or *volupté*. It was overrun with prostitutes—"whores de combat" Hemingway punningly called them—and all night long the corridors churned and doors kept slamming. Its restaurants barely functioned: food was scarce in Madrid, and provisions, even provisions for Ernest Hemingway, had to be scrounged. Hem and his party usually had lunch and dinner at a nearby restaurant called the Gran Vía, the de facto press club of Madrid, a basement cave, blue with smoke during the late Spanish dinner hour, and loud with the shouting of opinion, ambition, and ideology, a dank space with a honky-tonk feel, a little gaudy with rippling pink lights and the stink of the prostitutes' perfume. Bisecting the dining room was a long table where Hemingway was usually installed, drinking and holding forth. Around the rim of the room were alcoves big enough for two or a few, lairs for lust, love, or conspiracy. The Gran Vía was the one restaurant open in the city, and its food ranged from the fundamental to the revolting. Sentries had been posted at the doors, pistols at their waists and rifles in their hands, guarding this foreigners' haven from the women of Madrid, who clustered around, begging for scraps. Though the Gran Vía often ran short of food, its cheap liquor seemed to flow from an uncappable artesian source. You were much more likely to leave the Gran Vía drunk than full, and of course that suited Hem to a T.

At the Florida, Hemingway was installed in room 108, which connected to room 109, where Sid stayed. Room 108 was supplied with provisions impossible for other guests, stored in a large wardrobe. Hem was generous with them, and his room soon became a favorite meeting place, the one place in the hotel where you could get a real breakfast, and once Sid was there to cook, the aroma of the eggs and bacon and real coffee transfixed the building each morning. Hem had a gramophone and a supply of Chopin records, which he played incessantly and at all hours. Polonaises and nocturnes were heard while Franco's shells whizzed over the Florida, aimed mostly at the Telefónica building almost across the street, the tallest edifice in the city, its communications center, and a standard target for Franco's gun emplacements in the western suburbs.

Hemingway's first visit to the front was to the battlefield of the Guadalajara triumph. Driving through biting cold and flurrying snow, he and Ivens were taken to a field about fifty miles from Madrid, guided by a German Comintern general named Hans Kähle. There they found the ground strewn with the corpses of Franco's Italian volunteers. The victors' task of cleanup—cleanup of corpses—had not yet begun. The bodies of Italian soldiers lay strewn across the field like broken dolls flung down in the tantrum of some gigantic child, gape-jawed corpses staring upward into the falling snow and glacial rain, never to flinch again. Scattered around them in the battle-mud was their equipment. Shovels especially. When the assault got heavy, the Italians had begun trying to dig in for defense. And then there was . . . paper. For some reason there was paper everywhere, fluttering in the uncanny silence. "Why *paper*?" Hem wondered. Every now and then one of Franco's bombers would fly over the field of the fascist defeat, as if poking around for something to hit in vengeance. This was the first scene of the war that Hem and Ivens witnessed together. Hem described it in a NANA report, but it was a little downbeat for propaganda. The scene does not appear in *The Spanish Earth*.

Martha Gellhorn arrived in Madrid five days after Hemingway, and she arrived with Sidney Franklin at her side.

One of the issues about which Gellhorn would later accuse Franklin of lying was the significance of their simultaneous arrival. Franklin claimed that they arrived together because he had been helping her on her way from the start. He claimed to have met her in Paris when she arrived, and to have accompanied her to Toulouse as she set off for Spain, putting her—and a large amount of luggage—into a taxi for the first leg of her trip. Next, though they entered the country by different routes—why, one wonders?—they arrived in Valencia at the same time and were driven to Madrid in the same car, checking into the Florida side by side, and walking together to greet Hem in the Gran Vía side by side.

Sid thought this was proof he had helped Martha get to Spain.

Lies, Gellhorn sneered. More Hemingway lies.

Martha Gellhorn insisted that every step of her trip to Spain had been made strictly on her own. She had not one speck of help from Hem, and still less, if less be possible, from Hem's Brooklyn flunky. Hemingway had nothing—*nothing*—to do with her trip to Spain. When the biographer Bernice Kert asked Martha about Franklin's claims to the contrary, Gellhorn laughed them off. Absurd, she said. Impossible. Proof of the absurdity, she claimed, was that she hadn't even *seen* Hemingway since leaving Key West and Jacksonville, insisting that Hemingway had left New York for Spain without making any kind of contact with her. So how could Franklin possibly have met her in Paris? He had no idea when she would arrive.

Kert had to concede that this sounded true.

Except that it wasn't true. Hemingway, and therefore Franklin, almost certainly did know exactly when she would arrive. Martha Gellhorn had been with Hemingway in New York every day throughout the end of February, when all the bookings had being made. Gellhorn saw Hemingway the day he sailed; each of them surely had the other's coordinates. She herself sailed on a different ship only to avoid public suspicion.

Did Franklin put her, with lots of luggage, into a taxi in Toulouse? Another preposterous falsehood, Gellhorn claimed. She had left both Paris and Toulouse alone, crossing into Spain wearing only the clothes on her back, equipped with one small knapsack filled with canned goods, and carrying only fifty dollars in cash.

So there.

Really?

After leaving Toulouse, Gellhorn undoubtedly crossed the Spanish border on her own. But was she carrying no change of clothes and a mere fifty dollars? One can wonder. Even in 1937, for an affluent young American to enter Spain carrying only fifty dollars in cash—unless of course she had access to funds within the country—would have been simply stupid, a charge rarely leveled against Martha Gellhorn. Did she cross with only the clothes on her back? So Spartan a style of travel would have been very unlike her. Virtually every witness to Martha Gellhorn's stay in the Hotel Florida notes that she was invariably impeccably and even stylishly dressed, provided with many changes of clothing that seem unlikely to have been stuffed into one small knapsack filled with Spam.

Then there's this business about the fifty dollars. Martha Gellhorn always insisted that she paid her whole way, refusing to accept a cent from Hemingway. This is plausible, if unprovable: Gellhorn seems to have been quite scrupulous about money. Yet the few available scraps of her Spanish diary show that, once in Madrid, Martha Gellhorn spent many hours shopping. The city was filled with bargains. She ordered several sets of shoes to be made—and gave the shoemaker a nasty tongue-lashing when the results displeased her. She at least priced having a silver fox fur coat made to order, and she may even have gone ahead with the deal. Certain it is that Martha Gellhorn left Spain wearing a stunning silver fox coat. She always claimed the coat had been a gift—a tribute—from the men of the International Brigades. Another oddity. A conspicuously luxurious silver fox coat is a strange—and mighty expensive—gift for a set of mainly penniless leftist soldiers to offer any reporter, however sympathetic and good-looking. So how did Gellhorn really get her fur? We don't know. But it's not likely that she got it with the change from fifty dollars.

The point of all these slippery claims was to prove Gellhorn's intrepid independence from Hemingway. That is why she told Carlos Baker that when she stepped into the Gran Vía on the night of her arrival, Hemingway's greeting left her secretly enraged. "I knew you would get here daughter, because I fixed it so you could." Fury. *She* knew that Hemingway had done nothing at all.

Unless Sidney Franklin's claims were true, and Hem *had* helped. Interestingly, Gellhorn's most recent biographer, Caroline Moorehead—with her unique access to the archives—quietly drops this last anecdote, saying only that Martha shrugged off the braggadocio in Hem's greeting as one of the "foibles of genius."[4]

In truth the whole story of Gellhorn's totally "independent" arrival in Spain is highly improbable. Martha and Hem were together before they left the States. Before and probably after that, they stayed in touch with countless letters and telephone calls. Their rendezvous in Madrid had been an obsessive topic of discussion since January. Even if they somehow lost touch, contact could have been reestablished with one phone call. The Madrid telephones worked, and since every newspaper reader in the world knew that Hemingway was staying in the Hotel Florida, it seems unlikely that Martha Gellhorn did not. Sidney Franklin was in Paris when Martha was also there, and Sid knew exactly where Hemingway was. No known fact challenges his claim to have accompanied her to Toulouse. Martha's claim that their simultaneous arrival in Spain was pure meaningless coincidence is therefore quite difficult to believe. And if Martha was really angry with Hemingway, she kept the fact well concealed. Those who saw the pair at the Florida saw a couple rapt in mutual adoration.

He promptly introduced her to the privileged people gathered around him. Not least among these was Mikhail Koltsov. Koltsov's effect on both Hemingway and Gellhorn was profound. The awestruck Martha, impressed by the Russian's "quiet manners of complete confidence," recorded in her diary that he was "Stalin's man, Stalin's eyes and ears on the spot."[5] At the Gaylord—the luxury hotel were Soviet "advisers" were billeted—the waves parted around Koltsovs comings and goings. Here is Hemingway describing the arrival of Koltsov's car at the hotel. The sentries at the Gaylord's doors snap to salute "a little man . . . wearing black riding boots, gray breeches, and a gray tunic. With tiny hands and feet, puffily fragile of face and body, with a spitting way of talking through his bad teeth, he looked comic [at first] . . . but he had more brains and more inner dignity and outer insolence and humor than anybody he had ever known."[6]

Koltsov's people had surrounded Hemingway from the moment of his arrival. Ivens was a Koltsov protégé. Gustav Regler, who became very close to Hemingway at this time, was, too. The business of keeping Hemingway seeing and saying what the Popular Front wanted him to see and say was in the hands of these three apparatchiks: Koltsov as mentor, Ivens as collaborator, and Regler as friend.

Hem was especially impressed by the way Koltsov toyed, verbally, with totalitarian power, by the urbane way Koltsov played with terror. "We detest with horror," Koltsov would intone in lilting sarcasm, "the duplicity and villainy of the murderous hyenas of Bukharanite wreckers and such dregs of humanity as Zinoviev, Kamenev . . . and their henchmen."[7] Hemingway would watch the crooked smile on Koltsov's lips, waiting for the punch line. "Because I make jokes sometimes," Koltsov continued, "and you know how dangerous it is to make jokes, even in joke?"

Koltsov "joked" about the Terror. He was also a part of it, as perpetrator and victim-to-be. It was Koltsov who concocted the disinformation used to destroy Andrés Nin; his articles in *Izvestia* provided the Popular Front with the smears described by Orwell in *Homage to Catalonia*. But Nin is only one of the more famous cases. Koltsov regularly filed top-secret reports with the NKVD denouncing—thereby killing—"Trotskyite scum" in Spain. He must surely have been aware of the Robles case. Gorev was Koltsov's close associate; they had been together constantly during November; they lived in the same hotel. Koltsov had made manipulating Hemingway a priority. Just as he shunned Dos Passos. No surprise there. He knew exactly how the regime had turned against Dos: he was a close ally of Radek; he had been an interpreter and aide to Rodek at the All-Union Congress when the new policy was announced.

He was the master-muse of the Popular Front.

He was also a dead man walking.

We now know that at precisely this time—May 1937—Stalin laid plans to wash his hands of Koltsov. The propagandist only had just barely escaped execution in the first purge trials. His own prime patron had been Lev Kamenev, and Kamenev was a prime defendant in the first round of the Terror trials. Yet to the surprise of many, Stalin spared Koltsov, deeming him too valuable in the Popular Front to kill. Yet.

In May 1937 Stalin was naturally planning how to handle his forthcoming alliance with Hitler. Once the deal was in place, Stalin would of course want to rid himself of once-useful people whose main claim to fame was their now redundant "antifascism." The plan, therefore, was to stage a fifth wave of Terror trials, liquidating this "antifascist scum." Stalin had already picked the star monsters for the last murderous phase of his great deception. Chief among them—alongside his Jewish foreign minister, Maxim Litvinov—was to be that jackal, that "cosmopolitan" (read: Jewish) monster, Mikhail Koltsov.

It was only Hitler's invasion of the USSR that prevented this last terror trial from taking place. Not that the German invasion saved Koltsov. In 1942, Stalin ordered him shot anyway.[8]

It was into this cauldron of compromised celebrity that, at the beginning of April, a weary, wrenlike, worried woman from New York arrived. Helped by nobody, she hauled herself into the frigid lobby of the Hotel Florida and dropped her bags.

Josie.

Josephine Herbst was a novelist and journalist who in her time occupied a more or less respectable place in the New York literary scene's second or third rank. She was reasonably prolific, and the critics found her books sort of interesting, if a little too much indebted to Hemingway. She was mainly known, when she was known at all, as a hard-left journalist and polemicist. She wrote tough articles for semi-visible leftist publications, and her prose was considerably more sophisticated and well turned than the general run of Stalinist boilerplate. Quietly but decisively, she served the Stalinist propaganda machine, and it in turn kept her in business—just barely—as a writer.

People liked Josie, and she knew "everybody." The index to her letters reads like a literary Who's Who of the era. Chief among her famous friends were Dos and Hem. Josie and her beloved—but by 1937 lost—husband John Hermann had started out together with Hem and Dos in Paris during the twenties. In the Parisian springtime, they had all drunk together at the Dôme. They were all going to be great writers together. That was the dream, and Josie had dreamed it, after all, with the best. Behold! Hem had become Ernest Hemingway. Dos had become John Dos Passos. And Josie? John?

When it was time for the exiles' return Josie and John came back to New York. There Josie did at least publish quite prolifically, and developed a certain dun-colored reputation. (John Hermann did not do as well: he published one indifferently received book that sank almost as soon as it saw light.) The whole thing was a little sad.

Yet both Hem and Dos genuinely loved Josie, and loved her right up to the end. Pauline remained especially close to her. John and Josie used to go down to Key West, and though Hemingway—Hemingway!—thought that John drank a lot more than he should, everyone always had a good time. There was real affection there.

And now, somehow or other, Josie had got herself into Spain.

It is almost physically painful to contemplate the face that stares out of the passport photo that Josephine Herbst took with her to Europe that year. From under heavy eyebrows, a chinless, bird-like woman stares, connecting to the camera with huge, hurt, smart, defeated eyes. Is she angry? Or are they tears that she's fighting back? She is dressed without style, and maybe she doesn't care. More likely, she cares beyond caring. She looks determined, and yet the determination in those eyes is un-touched by anything like hope. Here is a face that says many things, but maybe the most important of them is that being Josephine Herbst hurts, hurts a lot, and hurts almost all the time.

The real question over Josephine Herbst's trip to Spain is its sponsorship. Under whose auspices did Herbst gain access to the country? Who paid her way? She did not represent any Ameri-can publications capable of incurring the expense of sending her, and she had no money of her own. Martha Gellhorn's press credentials from *Collier's* magazine were pretty shaky, but she did at least have a real letter from an important editor to present at the border. She could afford to pay her own way—though not on fifty dollars—and in due course did produce some very con-spicuous and well-paid journalism for *Collier's*. So far as is known, Herbst had no press credentials at all, and she filed no dispatches from Spain with anyone, though she did make some stirring radio broadcasts to America from the front. So how did she get to Spain?

The evidence is pretty conclusive that Josephine Herbst got to Spain under the covert auspices of the Soviet propaganda apparatus.

Sometime in the early spring of 1937, Herbst received an invi-tation from the broadcasting arm of the Spanish Republic's pro-paganda office, asking her to come to Spain and do her broadcasts about the Spanish struggle. It is possible (though not certain) that the Republican government paid Josie's passage to Europe and all or part of her hotel bills. Why Josephine Herbst of all people should have been asked to make these broadcasts is far from clear: hers was certainly not a name well known to the American radio public. Any number of American spokesmen for the Popular Front would have had more impact. Yet they were not necessarily part of the Soviet propaganda apparatus. Josie was.

The highest-level Spanish official to interest himself in Herbst's presence in the country was Julio Alvarez del Vayo, who in addition to being (off and on) foreign minister of the country was deeply involved in all the Republic's propaganda in the democracies. Josie's invitation to Spain would have required his approval. Alvarez del Vayo's closest associate in the Comintern apparatus was Otto Katz, who was the prime lieutenant in Spain (and elsewhere) of the Comintern's propaganda czar, Willi Münzenberg—and Katz was Josie's highest contact in the Soviet *apparat*. And it was through Katz that Josie met Alvarez del Vayo.

Josie's first move, once she had been invited to Spain, was to contact Otto, sending him a letter, which Katz's wife, and fellow Soviet agent, Ilse Katz, acknowledged March 20, 1937, noting with pleasure Josie's plan to go to Spain and offering her help. Ilse told Josie to contact her in Paris at Agence Espagne, a press office that was in fact a Comintern front run by Otto Katz in close association with Alvarez del Vayo.

Six days later, Agence Espagne provided Josie with a letter of introduction to Alvarez del Vayo, who was then the foreign minister of the country. The letter made a number of fictitious claims about Josie's importance as a journalist. It was to be hand-delivered to Alvarez del Vayo. Personally.

And so an obscure, seemingly unconnected American journalist was handed a passkey letter from the Comintern, on the strength of which she proceeded from Paris straight into a protracted private interview with the foreign minister of Spain—who was also an agent in the upper hierarchy of the Münzenberg political machine.

When Josie was admitted to Alvarez del Vayo's office in Valencia, they settled in for a long, private meeting behind closed doors. They doubtless discussed many things. One prime topic, however, was the death of José Robles. They talked about how to handle it. And they talked about it with a candor denied to everyone else in this story.

In this meeting, Alvarez del Vayo forthrightly told Josie that José Robles Pazos was dead, executed. He had been a fascist spy. Fascist spy? Josie knew Robles was a close friend of Dos, whom she would be seeing in a matter of days, and that he was well known for his devotion to the Republic. Yet she asked Alvarez del Vayo no questions about this claim. Nothing about evidence, or about a trial, or about a record of any sort of legal proceeding. She and Alvarez del Vayo did discuss Dos. "Some of the Spanish," she was told, "were beginning to be worried about Dos Passos's zeal, and fearing that he might turn against their cause if he discovered the truth, hoped to keep him from finding out anything about [the Robles killing] while he was in Spain."

Josie's claim about "the Spanish" doubting Dos Passos's "zeal" is puzzling. This conversation was taking place well *before,* not after, Dos Passos's arrival in Spain. Dos Passos had as yet no clue about Robles's disappearance and was still fully "zealous" about the Spanish cause.

Herbst, moreover, claimed that Alvarez del Vayo had confided the state secret of Robles's execution to her out of some sort of "concern" for her friendship with Dos. *Compassionate* concern? Given the lies and crass evasions that Alvarez del Vayo would soon be spreading about the case, this seems unlikely.

Whatever was decided at this meeting, it is clear that its purpose was to discuss how to handle—how to manipulate—John Dos Passos's response to his discovery that his friend had vanished from the face of the earth. One key fact: Josie was told that she must not, under any circumstances, let it be known that her source for "the truth" about the killing—that is, the lie that Robles had been executed as a fascist spy—was Alvarez del Vayo himself.

Josephine Herbst walked out of the foreign minister's office having been given a mission and a weapon to accomplish it. The mission was to "handle" Dos. The weapon was the lie that Robles had been executed for being a fascist spy.

From Alvarez del Vayo's office, Herbst was driven directly to the Hotel Florida in Madrid. When the car left her off at the door to journalism's celebrity haven, there was nobody on the sidewalk to greet her. She was no celebrity. Nobody helped her with anything. Nobody ever did. She struggled to haul all her luggage into the soaring art nouveau lobby. Battered by her long trip, she dumped her junk.

That was when, like a miracle, he was suddenly there, dressed in a khaki uniform, striding toward her in shining black boots, a wide welcoming smile on his face. "Josie!" Her name sang across the lobby. His arms were opened wide.

"Josie!"

It was Hem.

chapter 6

FONSECA, 25

As for Dos Passos's greeting, he found something a little strange—off, somehow—about it when he got into Valencia. He had no way of knowing how very different his own meager reception was from the lavish welcome that Valencia officials had spread over Hemingway two weeks before, or from Josephine Herbst's long, confidential conversation with Alvarez del Vayo a week after that. Dos Passos was aware only of something pinched and evasive in the way the people in Valencia were responding to him. It was nothing more than a slight, but the slight was real, and it was hard to miss. If his every move was being watched, his experience was one of being ignored. Actively ignored.[1]

It *was* odd. Dos Passos was, after all, a famous man, potentially a key figure in the Republic's English-language propaganda effort. *The Spanish Earth* was his film—he thought—and it had a high government priority. Dos had been told that on reaching Valencia, Julio Alvarez del Vayo, the minister of foreign affairs no less, would be waiting to meet him. And so he dutifully presented himself in the grand official building that housed the ministry, where he was shown into a dimly lit waiting room, and sat twiddling his thumbs for what seemed hours, watching a steady stream of important-looking folks with briefcases going before him into the bright rooms beyond. Sitting in the waiting room's dimness, Dos would see the baize-covered doors disclose the brilliance within: then he would watch them close in his face again. Dos had long since sent in his name. It was obvious that anyone and everyone had priority over him. At last even his patience snapped. He pushed his way out of his dim Siberia into the minister's bright outer office. There an officious young major domo, speaking to him through a British accent that was almost comical in its perfection, feigned surprise. Was it *possible*? Had Mr. Dos Passos not seen the minister *yet*? He would see to it at once.

The young man vanished into the sanctum beyond. He soon returned.

The flunky's feigned surprise had been transformed into feigned regret. "I am really distressed. The minister will be distressed. He has been called away on a matter of supreme importance. . . . Tomorrow . . . if you will be so kind as to accept an invitation to lunch with the minister, a car will call for you at . . . twelve noon."

Whereupon the confidential clerk clamped Dos's hand in a power grip that he used to propel Dos out the door and toward the street, keeping his plumy chatter flowing as they walked. Tomorrow's lunch would be "a little affair for foreign correspondents"—in other words, *not* a private meeting—"and in the meanwhile you must understand that we greet your project"—that is, *The Spanish Earth*—"with enthusiasm. Mr. Hemingway and Mr. Ivens are already at work, with cameramen, porters, assistants for transportation, filming the defense of Madrid."

This high-toned bum's rush ended at the curb with a "stiff little bow."

As Dos and the major domo parted, the young man gave his name: Alfredo Posada. Then he offered a controlled little smile. "I believe you know the name."

Dos lifted his eyebrows.

"Weren't you a friend of my brother Juanito?"

Juan *Posada?* Of *course* Dos Passos knew Juan Posada! Back in graduate school, Juan had been one of those bright Spaniards in Dos's and José's bunch at the Instituto.

"You'll find him the Chief of Police in Madrid."

Chief of Police? In the old days, Juan had been a brilliant young law student. He and Pepe Robles and Dos used to go mountain climbing together, shouting at each other about how to transform Spain as they made their way up the north face.

Alfredo Posada returned Dos's handshake with a smile that was a mask of ambiguous delight. Then he vanished.

Even the quarters where the government billeted Dos had their creepy side. Instead of the usual effort to ingratiate the visiting celebrity with a grand hotel, Dos was shunted to a room in the Casa de los Sabios (House of the Wise), a dank little rooming house for retired academics, filled with sad, shuffling, superannuated, highly educated Spanish gents. None of them seemed willing to engage Dos Passos in conversation of any sort. Meals with the elderly educators were eaten in a silence that seemed to seep upward like water filling a sinking ship, until it finally closed over the last pretense of exchange. It seemed to Dos that this was not the silence of formality, or even senility. It felt more like fear.

The noon lunch the next day, that "little affair for foreign correspondents," turned out to be a huge crowded event thrown to entertain, it seemed, every reporter in Spain. Dos had expected perhaps three or four other people to be present. This clamorous bash took place in a glassed-in restaurant overlooking the beach at Valencia harbor, the lunch a lavish paella served in pretty brown earthenware dishes, accompanied by even more lavish amounts of wine. As promised, the minister himself was there: presiding at the head table fifty feet away from Dos, "with a subtly contemptuous smile on his face." But now Dos *remembered* the guy. He'd met Alvarez del Vayo with Pepe several years back. He was a *good* friend of Pepe's—some sort of obscurely connected liberal journalist. How did such a man become the foreign minister of Spain?

After lunch, Alvarez del Vayo got up and made a speech: quite a good speech, Dos thought. At least it kept the reporters laughing. Yet there was something troubling about the man, something about that contemptuous smile of his. . . .

After the meal, Dos made another stab at speaking to his Excellency, pushing his way through the departing crowd to catch up with Alvarez del Vayo just at the restaurant exit.

Dos introduced himself. "I'll only detain you for a moment," he said.

"Indeed, indeed, we must see much of each other," Alvarez del Vayo whistled back, speaking English in Oxbridge tones almost—but not quite—as perfect as Alfredo Posada's. "If it weren't for this dog's life of a public official."

Dos persisted. "Shouldn't we confer about the film?"

"Everything," said Alvarez del Vayo, while slithering in the opposite direction, "is going smoothly. . . . Just ask for what you want, and you shall have it. Arrangements have already been made for a car to Madrid when you want to join Hemingway. . . . My secretary will call on you tomorrow."

Not so fast, Excellency. Dos had one more question. "Tell me, where can I find José? . . . I am sure you know him. . . . José Robles. . . . It seemed to us in New York, José would be just the man to act as a sort of liaison officer."

The mere utterance made Alvarez del Vayo freeze: *Robles*. Dos was sure he saw sudden beads of sweat oozing out among the freckles on the minister's forehead. "Ah yes, yes, the Johns Hopkins professor. . . . We'll have to get in touch with him a little later."

Lie number one. Alvarez del Vayo was at this moment fully aware that José Robles was dead. At least six days before, the Minister had told Josephine Herbst—for whom he had easily found time—that Robles had been shot as a fascist spy. *Get in touch with Robles later?* After telling lie number one, Alvarez del Vayo dismissed the writer with a handshake of almost painful vigor. "Begging your pardon . . . the official life. . . . You can take my word for it, your friend is quite all right."

Your friend is quite all right?

Lie number two.

Why in the world would Alvarez del Vayo be assuring Dos that José was "quite all right"?

Dos had only been asking where José was.

But where *was* he?

Dos Passos knew that his next step was to find Pepe, find Márgara, find somebody. But how to find the apartment where the Robles family was living?

The traditional account is that faced with official stonewalling, Dos simply made his way through the streets of Valencia—asking and asking, feeling his way until somehow he found the cramped, huddled apartment in a grimy Valencia side street where the family was billeted. Dos Passos himself gave an altogether different account in *Century's Ebb*, though it is maybe a little too dramatic for the measured tones of standard biographies.

In *Century's Ebb*—autobiographical fiction—Dos Passos wrote that after Alvarez del Vayo's brush-off, Dos followed the throng of departing reporters to the restaurant checkroom, where he stood in line, waiting to retrieve his hat and coat. When he was handed his hat, Dos noticed a small piece of crumpled paper nestled in the crown. He was about to toss the paper away when he saw something scribbled on it. Smoothing out the rumple, he read:

Dirección de la Señora Márgara Robles Pazos
Fonseca 25, Valencia.

It was Pepe's address.

Somebody was watching him. Somebody was trying to help.

Fonseca 25 was an address on a bleak little slum street crammed with stone houses, where a surly, illiterate concierge was on guard and wanting only to give him grief. Getting past this harridan took effort; and then came the climb between clammy walls up stairs slippery with oily grime. Dos Passos's knock on the Robleses' door, was met with silence. The door was locked, and it *felt* locked. Locked tight. He knocked again. The door felt double-locked. It felt . . . sc*ared*. Dos rapped as loud as he could.

At last he heard a slow, delicate, hesitant fumbling at the lock. After a final click, the doorframe was creased by the narrowest possible crack, just enough for the person within to peer out without being seen.

And then he heard the relieved voiced of Márgara Robles whispering, "*Dos. Qué maravilla.*"

Márgara opened up just enough to let Dos squeeze through. Then she pressed the door shut again and snapped down the locks as fast as she could.

Inside, Dos Passos found himself looking into the face of staring terror. Márgara's face was so drawn that it looked like a skull. The apartment was as dank as the stairwell: closed, airless, and comfortless. Márgara walked to a cot in the middle of the room, slumped down on it. Her reddish tinted hair was unkempt. She kept looking down at the floor. Her hands were clamped on her knees.

There were no words of welcome. When Márgara spoke, she looked up and spoke very quietly.

"For now," she muttered, "we can speak freely. The children are at school." Then she asked Dos what he knew.

Knew about *what*?

Márgara suddenly understood: Dos still had no idea what had happened here.

José had been arrested. Men—she did not know who—had come in the night and taken him away for questioning. They took him to some sort of police station. They were going to charge him with something. But whatever it was, he hadn't been charged yet.

Charged? "What possible reason could they have?"

Márgara had no idea. In the classic reflex of the accused, she had been ransacking her mind for something, anything, her husband might have "done wrong."

And what had she come up with? Well, there was José's brother, who was fighting on Franco's side, and was now a prisoner in Madrid. Could it be that? José and his brother had never got along; they hadn't even seen one another since their father's death, which was many years ago. They had never agreed on politics.

There was another thing: José had been working, secretly, with the Russians. It was something important. He had told her he wasn't free to discuss what he was doing, not even with his wife. "He turned off her questions with his usual sarcastic sayings, but she could see he was worried and harassed." But he had unquestionably connected to the Russians in some secret way. There was that.

And then, the nighttime knock at the door.

Dos Passos's reactions to these revelations were those of a lawyer's son. He instantly decided to intervene. If José had been arrested, there must be some charge. Pepe would be needing a legal defense. Luckily, Dos knew some Spanish lawyers, some pretty important ones. He even knew a little about Spanish law. And a little celebrity pull in the right place right now would do no harm. *Qué maravilla*, Márgara had said it in relief the moment she saw Dos's face. But could José be saved with Dos's methods? Out came a notebook, and Dos's questions began. Márgara shook her head in frustration. She knew so little. José had been so secretive. She knew that he had started out at the Ministry of Information. . . .

Alvarez del Vayo, Dos thought. Him again. Alvarez del Vayo had been minister of information before he became foreign minister.

And then, Márgara went on, José had been moved to the Ministry of War. Lately he had been involved in some sort of secret negotiations. About what she did not know.

All right. What about José's enemies? He must have had some. "He was pretty freespoken."

Freespoken? Márgara didn't think so. "Not recently. You wouldn't have known him. He became quite careful about how he talked."

"It's ridiculous," Dos said. "There must be some way of appealing to the law."

Márgara stared back at him. "Law! You don't know the Spain of today!"

At this point the two Robles children entered the apartment, home from school. Coco Robles was seventeen; his sister was twelve. Though both were attending school in Valencia, Coco also had a job, a real job, working for the *causa*. Because Coco, like his father, knew Russian. Back in Baltimore, when his father set out to learn the language, Coco had joined him. They had taken lessons together, and in the end Coco was almost as good as his dad, good enough to translate documents in Alvarez del Vayo's propaganda office. They'd even given him a desk. The two children stood silent in front of Dos.

Instead of rushing to him as they usually did, the two young-
sters stood there, staring at their feet.

When Márgara asked if they didn't remember Uncle Dos, the
two of them nodded yes in a frightened little way. That made Márgara burst into tears and run to a corner, trying to hide her face.

Dos Passos had heard and seen enough. He was going back to
the ministry.

"I'll be back!" he shouted as he vanished into the lightless
stairwell.

Leaving Márgara and the kids at the Calle Fonseca, Dos Passos
went straight back to Alvarez del Vayo's office. And there, a new
and different runaround began.

Yesterday he had been insulted in the dim waiting room and
then brushed off with unctuous pseudo-deference. Today at
lunch he had been treated as a not-quite-important-enough
man, one for whom unfortunately the minister had no time. In
the space of one afternoon, Dos Passos's status had plunged
from celebrity to non-person.

He was informed that the minister, accompanied by Alfredo
Posada, had left Madrid an hour before. So sorry. What Posada
and the minister had left behind was a bureaucratic stonewall.
His questions about Robles were urgent. Robles? Nobody behind any desk in the place had ever heard of a José Robles. For
that matter, it was hard to find anybody who would admit to
ever having heard of a John Dos Passos. Dos Passos had been invited to Spain because he was a celebrity making a film that had
high government priority. After a decade or so of gathering
world renown, Dos was used to his name having at least some
small impact. No more. Not in the Ministry of Foreign Affairs.

"Losing contact with the higher-ups," Dos would write,
"gives you a damn funny feeling."

Someone *was* watching. Seeing but not seen, at a desk at the back of the propaganda office, sat an American communist apparatchik named Liston Oak. Liston Oak had been doing a lot of silent watching lately. Among other things, he had been watching the pain of young Coco Robles, coming into the office every day to translate Russian documents, sitting at his little desk nearby, and asking, asking, asking if anybody knew anything about his father; and then listening as everyone there told the boy no: oh no, they knew nothing. It was touching, seeing Coco's concern, seeing Coco's simple faith in the comrades in the office, and seeing them all lie to Coco.

And now Coco's story was beginning to merge with Liston's job. Were it not for Alvarez del Vayo's decision to sideline and isolate Dos Passos, Liston would have been the man assigned to squire the visiting writer around. That was what he had done with Hemingway and plenty of others. Liston's official title was to be Director of Propaganda for the United States and England in Alvarez del Vayo's office.[2] (That Alvarez del Vayo would appoint an American communist unable to speak Spanish to such a post offers a remarkably clear perspective on Alvarez del Vayo's priorities.) Liston's job was to act among the Americans as errand boy, censor, ideological watchdog, and informer. In Hem's case, a big part of the job consisted in keeping the great man supplied with enough good liquor and food. But Dos Passos? He had been told to steer clear of Dos Passos.

Liston and Dos already knew one another, vaguely. They had met in 1931, when Dos Passos had traveled with Theodore Dreiser to Harlan County, Kentucky, on a Communist Party–sponsored fact-finding trip during a labor dispute. Manipulating cultural celebrities had been Liston's work then as now. He was so very good at it that the party had recently sent him straight to Moscow, for real promotion.

The Moscow Liston reached in 1936 was the Moscow of the Terror, and as the purges unfolded around him, even this staunchly Stalinist former schoolteacher from Monterey, California, felt something . . . stirring inside. The American party's pride and joy had been granted an interview with none other than Stalin's propaganda czar, Mikhail Borodin himself, who offered Oak a major job, working on *The Moscow News,* the Soviet Union's English-language daily. It was the pinnacle of Liston's career as a communist. Yet something was turning this triumph into ashes. Something was eating at Liston. Maybe it was moral revulsion. Maybe it was mounting fear. Maybe it was the hard, heavy work of rationalizing mass murder. Maybe it was some combination of them all. Life in the Soviet capital, with its Byzantine intrigue, its blackout of news, its lethal gossip, its constant obsession with treason, its endless procession of once-famous revolutionaries crawling as abjects, confessing, and confessing, and confessing, all condemned to be shot—even if it *was* revolutionary justice, it was giving Liston the creeps.

The rule required that before Liston Oak could take possession of the poisoned apple that Borodin was holding out before him, the American party back in New York would have to vet him and vouch for his reliability, a process that turned out to be long. The wait became an unexpected lucky break. For the first time in a long time, Liston Oak found himself at liberty. He could leave Moscow. He could go anywhere. He could . . . go to *Paris!*

It was the fall of 1936, and Paris is exactly where Liston went. In Paris, he was miserable. Miserable that the life he'd glimpsed in Moscow, scene of the brilliant career he'd been offered, was also the scene of the Great Terror. Miserable with fear. Miserable with doubt. Agitated and uncertain, Liston found himself trudging through the streets of Paris night after night, unable to sleep, long after those beautiful streets had gone black even to night life. More than once, the American caught the dawn happening over the Seine. It was the late fall of 1936; Christmas was coming. In Moscow: trials, terror shrieking from every headline—headlines Liston would soon be writing—the heroes of the revolution crawling, exposed as fascists and enemies of the people, begging for death, imploring the court to shoot them, please, please shoot them like the mad dogs they were. On the other hand, there was Spain and heroism. Spain where the November defense of Madrid was entrancing the romantics of the world. In Moscow, Terror. In Spain, a great, heroic battle against the march of fascism. He couldn't quite admit that his beautiful revolutionary dream was being mauled and murdered in Moscow, and yet Liston wanted the dream back. Liston wanted to get back to the good gratifying business of transforming the world. Liston wanted Spain.

Luckily, Liston had influential friends. He would never have gotten in to see Borodin without them. Liston confided at least some of his anxieties to Louis Fischer, then the most important Stalinist fellow traveler in American journalism, and a man with real influence in the Comintern propaganda machine. Fischer quickly grasped Oak's conflict and recommended that Oak turn down the spectral big job to follow his dream of heroism. Say "no" to the Communism of the Terror; say "yes" to the Communism of revolutionary heroism. Simple. Louis Fischer would use his influence. Stop worrying. He would be glad to write a letter to the people who counted. *Really* counted. Consider it done.

The gesture was shrewd, and, in its way, kind: it may well have saved Oak's life. American communists sent on to Moscow did not always leave their assignments alive. Fischer arranged for Liston to be seconded to Spain and set up in the propaganda office run by Julio Alvarez del Vayo. Liston would be in Valencia, a city that (apart from the fact that almost every person in the street spoke a language he did not understand, and was packing a gun) looked a lot like home. Just like Monterey: same blue bay, same orange groves rising in ranks up the purplish hills, same soft, sweet air blowing off the sea over beaches where people wandered, buying cheap irresistible food from open stands. All that, and revolution, too.

And that is where Liston was in April 1937. Coming through Valencia, Dos had not spotted Liston. But Liston had spotted Dos.

Liston Oak not only knew what had happened to José Robles; he knew that something a lot bigger and bloodier than the death of Robles was brewing inside the communist operation in Spain. There was going to be terror. There was going to be a coup. Liston knew the general substance of impending events, if not the exact timing and details. Spain's Soviet "advisers"—using Alvarez del Vayo as their prime political front man—were preparing to purge their political enemies in Spain in a wave of provocations and killings that would begin in Barcelona and come to be known as the May Days. These events had been recommended and planned by Gorev since his arrival with Koltsov in August.

Did Robles know or guess anything about these plans? We may never know, but their moment was coming up fast: it was a little over two weeks away. The May Days would be the occasion for the legalized coup through which the Soviets would oust Prime Minister Francisco Largo Caballero and replace him with their obedient servant, the corrupt finance minister, Juan Negrin.

Knowing some if not all of this, Liston sat at his back desk. Every day he saw Coco, coming in after school. Every day he heard about Dos Passos's bewildered search for just one or two simple facts. And every day Liston Oak became a little more afraid.

At long last, Dos Passos found someone who would tell him something. There was a polished but ruthless secret policeman moving between Valencia and Madrid named Pepe Quintinilla. His full title was Commissar General of Investigation and Vigilance, and he has gone down in the history of the period as a chilling figure: smooth, cruel, all too delighted with his work tracking down traitors, a sadist with a sentimental side: Hemingway became fascinated with Pepe Quintinilla, studying him with a mixture of awe and loathing, and assigning him a large role in his dark play *The Fifth Column.*

"The Executioner of Madrid," as he was called, happened to be the brother of Luis Quintinilla, a left-wing painter for whom Dos Passos had done many helpful favors back in the States. Dos Passos had collected and promoted Luis Quintinilla's work for years; and when Quintinilla's radical politics got him into a nasty legal scrape in Spain, Dos and Hem together had raised money for the painter's legal defense. (Raising funds for people in trouble was typical of Dos, and he was quite good at it—a fact that's all the more striking in view of his personal finances: Dos was perpetually in a bind, forever a day late and a dollar short, unlike Hem, who managed his vastly larger cash flow shrewdly and with success, and who tried less and less to conceal his irritation with what he viewed as Dos's fiscal incompetence.)

The Quintinilla family owed one to Dos. They never paid it, but at least Pepe Quintinilla was in no position to claim he'd never heard of John Dos Passos.

Dos Passos first met with Quintinilla either in Valencia before he went on to meet Hemingway in Madrid, or a few days later in Madrid. (The Republican officials regularly shuttled between the two cities.) Wherever the venue, the substance of their encounter was a new pack of lies. Some problem with Pepe Robles?

Yes, Quintinilla had heard something about it. A minor matter. Sure to be cleared up soon. Not to worry. A trivial business. A technicality. Set your mind at rest.

Except that Quintinilla could not let the lie rest with this simple denial. Probably to prepare a scapegoat—and ignoring the incompatibility of the two claims—he added the thought that Robles might possibly have been the victim of the anarchists, the crazies from Barcelona whom communists like Quintinilla had labeled "uncontrollables"—and whom they planned to wipe out a little more than two weeks later in the May provocations. Robles might have run afoul of the uncontrollables. They were ruthless, treacherous. They'd have to be dealt with, sooner or later.

Coco's daily suffering was beginning to wear Liston down; he was finding it harder and harder to listen day after day to the boy's questions and the comrades' answering lies.

One day, perhaps without quite knowing why, Liston took just one small step. Maybe he just couldn't endure the pain of watching the kid any longer. Maybe he was trying, by this strangely indirect route, to get the truth to Dos. All we know is that one afternoon, just before Dos Passos left Valencia, Liston called Coco over to his desk, and he told him the simple truth.

He told Coco that his father had been shot, and that he was dead.

The boy stared at him.

That's the truth: Coco Robles's father was dead. Liston was terribly, terribly sorry; it was a horrible thing and it was a horribly sad thing, but there was nothing, nothing, to be done about it.

Coco Robles turned and flew out of the office, racing for the Calle Fonseca and his mother. Liston stood silent and frightened, watching the boy disappear.

Denial is a potent force. After Quintinilla's assurances, perhaps Dos Passos wasn't sure he believed the diametrically different story Coco had brought home from the office. He seems not to have grasped that it came from a man he already knew. In any case, Dos did not go to Liston Oak, asking for clarification. He seems to have decided that Coco's story was gossip: very alarming gossip, of course, but still not the definitive word.

Dos Passos had heard that the president of the Spanish Republic, Manuel Azaña, a man he had interviewed and known, was in Madrid. Torn between the conflicting accounts, he decided to go to the top. He would proceed to Madrid and demand an audience. If he could not get access to Azaña (and he never did), he had other friends: Juan Posada, for example, whom he'd just discovered was Madrid's chief of police. He would go to Madrid, join Hem, and try using a little pull.

Dos Passos left for Madrid not long after dawn the next morning, in a swank, chauffeur-driven Hispano-Suiza, riding with a bibulous French journalist—who was not, as some biographies claim, André Malraux—who had loaded the car with packages of food and boxes of chocolates. Their ride through the blooming spring landscape and "story hilltop villages" lasted until dusk, and what had been a day of azure skies and orange blossoms and scenes not unlike what you see in a triptych from the Spanish Renaissance. But as the big car drew near to Madrid, all that gave way to a "steely" twilight and air choked with dust. Dos felt the French journalist scrunching down beside him. This car was driving into a war. A real war.

They went through a town near Madrid, Alcalá de Henares— "the home of Cervantes," Dos mumbled reverently, while the Frenchman stared back at him, blank about Cervantes. The roads were filled with "military trucks, troops marching, horse-drawn field kitchens." Peering from the window, Dos noticed that all the Spanish soldiers were wearing helmets not from Spain but from other countries. Some were in the "tin hats with a keel down the center" that the French wore in the trenches of World War I; others were in the "mushrooms" that the Germans had worn. Surplus. At the outskirts of the city, at sunset, the car pulled past a building filled with kids in makeshift uniforms, doing drills while holding broomsticks for rifles. And as the dusk deepened, he saw Madrid, lightless on its high plain, bleak with a "grim look, as if it had been stamped out of iron."

And then the darkness was really falling and they were in Madrid itself. The city was under a strict blackout. Madrid's daytime carnival of war had become the deathwatch of its night, a night darkness that seemed to Dos to be "pouring" into the city. The silence of a city under curfew is not just quiet but truly silent, and that true silence can be eerie. Lights off, the limousine crept through the streets to the Gran Vía and the Plaza de Callao. Getting out of the car in front of the Florida, Dos stood still in the darkness, listening hard. The silence was not absolute: he could hear one remote sound, something seeping under the blanket of the urban hush: sharp, hard cracks, distant and unmistakable. Rifle fire. Very far off, but perfectly clear. Next came machine-gun fire. Lots and lots of sharp hard cracks, close together. They too were quite unmistakable.

"Shit." The frightened Frenchman muttered under his breath, catching on.

Just then Sid Franklin appeared in a sulk, sent to carry Dos's bags. Sid waited patiently as Dos Passos checked in, and then he glumly led him up to Hemingway's celebrity suite.

"Papa has been waiting for you all day," he said.

chapter 7

THE AIR OF MENACE

Hem started a fight the moment Dos came in. Sid ushered Dos Passos into Room 108. There Hemingway lay in bed, installed in regal fury, nursing a glass of wine, a blanket over his legs, and his eyes glaring.[1]

"How much grub did you bring?" he snapped.

Oh, the *food*. The Hispano-Suiza downstairs had been loaded with provisions being sent by the government to the hotel; and the frightened Frenchman had loaded the trunk with all kinds of specialties. But Dos remembered now. Provisions were very tight in Madrid. He'd been urged to bring extra supplies of his own. But after what had gone down in Valencia, he'd had other things on his mind. He had to admit it.

"Then how do you expect to *eat*?" Hemingway shouted.

Dos stood speechless.

"Martha!" Hem roared, calling into the adjacent room. "He hasn't brought a goddamned thing!"

At this point a sulking Martha entered the room, draped in her silver fox coat. *The* silver fox coat.

"We might have known," Martha said, drawling with contempt. Gellhorn did not waste so much as one welcoming smile on Dos Passos but gave him instead a steely stare. The room was cold. Gellhorn tightened the fur around her shoulders. "I'm still chilly," she muttered. "Madrid's the coldest place in the world."

Hem at least managed to pour the newcomer a glass of wine. Dos glanced between Hem in bed and Martha at a vanity table where she was settling in without one word more. Dos could not refrain from lifting his glass: "To the happy pair," he toasted, dryly.

Martha did not glance up from her business, which was filing her nails. She seemed very interested in her nails.

On a hunch, Dos Passos asked if Hemingway had by any chance run into either of the Posada brothers.

"Sure," Hemingway said. "See 'em all the time."

Of course he had seen them. So there was a good chance that Hem might already know about Pepe.

Hemingway pulled himself out of bed and stood up, the better to point his wrath at Dos, and locked gazes with his old friend.

"What are you worried about, Dos? The Fascists don't shell the hotel until morning. Even then his gunners are aiming at the Telefonica. Damn poor shots. If they aimed at us, I'd feel better." It was Hem's first step into what became a favorite fiction: that Dos Passos was afraid in Spain.

"I'm not worried about that," Dos smiled. And he wasn't.

Hemingway's segue was quick. "If it's your professor bloke's disappearance, think nothing of it. . . . People disappear every day."

So somebody *had* got to Hem. Dos Passos said nothing.

"Sid," Hemingway snapped, summoning the Brooklyn bull-fighter. "Where's Joris? See if you can find him, will you?"

That got Sid out of the room. Martha kept working on those nails.

The moment the door closed behind Franklin, Hemingway began to shout into Dos's face. "Don't put your damn mouth into this Robles business . . . not even in front of Sid. Sid's the rightest guy in the world, but he might get potted some night. The fifth column"—covert Franco sympathizers in Madrid—"is everywhere. Just suppose your professor took a powder and joined the other side."

Joined the other *side?* This was the first time in a week of listening to lies that Dos had heard anyone, no matter how obviously lying, suggest that Pepe might been involved in treason. Not even Quintinilla had hinted at such a possibility.

Dos swung back in dismay. "That could not be. I've known the man for years. He's absolutely straight. Nobody forced him to give up a perfectly good job to come over to help his country."

Without looking up from her nails, Martha now joined the discussion with a voice that was like a "blast of cold air." "People have different ideas about how to help their country. Your inquiries," she frigidly added, "have already caused us embarrassment."

(Embarrassment? Caused us *embarrassment?)*

Sid had been quick to find Ivens, who entered the room boyish and beaming, all affability, talking about how wonderfully the film was going, and how the important thing now was for Dos to go back to New York and raise lots more money for it. *(His film. Dos had told Carlo it was his film. His and Hem's.)* As for the rushes, maybe Dos could be shown them sometime. Not now but later. Maybe in Paris. *(He'd told Carlo he'd been repeatedly assured that they would be completely in charge of shooting* The Spanish Earth.*)*

Paris. Not now. Maybe in Paris.

(Tresca laughed in his friend's face. "Completely in charge?" Would Dos perhaps be interested in knowing that his "cameraman" was a crypto-communist apparatchik?)

In the days to come, the rumble of Hemingway's hostility may have softened here and there, but it never really let up. In fact, it grew more raw and bitter as Dos Passos proceeded with what he considered his business in Madrid. Dos kept doing his reports for *Fortune*. He insisted on going on location with Ivens. And in defiance of Hem's shouted command, he did not "keep his damn mouth out of this Robles business."

One trip to "the front" was with Hem and the visiting British celebrities that Otto Katz had brought to Madrid. The site was a bombed-out apartment building—Hem called it "the Old Homestead." This perch offered a quite safe point of high perspective on the fighting going on in the Madrid suburb of University City. There Hemingway exasperated Dos Passos by showing off, just as he had earlier, on a contested spot on the Madrid-Valencia road, where he'd made a merry show of his fearlessness, conspicuously prancing with the film crew over a stretch of the road exposed to fire, knowing well that they were perfectly safe: it was siesta time, and even the fascist marksmen could not tear themselves away from the habits of a lifetime. There was a smirking, juvenile side to Hemingway's bravado. It irked Dos Passos.

The tensions thickened when Dos Passos went with Joris Ivens to the town of Fuentedueña, a nearby village that had become a showcase socialist commune. Fuentedueña was an impoverished little place that had been released from feudalism only months before. "The minute you step off the road," Dos wrote, "you are back in the age of packmules and twowheeled carts." It was being transformed, and Dos wanted to see its transformation featured in the film. Hemingway did not. Hem wanted to play down radical social change in the Republic and play up the heroic military struggle against fascist militarism. This was more than a mere clash of temperament: macho Hem wanting battle scenes versus fervent Dos plumping for social change. True, radical social change thrilled Dos Passos and bored Hemingway. But as Ivens knew, the real issue was Comintern propaganda policy. The directive was to portray Spain as a beleaguered democracy fighting fascism, and—above all—*not* as a revolutionary state. Too much talk about revolution might scare off the democracies. Alvarez del Vayo, for example, had instructed Liston Oak to see to it that "not one word" about the Spanish social revolution was left standing in any press report leaving the country.[2] Scenes of wholesale expropriations and left-wing communes were out. Hemingway followed Ivens's lead in wanting to play them down. They also wanted to play down the war of Spaniard versus Spaniard, and play up the wider fascist menace, above all the Italian and German intervention.

Yet Fuentedueña was a flowering example of something important, and Dos Passos was able to shoehorn something of its new life into the picture. "Our Dutch director," Dos wrote, "did agree with me that, instead of making the film purely a blood and guts picture we ought to find something being built for the future amid all the misery and massacre. We wanted cooperative work, construction with the profit motive left out, to be the theme." Here is Arturo Barea, in *The Forging of a Rebel*, one of the classics of the Spanish left, speaking of Dos at this moment: "We had a guest whom I liked and respected, John Dos Passos, who spoke about our land workers and peasants with gentle understanding, looking from one to the other out of wondering brown eyes."[3] Dos finally got Ivens to include some innocuous footage from an irrigation scheme being developed at Fuentedueña: it wasn't much, but it was something other than war.

And it thrilled Dos. When he got back to the States he wrote and published a glowing report, far more detailed than anything in the film, on this piece of grass-roots social transformation.[4]

And Dos did not stop his search for Robles. Despite Hem's snarled warning, Dos Passos saw no reason to make a secret out of his quest for information about José. *("Caused us embarrassment?" "Us?")*

On the contrary, Dos talked steadily and insistently about his quest. Clearly, silence offered no protection to anyone over anything. Whatever trouble Pepe was in, it could not be made worse by John Dos Passos asking what it was. So he asked and agitated.

In *Century's Ebb*, Dos Passos says that he ran into his old friend Juan Posada on maybe his first night in the Gran Via restaurant. Dos hated the Gran Via, with its "honky-tonk" atmosphere and its smell of "scorched milk," but it was a relief to spot Posada there, even if his old friend the chief of police looked transformed. Juanito's face seemed stamped with age. In place of its old ruddy color, there was something "waxen" about it.

Dos was up in a flash, talking about the old days, remembering how they'd climbed the Maliciosa—a peak in the Guadarrama mountains—and their ferocious long-faded debates about revolution and the Spanish Civil Code.

Surveying the room, Posada laughed a dry laugh. "That was in another century."

Juanito radiated a message: Be discreet. Everyone was listening. Be careful, even here. Dos ended his greeting with a vague smile. "There will be," he said, smiling but in a low voice, "other problems of law. Problems that I shall want explained."

Posada picked up Dos's significant glance. He "pressed the air down with the flat of his hand in a gesture of silence. 'Later,' he said. 'As much as you want.'"

Dos Passos did of course see the need for discretion. He was not willing to keep silent about the Robles business, but he did recognize the air of menace surrounding the entire subject. Right around now, Dos began to suspect that his frequent letters to Katy might be being intercepted. He began to leave out names, places, and private thoughts, relying instead on generalities and a kind of impromptu couple's code. He saw that however much José's vanishing mattered to him, in some sinister way it mattered no less urgently to the people on the other side. Hem had tried to dismiss Pepe's disappearance as somehow unimportant. Dos saw it was plenty important—all-too-important—to the many officials high and low who were so busy evading the simplest questions about what was going on. The air of menace congealed over any question connected to José. Dos began watching every move.

At that moment Juan Posada, though Madrid's chief of police, knew nothing about the fate of José Robles. Dos Passos continued to agitate for the missing answer in the Hotel Florida, which was, let's remember, one crawling swarm of professional gossips. It didn't take long for the story to spread.

Including to Josephine Herbst.

Dos had been particularly delighted to see Josie. Back in New York, he'd suggested she look up Robles in Valencia, so he must have asked if she had. If he did, Josie must have lied. Dos Passos had arrived in Madrid on April 11. For the next eleven days—up until April 22—he saw Herbst on the friendliest possible terms, every day, and she listened to his concerns about Robles while keeping her secret about Robles carefully concealed. The moment had not yet come to use the weapon she'd been given. Herbst stayed silent, taking in Dos Passos's mounting concern, waiting for the time, the place.

They were together a lot. With hope jostling against uncertainty and despair, Dos started having breakfast with Josie many mornings. That cup of exhausted tea with a stale roll became something he looked forward to. They would sit in the little restaurant off the atrium until the odor of sizzling ham and fresh coffee and maybe even scrambled eggs would come seeping down from the balcony up by the Hemingway suite. Sid Franklin was at work again at his hotplates, and soon Hemingway would appear at the balcony shouting at people to come up and eat. "There was a kind of splurging generosity about Hemingway at the Florida," she wrote. Sid Franklin and Liston Oak, by constant scrounging, kept the master of the well-supplied room 108. "There was a tall wardrobe in Hem's room," Herbst wrote, "and it was filled with tasty items, ham, bacon, eggs, coffee, even marmalade. These tidbits were the result of Sid's ability to scrounge around and lay his hands on essentials nobody else could have touched."

And yet Herbst was aware that Hem's splurging generosity "had an underside . . . a kind of miserliness." As she waited and watched, Josie was assessing the tensions between two friends: the early pages of her "Spanish Journal" are devoted as much to their relationship as they are to the political situation. She dutifully noted Hem's tirades against Dos: Dos was not good in war, Hem claimed, because he was not a hunter. He didn't know how to take care of himself in the wild. That's what had made him show up with no food. Dos had no balls; Dos had no understanding of war. Then, inevitably, he threw in his standard insult for any male friend: Dos was dominated by his wife. "You could feel the irritation growing between the two men," she wrote, focusing on the psychological undertow between them, making notes about it and observing it with some acuity. Hem's infidelity to Pauline was also on her mind, and shrewd notes about the triangle are also in these pages, noting especially how torn Hemingway was between Pauline and Martha.[5]

She also noted that Hemingway was visibly glowing with that special intoxication that shines from a self-righteous ideological high. Something had happened in his thinking, and Herbst knew it. "In annexing new realms of experience, Hemingway was entering into some areas that were better known to people like Dos Passos or even myself," she said. "He seemed to be naively embracing on the simpler levels the current ideologies at the very moment when Dos Passos was urgently questioning them."[6]

The memoir suggests some measure of sympathy between Dos's "doubts" and her own state of mind. This may be a little misleading. The truth is that in early April 1937, Dos's doubts about "Stalinism," though real, were not all that urgent. Josie herself was still a devout Stalinist, and still closely and covertly affiliated with the Comintern propaganda machine. The Comintern had brought her to Spain in the first place. She was in confidential contact with its senior agents, such as Katz and Alvarez del Vayo. And "some of the Spaniards were beginning to have doubts about Dos Passos's zeal."

Dos's doubters were more Soviet than Spanish—more Alvarez del Vayo and other Comintern agents than men like Posada or Arturo Barea. In 1937, Dos Passos was unequivocally committed to the Republican cause. His view of that cause was broader than the platitudes of the Popular Front, but his zeal for a Republican victory was not hedged in any way. The days of Dos Passos's anticommunism and drift to the right were still wrapped in unimaginable mists to come. They would come only *after* he had lived through the Robles murder. It was as a friend, not an ideological guide, that Dos trusted Josie. Josie continued to play the friend to him, sweet and supportive, though she carefully kept her knowledge about Robles concealed. She was waiting.

Josie's seeming kindness stands in stark contrast to his treatment by the other American Stalinists. When Dos left New York, officials of the American party had been still treating him with deference. In Madrid, American communists suddenly turned hostile and abrupt, filled with hate, openly malevolent. The change took Dos off guard, "stuttering like a schoolboy who has forgotten his lesson."

"You social fascists," one party-liner snapped at him, "would be funny if you weren't so dangerous."

Yet Dos was still marginally protected by his fame, his connections to *The Spanish Earth* and to Hemingway. Such was the force of the Comintern's desire to enlist Hemingway as its spokesman that if Hem had not turned against Dos in 1937— that is, if a communist attack on Dos would still have risked alienating his dear friend Hem—that attack might not have taken place. Even as things stood, so long as Dos was still connected to Hem and to *The Spanish Earth*, the American Stalinists were not quite ready to cut him loose. As one rock-ribbed American apparatchik confided to Dos in awestruck tones, "even our friends in the East"—that is, the Soviets—"are enthusiastic about the film. One of the responsibles told me a documentary filmed by Ivens and narrated by Hemingway would be worth a truckload of machine guns."

The handwriting was on the wall, even if Dos couldn't quite decipher it yet. The Comintern was washing its hands of Dos Passos and his petit-bourgeois compunctions. He'd been an ideological marked man since Radek's attack. Yet then, a full-court smear might have compromised the smiling double-talk of the Popular Front—and it might have alienated Hemingway. But now? Hemingway's emergence as a new hero of the Popular Front might be used to *spearhead* an attack on Dos Passos.

That would eliminate the need for caution, wouldn't it?

Josie kept making her notes on the tensions between the two men.

Meanwhile, the Comintern did not leave her alone with her mission. It was just at this time that Otto Katz checked into the

Hotel Florida. Not many people knew who Otto Katz was—apart from people already in his apparatus, people like the British journalist Claud Cockburn and Josie. Otto Katz was the Comintern agent and NKVD officer whom Josie had approached before leaving. Otto Katz was the secret agent who had issued the order that admitted Josie to the country and put her in Alvarez del Vayo's office, behind closed doors. Otto Katz was Willi Münzenberg's second-in-command, and as such one of the most senior propaganda agents in the world. Otto Katz had for years managed the apparatus's covert role in filmmaking. Otto Katz had been an intimate ally, cultural adviser, and protégé of Karl Radek. Otto Katz was close to Koltsov. Otto Katz had been Joris Ivens's employer in Moscow. Otto Katz was Alvarez del Vayo's partner in Agence Espagne and was probably Alvarez del Vayo's superior in the apparatus. Otto Katz was—apart from Koltsov—the most fully informed propaganda agent in Spain.

And now, using the pseudonym André Simone (despite his strong Sudeten-German accent), posing as a German antifascist correspondent, and guiding a group of British celebrities through the theater of war, Otto Katz was in the Hotel Florida, perfectly placed for all that was to come.

chapter 8

BOMBARDMENT

O n April 22, 1937, two shells hit the Hotel Florida just as dawn began to break over Madrid. In her room, just down the hall from Hemingway's suite, the sleeping Josephine Herbst was snapped into wakefulness by "two enormous thuds." She sat up, instantly aware. Bombardment. The blast woke her like a slap in the face. They were shelling the hotel, and they were scoring direct hits. The sound of impact was followed a moment later by an incomprehensible noise that seemed to be coming from inside the walls of the hotel, like a "heavy wall of water . . . crashing down with an iron force." This was an attack.

As quickly as Josie grasped that that these were shells hitting the building, fear, pure fear, started surging through her. She clutched her blankets, rigid with panic. The thing tearing loose inside her seemed to pass almost beyond mere emotion. It was like some alien animal assaulting her from within, palpable and violent, ripping up her very being with a strength she had not imagined possible. This was just plain terror—just true pure blank blind speechless terror—and it was all Josie could do to hold on tight as it took possession of her. She seemed to turn to stone in that bed, waiting for whatever was coming next.

She didn't have to wait long.

What was that? Several floors above, John Dos Passos also snapped awake. He had been too deeply asleep to identify that first crashing sound, but it made him sit up in the bed, struggling for orientation, listening hard to what seemed only confused night noises, staring out at the "light indigo oblong" of a window across the way from his. *Something* had hit *something*. And hit it hard.

Then came the next round of shelling and the guessing was over. They were shelling the hotel. A new shell came streaking toward the building. As it cut through the air, it made a sound like tearing cloth, as if an immense piece of silk were being ripped in two by an invisible giant in the sky. The shell was sundering the fabric of the night as it raced toward the building, getting louder and louder until, after an almost imperceptible split second of silence, there was the jolt of impact and a shattering explosion that made the whole building shake. Then, as the boom of impact seemed to float away like sonic smoke, Dos heard the sound of breakage: the crash of smashed tiles and broken glass raining down, splintering granite, stone clattering onto ledges and into courtyards.

The fascists were shelling the hotel. They were not just missing the Telefonica. They were *aiming* at the hotel. They were probably firing from the Casa de Campo, about two miles away on the western edge of the city.

Dos Passos jumped out of his bed and went to his window, peering out into the dark, trying to get some bearing on where or what had just been hit. The Florida was built on a hill; the still-sleeping city stretched out in the night down below: "narrow roofs, smokeless chimneypots, buff-colored towers with cupolas." Peering into the murk, Dos Passos strained, searching the darkness nearby for some sign of impact, smoke, fire. In the remote distance, the dawn was just starting up.

Then while he stood there, once again that sound of ripping silk came streaking toward him, immense and high-pitched, racing straight toward the hotel. Then the impact shook the place again, followed first by the shattering sound of hard things breaking, and then by a piercing wail, the howl of agony. It was not a human cry. It was the howling of a dog: some poor hurt terrified beast eight floors down, its shriek yipping up and up and up, faster and faster, terrible. As that cruel howling cut into him, Dos Passos saw what he'd been looking for: smoke, a plume of it rising from one of those pretty rooftops down below. The smoke wasn't coming from the hotel, but it was very nearby, and as the smoke rose up the screaming dog's cries died down to a moribund whimper, and then stopped.

The sliver of dawn was widening.

Was the attack over?

First Dos Passos went out—still in his bathrobe—to see what was happening with the others in the hotel. People were gathering: Martha Gellhorn was there in her pajamas and an overcoat. It is testimony to some sort of rather special sang-froid that Dos decided not to spend time milling with the agitated folks in the hall: he decided to try for a little more sleep. He returned to his room and clambered back into bed, and he actually managed to drift off for maybe a few minutes, until the giant outside started ripping the silk again—and again and again and *again*. No good. By now, the giant was tearing the silky sky to tatters; the shells were coming in too fast to count, and fear finally got to Dos, clutching his throat and yanking him out of bed. The damn things were coming in all over the place. Most weren't hitting the Florida, but they were all *very* near. So much for sleep.

Dos Passos went to his bathroom and tried the water. There was no hot water, but there was plenty of cold. He decided to shave and bathe. Cleanliness and order might not confer safety, but they did help sanity. After taking his chilly bath, Dos dried off and then he stood at the sink, shaving to the rhythm of shells rocking the hotel. Next he got dressed, in a suit. He buttoned up his shirt. Then he selected a tie. Then he went to a mirror, and he tied it. The shells kept flying in.[1]

Downstairs, Josie's panic had been in full command, shrieking at her get *up!* Get up and get *out!* Get *out!* Get *OUT!* Fear flung her out of the bed, and she was in the dark, scrambling for her clothes. When she at last found herself clutching something she could wear, her hands were shaking so uncontrollably she couldn't do the buttons. Impossible: to hell with getting dressed. Josie grabbed a bathrobe and rushed out of her room onto the balcony that curled around the atrium.

All the balconies were filling with terrified people in pajamas and underwear and bathrobes, all crowding toward the rear of the hotel. Once again, Josie could hear that incomprehensible *sound* filling the air: "A strange sound like the twittering of birds at dawn in the country." Martha Gellhorn, rushing out of Hemingway's room, heard a sound she identified—rightly or wrongly—as the squeals of prostitutes scurrying out of journalists' rooms on every floor, "crying in high voices like birds."[2]

Everybody was pushing to the rear of the building, as far as possible from the façade that was taking the hits. Everyone except Hemingway. As Herbst was being swept along with the crowd, she passed Hemingway, fully dressed, heading toward where the shells were hitting, beaming, buoyant, absolutely bouncing with excitement.

"How are you?" Hemingway hollered as he swept by.

Josie tried to speak. Her lips struggled to shape the word "fine." Nothing came out except mute paralysis and fear. The people around her were dragging suitcases and even mattresses, and jostling her along with them while Hemingway was heading straight into the trouble, hot for action, and suddenly she felt something other than fear. She felt fury. Fury at Hem.

"Fine!" she hollered after Hemingway. "But, I didn't come here to die like a rat in a trap!" Hem tossed her a backward glance and then was gone.

And Josie felt the pang of an emotion other than fear: Shame.

What had she *done*? She had shown her fear to Hemingway. She'd shouted it out. Now she was being jostled by everybody else toward the rear of the hotel, away from Hem's vanishing back. But Josie was immobile with mortification. She held still, and then turned against the human tide, wedging through the rush of people going the other way, pushing her way back to her room. She had let her terror show. How *could* she? Josephine Herbst pulled the door to her room shut behind her, and once she was alone again, she pulled herself together. She was bitter and ashamed, but she found she was shaking much less. She got dressed.

When Josephine Herbst stepped back out into the atrium again, fully dressed, she found a new scene forming around her. The British journalist and Stalinist propagandist Claud Cockburn, Otto Katz's close friend and colleague, went by rather grandly carrying an electric coffee maker, though Cockburn didn't seem to know quite what to do with the thing. The French writer and aviator Antoine de Saint-Exupéry, the author of *Wind, Sand, and Stars* and *The Little Prince*, emerged from his room in a "vibrant" blue satin bathrobe and a guilty box of grapefruit that he had stashed in his room; he was now intent upon handing out grapefruits, with a wordless but a gracious

flourish, to every person—some claimed it was every *woman*—
who passed his door: *Voulez-vous un pamplemousse, Madame?*
The bombardment seemed to be letting up. Down in the
lobby, guests had begun to gather, balancing their wish for
breakfast against the horrors of war in a way even those present
found a little funny. Here and there, some recently very frightened people could be heard to laugh a little. Claud Cockburn
had just blown a fuse with his damn coffee pot. Herbst strode up
to him, seized control of the pot, somehow fixed the fuse, and
got some coffee perking. Meanwhile, a number of women were
standing around holding grapefruits.

The ripping silk, the explosions and architectural jolts were
not flying toward them quite so often. They'd maybe even
stopped, though Josie could still hear that other strange sound
inside the walls. Whatever it was, it sounded vile to her. It
sounded like some sort of scrambling. It sounded *alive*. What
was it? Rats? A waiter from the Florida's restaurant was going
from room to room, knocking on doors, and bringing the
women he found there out into the common space, his arm
around each. Some of them were giggling. Some were weeping.

In the new creepy calm, the air thickened with a sandy plaster
dust drifting down to the lobby floor, and a communal breakfast
began to be assembled from everyone's hoard—stale bread, the
coffee in Claud Cockburn's coffee maker, and Saint-Exupéry's
grapefruits. Then somehow a toaster was produced. Josie was
pouring coffee into little water glasses when she looked up to see
John Dos Passos standing before her, very calm, smiling, and by
now wearing that jacket and tie.

Good feeling started to surge. People started to talk, and the
toaster started to smoke, and for now at least the only burning
smell was burning bread. Even Herbst, not normally an optimist about humanity, paused to reflect: "It was consoling to see

everyone behave so well and to wonder if, within, the turmoil in others had been as hard to quell as it had been in me."[3] People gathered round, among them the British visitors that Otto Katz, as André Simone, was leading through a fellow travelers tour: the Duchess of Atholl, along with the feminist labor politician Ellen Wilkinson, the scientific popularizer J. B. S. Haldane, who had visited "the Old Homestead" with Dos and Hem, and the Dean of Canterbury Cathedral, a committed fellow traveler named Hewlet Johnson. Otto Katz himself? He was probably there, too, even if a number of his close friends kept his presence quiet.

In any case, the bombardment was over, and the grapefruit and coffee were gone. As plaster dust sifted down out of the atrium and onto the lobby floor, some people were drifting into political arguments, while others just drifted away. Dos Passos announced that he for one was going back to his room and see if he could catch up on a little of that sleep that Franco's fury had wasted. Hemingway ventured out into the big square in front of the hotel. It was now well past dawn. The Plaza de Callao—then as now a major center for Madrid's principal movie theaters— was strewn with pulverized rubble. The air billowed with the polluted dust of bombing, and the pavement was littered with the broken pieces from all the stricken buildings, much of it smashed pinkish grey stone that made Herbst think of animal guts in a slaughterhouse. Hemingway was impressed by the damage done to the Paramount Theater across the way, where a sign for Charlie Chaplin's *Modern Times* had taken a direct hit, smashed as if the bastards were taking revenge on a leftist masterpiece. The British visitors picked through the stones, looking for pieces of shrapnel to take home as souvenirs.

When people at last decided to disperse and go on with their day, Josie Herbst found herself standing beside Hemingway in the lobby of the Florida, still ashamed of having shown him her fear, and a little down in the mouth.

Hemingway picked up on it, of course. Why so glum? His tone was slightly needling.

Josie bristled. What was she *supposed* to feel under artillery barrage? "I don't feel like a girl scout," Herbst snapped back, "and I don't care who knows it."

That made Hemingway "relent." After all, he was Hem, her pal, her big brother, her host. Take it easy, Josie. Come on up to my room. Let's have a drink.

The hour must have been somewhere around eight in the morning, but of course Herbst said yes. People did not turn down drinks with Ernest Hemingway, even at eight in the morning.

When they got to room 108, Hemingway went to his famous wardrobe and produced two snifters and a bottle of Spanish brandy. They sat down: Hemingway tilted his glass to Herbst's health.

Then he got down to business. He was especially anxious to have this little talk with Josie not just to calm her nerves but also to discuss this problem with Dos.

Herbst leaned back to hear him out.

Something, Hemingway announced, had to be done to make Dos stop yammering all the time about this man Robles. It was becoming a serious embarrassment. What was Dos's problem, anyway? Doesn't he understand that this is war? OK, his friend has managed to get himself into trouble. That's tough. That's also what happens in wars. Dos's incessant whining about it was throwing suspicion on all the people in the Florida. It was fouling up *The Spanish Earth* project; it was going to foul up everybody's standing in Spain. Did Josie know what happened between Dos and Pepe Quintinilla? Well, it was a tale to tell. Quintinilla, a wonderful man, a real insider and a great guy, happened to be one of Hemingway's particular friends in this town. Josie should get to know him. And it was only natural that Dos take his problem with Robles to Quintinilla. Well, Quintinilla met with Dos right away, listened to all his questions, made the proper inquiries, and got back to Dos and told him straight from the shoulder that it was quite true, this Robles guy had been arrested all right, there were some questions about him that had to be cleared up, but that there would be an inquiry and a fair trial and if Robles was innocent of whatever it was then everything would work out just fine.

That was that. Now Hem simply could not understand what the hell more Dos wanted. This reassurance came straight from the top. You just can't get better information in Spain than from Quintinilla. And what did Dos do with Quintinilla's answer? He'd been going around saying he didn't *believe* the man. Didn't believe Quintinilla *himself*. That Quintinilla was lying, that his answer was just more of the same old runaround. It was just intolerable. Didn't Dos understand that smearing a man like Quintinilla could only bring down big trouble on them all? Something had to put a stop to this crazy meddling, and now. Hem was at the end of his rope. Dos liked Josie; Hem had noticed that they had tea together most mornings. Couldn't Josie do *something*? Maybe Dos would listen to her.

It was the moment Herbst had been waiting for. The time had come for her to produce the weapon she had been concealing since she arrived in Madrid.

"I put down my drink and said: 'The man is already dead. Quintinilla should have told Dos.'"

Hemingway stared back, thunderstruck.

Already *dead*?

José Robles had been executed.

But why?

Because he was a fascist spy.

But how could *Josie* know *that*, when even a man like Quintinilla . . .

Quintinilla was lying. Dos was right about that part. Josie had already pointed that out.

Hemingway stared at her.

Josie had been told the truth the day she got to Valencia, during a meeting she had there with an Important Official, who in turn had the information from someone even higher up. Both of her informants insisted upon anonymity. She couldn't tell Hem who had told her because she had given her word, but Hem could rest assured that her information was accurate. Robles was a fascist spy, and he had been shot for it. He was already dead by the time Dos arrived in Spain.

Hemingway took it all in. This changed everything. As she spoke, Josie noticed how easily Hemingway accepted the charge that Robles was a fascist spy. It was not a claim or even a suspicion mentioned thus far by anyone known to Dos, but Hem bought it without a blink. He asked no questions about trials, or charges, or evidence, or circumstances. Robles was a fascist spy. Simple.

Later—much later—Josie claimed she herself had not been so sure. Robles, she knew, "was well known for his enlightened views, and there was the chance that he was the victim of personal enemies or even of some terrible blunder."[4] Really? If these really were Herbst's private thoughts, she kept them very private. She certainly did not share them with Hemingway or Dos Passos, either then or ever. Herbst watched while the lie with which she had been entrusted filled Hemingway's mind. For once, Herbst had the man's complete attention. She was no longer being patronized.

She continued.

The question now was what to do. She had thought the whole situation through with very great care, and she had developed a plan.

The most important issue before them was that somehow Dos must be told the truth. They both were Dos's dear friends. Dear friends like themselves could hardly leave Dos, as she put it, "in anguished ignorance." Decency demanded that, as Dos's friends, they do something.

But *who* should tell him? And how? What would be the right time, the right place?

There was a problem with Josie being the one to tell him. Although she felt free to tell Hemingway all about her conversation with the Important Official in Valencia, Dos must not know about it under any circumstances. Why? Well, she had *promised*. She had sworn she would protect the Important Official's anonymity. She had given her word. If she was tossing her promise aside by telling Hem, it was only because she was so devoted to the truth. "Circumstances," she said, "seemed to me more pressing than any promise."

But since she was telling Hem, should she tell Dos, too? Well, no. She had given her *word*. Not that she was protecting *herself*, of course. It was a question of honor. If Dos found out the truth about Robles from her, he would naturally ask how she knew. He'd want to know whom she'd heard it from. Then what? She would have broken her *promise*. Honor, honor.

So since Josie could not tell Dos, who should?

Well, the answer was obvious. *Hemingway* should break the news to Dos.

Hemingway sat listening with rapt attention.

Yet who could they say had told *Hem* the truth about Robles? Until today, Hem had clearly believed Quintinilla's lie about Robles being arrested over some minor matter that might well be cleared up in a trial. Who or what changed his mind? He couldn't say it was Josie. That only deepened the problem they were trying to avoid.

Clearly, Hem would have to claim he'd learned the truth from somebody else. But whom?

They would have to invent a source. It would be a lie, but it would be just a *little* lie, and they would be lying for Dos's sake, too. They were lying so that Dos could be told the truth. They were lying *for* Dos. Their "source" should be "someone from Valencia who was passing through but whose name he must withhold."[5] After giving it careful thought, Josie was sure she knew exactly the right man to play this part. She just happened to know a man who was passing through; someone with access to information at the top; someone who would be willing to say he could talk to Hemingway but refused to talk to Dos. A German correspondent. That was perfect.

Hemingway was listening hard. A German correspondent willing to talk to him but not to Dos. The implication was clear: Hemingway could be trusted with this delicate state secret, while Dos Passos could not.

Herbst watched knowingly as this implication sank in.

The next question was where and when to tell Dos their lie. There was an obvious answer: at that very moment, Dos Passos was in his room, taking a nap. It would have been simple enough to walk up to his room, knock on the door, and then tell Dos the "truth" the German correspondent had just told them. Gently, privately, and with discretion. Friend to friend.

But Josie wouldn't even consider this option. Herbst had something a little more public in mind.

That very afternoon all three friends were to be driven to a castle outside Madrid for a fiesta and gala luncheon celebrating the "transfer of command" of the Fifteenth International Brigade to the Republic. Herbst, Hemingway, and Dos Passos would be going: *everybody* would be going. The entire press corps would be milling around, not to mention all kinds of literary celebrities, officials, generals both Spanish and Soviet, the Spanish Republican Army's commandant General José Miaja himself, all *kinds* of people in power and opinion makers. The visiting British dignitaries would also be present—and so would their guide, André Simone, who under that alias posed as a German correspondent, even if Josie knew him better as a collaborator in the Soviet secret services with Alvarez del Vayo.

Why not break the news to Dos at this afternoon's luncheon? Hem could tell Dos that he and Josie had met the German correspondent then and there. Simone-Katz would be at the luncheon with his British charges. The fiesta would have important people wall to wall. And all eyes would be on the two Americans, the most famous guests in the place. Whatever happened between the two men would be *seen*, and seen by people who counted. Where better to break the news to Dos? At the fiesta. In the high glare of publicity. In front of everyone. Or to be more exact, in front of Everyone. The ideal time, the ideal place.

There was no need to articulate the implications. John Dos Passos—the most famous leftist writer in America—humiliated in front of Everybody. Dos Passos—the collaborator on *The Spanish Earth*—exposed as the friend of a fascist spy. Dos—noble Dos—the protector of treason.

It was Hemingway's turn to put down his drink. Josie thought he looked almost *too* cheerful. He was beaming. He thought Josie's little plan was just *splendid*.[6]

Josie smiled, too. Her own back was completely covered. Either on her own or in collaboration with a senior Soviet propaganda agent, she had quietly and discreetly handed Hemingway the exact weapon she knew he was looking for. And then, just as quietly and discreetly, she had shown him how to use it.

chapter 9

FIESTA

The party was set to begin in just a few hours. The occasion Josie and Hem had chosen to blindside Dos was a fiesta celebrating the nationalization of the Fifteenth International Brigade, taking place in a chateau—a onetime royal hunting lodge—perhaps forty minutes outside Madrid, not far from the great royal residence of the Escorial. The cream of the Florida's celebrities—Josie just barely made the cut—was to be driven out to the chateau in time for a review of the troops, speechmaking by important generals, and a festive lunch in honor of a "transfer of command" of this most important of the International Brigades. The transfer in question was from the Brigade's former but illusory status as an independent militia to a new status, equally illusory, purportedly under the command of the Spanish Republican Army and its commandant, General José Miaja.

In truth, this entire event, with its blaring bands, sonorous, thick-throated speeches, and lavish entertainment, was just another piece of propaganda—and given its implications, a rather sinister one at that. The supposed transition of the Fifteenth Brigade from its prior status as an independent militia to its new status under unified Spanish Republican command was illusion.

The Fifteenth Brigade had never been an independent militia; it had been covertly organized by the Comintern, and operated under the unseen command of the Soviets. Nor were these concealed realities about to be materially changed by anything celebrated at the Duke of Tovar's chateau. General José Miaja was a figurehead; or in any case, the Russians treated him like one. In public, they ostentatiously deferred to the portly old commander, but this was mainly as a sop to Spanish nationalist sentiment: Shouldn't at least *some* of the Republic's generals be real Spaniards? Privately, the Soviets and their Spanish communist allies viewed the general with a venomous contempt that, even now, is a little shocking. As one Comintern general put it, "We tried to create an aura of prestige around him that he damn well didn't deserve."[1] The Soviets had no intention of giving Miaja or any non-Soviet effective control over their Brigades, and they never did. They merely wanted to make the Fifteenth *seem* to lead a parade of "independents" to a new "unified command."

The Soviets were promoting this illusion because in their propaganda they were simultaneously demanding that all the other, and more authentic, independent militias in the coalition submit to the same unified command. In late April, communist propaganda was pumping out a steady stream of invective against the other "independent" militias as packs of "uncontrollables," filled with renegades and traitors. Most of these independent militias were attached to non-Stalinist factions in the government's coalition; they were precisely the kind of fighting force that George Orwell writes about in *Homage to Catalonia*, groups bound to the doomed Spanish anarchists and the POUM. The Soviets wanted these organizations destroyed; after months of preparation under Gorev and others, the Soviet military machine and the NKVD (the ubiquitous secret police) were about to liquidate them all, breaking up their command, decimating their ranks, and murdering as many of their leaders as could be murdered. The Fifteenth Brigade's shift of command authority was based on a distinction without a political difference. As the Soviets alone were well aware, the provocations and killings of the May Days promised a collateral gain: the destruction of the Largo Caballero coalition in Valencia, and the establishment of a new pliant government that would put the "unified command" of the Spanish Republican army firmly under their own control. Meanwhile, chief on the hit list was that "Trotskyite" Andrés Nin. The purpose of the April fiesta was to help disguise May's intrusion of the Great Terror into the Spanish tragedy. The Fifteenth Brigade's embrace of "unified" command was to prepare all the *other* "independent" militias for the destruction that was now squarely in the Soviet crosshairs. In a little over two weeks, the killing would begin. In Barcelona, George Orwell would be handed the shock, and the story, of his life.

The Hotel Floridians were driven in style to this non-event at the ducal chateau. Hemingway and Josie went with their Spanish hosts, Rafael Alberti, the illustrious poet and committed Stalinist, and his wife María Teresa, while Dos was to be driven in another car by the Albertis' friend, a young Communist wunderkind named Gustavo Durán. The Albertis and Durán arrived at the Florida around 10:30, excited and celebrity-struck, determined to make the maximum hay out of their afternoon glowing in all this American fame. Rafael came striding into Hem's room wearing a military get-up that, despite the clatter of its polished high boots, could not hide from Josie's practiced eye the poet's unmilitary narcissism. Chattering "like a canary," María Teresa was dressed in "coral earrings, a brooch, and a filmy scarf" that made Josie feel "like a nun." At the Albertis' side stood the young, complex, multitalented Gustavo Durán. Until the outbreak of the war, Durán had lived in Paris, a well-connected, but not very successful avant-garde composer, a friend of the chic American avant-garde composer George Antheil and (incidentally) Hadley Hemingway. But music was not Durán's authentic calling; the war in Spain had helped Gustavo find himself as a political soldier and Communist apparatchik, both of which blessed him with the rapid rise denied to him in music. Even so, Durán was a real, living, breathing version of the soldier-artist who was so very dear to Hemingway's fantasies. Durán seemed sent from Central Casting. (He really did quite strikingly resemble Gary Cooper.) He had abandoned life on the Left Bank to enter the theater of war. Durán had looks and brains and talent and cool, and in short order, he and Hemingway became fast friends. Josie sized up Durán shrewdly, and didn't like the man much, while Durán, instantly assessing Herbst as a nobody, looked right through her. He struck Josie as "very compact, erect, and clear," with "rather cold blue eyes." He also struck her as the sort of man who habitually looked right through nobodies.

As a rising star Durán had already come far enough to be standing in Ernest Hemingway's hotel room. But the forthcoming communist near-coup in Valencia would soon lift him to even finer things. He had been, or would soon be, Spanish interpreter and adjutant to the Soviet General Emilio Kléber—a position very like the one Robles had held with Gorev, though with this all-important difference: Durán was a firmly committed Stalinist operative, serving the apparatus so flawlessly that he soon graduated to secret police work, in which he quickly became a favored protégé of the Soviet NKVD chief in Spain, Alexander Orlov, the man who, on Stalin's direct personal order, murdered Nin.[2]

The two groups set off. Josie and Hem went with the Albertis; Durán drove Dos Passos. The Albertis' ecstasies over their ride in the fame car came close to making Josie lose her mind. Josie had more than one good reason to be on edge, and as María Teresa chattered away, the American could gladly have

strangled her. As for Rafael, "I would rather read Alberti's wonderful poem 'Sobre los Angeles' quietly at home than go twenty
steps to meet him in his sparkling military boots and with his
camera in hand."

That damn camera, especially, drove Josie nuts. Rafael and
María Teresa were dead-set on getting a snapshot immortalizing
their moment in the sun with Hem and Dos—the perfect expression, so far as Josie was concerned, of the name-dropping
narcissism that made the whole celebrity-sick atmosphere at the
Florida so intolerable.

The cars' first stop was at the crossroads of a small village not
far from the chateau. As Dos described it, it was located "among
the ugly summer villas of welltodo madrileños that deface the
high boulderstrewn foothills of the Guadarramas." There, everyone got out and "stood at the edge of the road waiting in a little
crowd of guests" for the review of the troops. Alberti saw this as
the moment to get his picture. As people milled around, waiting
for the ceremony to begin, Alberti shepherded Hem and Dos and
María Teresa into a little cluster on the edge of the road, acting
on what Josie called "his propensity for arranging groups for pictures, then leaping into the center of the group at the last moment while he thrust the camera into someone else's hand."[3]

The unwilling hands into which Alberti shoved the camera
this time were Josie's. And as her heart swelled with bitterness,
she made the snap.

The picture still exists. It's not much of a picture, but does say
a great deal about its moment. To the left of the group, against
some scruffy crossroads greenery, stands Alberti, looking impressed and pleased. On the far right, a perfectly pleasant-looking
María Teresa beams, tickled pink. In between the Albertis stand
Hem and Dos. It is obvious that Hemingway has not yet un-
loaded on Dos Passos; that the two are still on good terms. The

smiling expression on Dos Passos's face is still cordial, still open, and still unhurt. The attack has not begun—not yet. The image of Hemingway, on the other hand, is unlike almost any picture of him in existence. The man looks almost sick with hatred. He is slouching, joyless and defiant. He doesn't even fake a smile. The group is arm-in-arm; Hem has draped one limp hand over Dos's shoulder in a kind of indolent contempt. This man is ready to strike. He is ready to inflict pain. His expression is at once enraged and afflicted. His eyes speak to the camera, but they have only one thing to say: *the hell with you. The hell with your opinion about what I'm going to do. The hell with you all.* Josie caught it in just one resentful click.

Next General Miaja rolled into the crossroads in a staff car, accompanied by numerous Russian officers and the Soviet general who went under the name of General "Walter." The French, Belgian, Italian, and German Brigadiers, vowing their allegiance to the Republic, assembled and made a snappy show of presenting arms while the band played (twice) "The Hymn of Riego," the Republic's national anthem. Then everyone walked down a dusty little road to a place where a platform and bunting had been set up for more martial music and speeches. A great many important people were standing around. Durán glanced toward the sky, muttering to Dos, "the fascists have supporters everywhere, but their espionage service is lousy. They ought to be bombing us this minute."[4]

When the last band had played the last anthem, the celebrities piled back into their cars and were driven to the chateau, where the Russians had established their headquarters. It was beautifully situated in the shadow of the snow-capped Guadarramas, approached only by going past a large square guard tower, beyond which the group assembled before the chateau on a lovely patio "lined with oleander trees in earthen pots." The group was led into the building through its enormous kitchen, which in addition to being vaulted and copper-hung and sumptuous with Mediterranean abundance—"we seemed to have stepped into a Bruegel painting"—was filled with food, and *good* food, moreover. After Madrid it seemed a miracle: "actual cooking was going on," enough to keep "a dozen sunburned soldiers . . . busy preparing the feast." Through the starched curtains at the kitchen windows, Herbst caught a glimpse of April lilacs in bloom. They were in a different world.

This was where Hemingway would strike. The guests were led through that steaming vaulted kitchen into a dining room that was better than large: it was splendid. From its seignorial walls superb ancestral portraits in ruffs and swords, a whole Spanish Renaissance of forgotten grandees, gazed down on the banqueting hall. There the guests were greeted by two high-ranking Russian military men whom Herbst was quick to point out "did not seem inappropriate substitutes" for the forgotten nobilities looking down on them from the walls.

Herbst was not, of course, seated at the celebrity table with Hemingway and Dos Passos. Yet for once obscurity suited her. She had been apprehensive about how her plan was going to play out. She was seated beside a Russian division commander, whom she was relieved to find could converse with her in German. While this chat went on, Josie kept a clear view of Hem and Dos, who were seated up near the head table. She was too far away to hear their voices, but judging from the expressions on the two men's faces, everything was proceeding exactly according to plan. And the plan was, after all, Josie's plan.

By now Hemingway was glowing with confidence and cruelty, cutting into Dos Passos with the "news" he had just "learned" from the "German correspondent." Despite silence, Herbst could easily follow the progress of his attack, watching Dos Passos struggling to keep his composure. He had, Herbst thought, an "abstracted air" that made her know Hem was hitting home. Yet as Hemingway slashed away at him—and as the other guests listened, attentive and appalled—Dos Passos "kept up his end of the conversation with considerable spirit."

Hemingway was grinding away especially hard on his own newfound certainty that Robles had been a *traitor*. José Robles was not simply a man in trouble: he had been shot as a proven fascist collaborator, a renegade, a dirty spy, a betrayer of his friends. He'd been exposed, tried, and shot for treachery. Fair and square. So it was time to stop the hand wringing and the whining. Dos's friend was a fascist, and he had gotten what he deserved. How did Hem know? It came straight from an impeccable source. The "German correspondent" was here in the room, just in from Valencia; a man with the best contacts you can have, and he'd given it straight to Hem: Robles is dead, shot for treason. There's no mystery about it. The "German correspondent" was perfectly ready to tell *Hemingway* the whole story; for that matter, he'd even told Josie. But the "German correspondent" drew the line at talking to Dos Passos. He had his standards. Dos was a friend and defender of a fascist traitor. The correspondent refused to have anything to do with Dos.

Josie watched the scene unfold: Hemingway hitting with all his sadistic fervor, Dos Passos struggling to hold his ground.

When lunch was over, the guests gathered for dessert and coffee in the garden. Herbst was chatting in German with yet another Russian officer when, painfully distressed, "with a little coffee cup in his hand, Dos came up to me and in an agitated voice asked why it was that he couldn't meet the man who had conveyed the news, why couldn't he speak to him too?"

It was a good question, and needless to say, Herbst did not answer it. "The only thing I could think of was to tell him not to ask any more questions in Madrid. It would be better to wait until he got to Valencia and then see someone like Alvarez del Vayo and find out what he could."

Dos walked away, uncomprehending.

And then came a final poignant touch, significant especially for Dos. Just before the event ended, a young Spanish officer escorted two women into the room, mystery guests here for a star turn at the end of the affair. Wearing broad straw hats and silk shawls, the two were seated at the head table. When they took off their hats and pushed back their shawls, the Spaniards in the room gasped at the sight of a well-known singer named Niña de las Peñas and . . . Pastora Imperio. There she was: "one of the greatest Spanish dancers the world has ever seen," the living flame of Dos's youth, whose all-but-mystical flamenco he had taken all his Harvard friends to see, the creature of fire whose dance the young Dos had discovered with José, and who had been for the nineteen-year-old Dos the incarnation of sex and death. Pastora Imperio was now a rather stout woman in late middle age, but she was still a star. The grieving Dos stared at her.

Everyone started to clap, demanding music. Pastora rose.

"I can't make speeches, but when I see you young men and how you are fighting for our liberty and when I think of my Spain . . . my heart breaks." She began to weep; she suddenly covered her mouth, and then sank down again in her chair.

The ride back to Madrid was smothered in silence. The Albertis may have tried to keep up their chatter, but Hemingway ignored them. After indulging in some particularly egregious cruelty, Hemingway often became sullen and withdrawn, probably warding off the first wave of guilt. Certainly Josephine Herbst had nothing to say. The stricken Dos Passos was in the other car with Durán, who complained as he drove about the insignificance of the afternoon. A waste of time. A stupid waste of time. When the first car pulled up outside the Florida, Hemingway was out the door in a flash. He bolted and fled, without so much as a goodbye.

The next to leave were the clueless and probably bewildered Albertis.

That left Josie standing alone on the sidewalk as Durán drove up with Dos.

Dos Passos was dazed, drenched in sadness. He had been clinging for days to a plausible denial of José's death, rejecting the rumor that Coco had brought home from the propaganda office in favor of Quintinilla's evasions. But now came this . . . this new, even more horrible rumor. Dos's hope was dying. These new claims were being asserted with such *confidence*. And by *Hem*. Hem was killing his hope. Hem *had* killed his hope. José Robles was dead. He was dead.

Dead—even if this nonsense about "treason" was an obvious lie. Treason? Nobody anywhere had spoken to Dos Passos about treason except Hemingway, and of course Dos did not believe the claim for a moment. But where was Hemingway getting this stuff? Was he just inventing it? And who was this German correspondent?

Dos was imagining the scene again, as he had already imagined it: *"They shove a cigarette into your hand and you walk into the courtyard to face six men you have never seen before. They take aim. They wait for the order. . . ."*

Standing in front of the hotel alone with Josie, Dos Passos suddenly turned to Herbst and made a strange request; he felt he could at least trust her at this moment. He didn't want to go back inside the hotel quite yet. It was nearing sundown, and Dos Passos wanted to take a walk. He wondered if Josie would very much mind walking with him.

He wanted to walk over to the Plaza Mayor. Had she seen it? A wonderful place. It was quite near, maybe half a mile from the Florida. Dos Passos knew the way well.

And so, though Herbst could hardly imagine why, they set out together.

The Plaza Mayor is an exceptionally magnificent baroque space in the heart of Madrid, built in the early seventeenth century, not long after the death of Philip II, during the reign of Philip III, when the Spain of the Hapsburgs was at the height of its cruel, imperial magnificence. Some of the most terrible episodes in the history of Spain have taken place in the shadow of these arcades. Three centuries before, this was the place where the Inquisition burnt heretics in the infamous *autos-da-fé*. It had also been the scene of Madrid's first bullfights, and over the centuries it had been filled with fiestas and rebellions, carnivals and religious revivals. The tangled narrow streets of the oldest part of Madrid surround it, and once you have stepped into the plaza through one of the many arches that open into it, you stand in a vast open square, ringed on every side with colonnades, which were then, as now, filled with vendors, tourist traps, shoeshine stands, urchins, and pickpockets.

At least in 1937, the Plaza Mayor was among the most magnificent and most proletarian places in Spain. It was a breathtaking slum. Twenty years before, Dos Passos had come to know it as a student of architecture in the Centro de Estúdios Históricos, back when Madrid felt like his city. "I feel as though I have lived here all my life," he'd told José. Learning to see Madrid, to hear Madrid, to feel Madrid had been for Dos Passos a founding event in his life as an artist. And much of that process had taken place at Robles's side. Under these arcades, they had gotten drunk and declaimed the epics at one another. Here they had held forth about love and God and Walt Whitman and revolution. Here Dos had seen Spaniards of the streets and street kids straight out of Goya. And now, now that Dos Passos no longer had any hope about José Robles, he wanted to see the Plaza Mayor once again. He walked with Herbst through the war-ripped streets. As they walked, they could hear shelling in the distance. They arrived at twilight.

The only thing somber about the Plaza Mayor that night was its immensity and its long reach into a dark history. In the dusk of April 22, 1937, it was rollicking with life, and not the life of celebrities and conspiracies, but the life of the poor. Dos Passos stood alone with his thoughts for a long time, silently taking in the whole wide teeming space. The Plaza had been hit hard by Franco's bombing. The façades of many buildings had been ripped away, leaving gaping honeycombs of inner rooms, "the front of a house sliced off and touchingly revealing parlors, bedrooms, kitchens, diningrooms, twisted iron beds dangling, elaborate chandeliers hanging over void, a piano suspended in the air, a sideboard with dishes still on it, a mirror with a gilt stucco frame glittering high up in a mass of wreckage where everything else has been obliterated."

Rubble was piled everywhere, and children were playing on it, shouting and laughing in the dusk. Those children still looked like they had come straight out of Goya. Yet in this war-transformed city, Dos Passos had been struck by how much everything looked the same: "the streetcars are the same, the longnosed sallow madrileño faces are the same, with the same mixture of brow bullet-headed countrymen, the women in the darkcolored shawls don't look very different. . . ." Even "the shellholes and the scars made by flying fragments and shrapnel have not changed the general look of the street." Yet converging on precisely this sameness, the terrors of war had made everything seem alien. Life's banality was unchanged in the face of death, and it felt terrible. "It's the usualness of it," he concluded, "that gives it this feeling of nightmare."

Was it that "feeling of nightmare" that Dos Passos was feeling when he stood beside Josephine Herbst under an arcade of the Plaza Mayor? In the center of the square, a grandiose equestrian statue, a magnificent statue of a triumphant Philip III, had been erected on the very spot where the Inquisition had burned its heretics. Now an anarchist flag on a pole had been stuck into the hand of that absolute monarch on his charging mount, and the banner was flapping in the evening breeze.

The Plaza Mayor had survived poverty, and now it was surviving bombing and death. It spread before them, shouting, laughing, arguing, and singing. Dos Passos and Herbst stood there in silence, Dos in the silence of his devastated hope, Josie in the silence of her guilty secret, watching the sun going down on its abashed magnificence.

In *Century's Ebb*, Dos Passos suggests that it was later that night, at a large famous-person party held in Juan Posada's apartment building in Madrid, that he at last got definitive— that is, official—word on Robles's death. Posada's apartment was rich and rather grand, and the service and liquor were lavish. Once again Everyone was there. Hemingway and Gellhorn were at the center of attention, and though Dos was avoiding the "happy pair," he could hear Hemingway's "rickety" Spanish and Martha's "dry laugh" coming from the heart of the elegant crowd. Alvarez del Vayo was there. Durán was playing Chopin on the piano.

Dos Passos had "slumped into a mood of desperate anxiety," and he had stepped out onto a balcony to stare out on what he now perceived as a "desert" of "tiled roofs and distant domes and spires faintly visible in the starlight."

Then he heard someone step out onto the balcony with him. "I brought you another Scotch." It was Posada. He was speaking in English.

Dos took the Scotch.

"Nice view," Posada said, to say something. "Isn't it?"

Dos couldn't speak.

"The man has been shot," Posada said, in a low, curt, voice.

Dos turned to look straight at his old friend. Why? *Why?* There must have been some *reason.*

Posada did not give a reason. "Dos, we are living in terrible times. To overcome them we have to be terrible ourselves."

Dos Passos ignored this bit of philosophy. In the room beyond, Durán was finishing the nocturne, and now applause came rolling out over them.

"Why has nobody told his wife?" Dos asked. He was speaking rather sharply.

Posada answered in a tone that was almost pleading. "Dos, you know this is not my fault. In spite of this life, I'm not more inhuman than I was when I was a dedicated student of the law, a boy, if you'll remember, of somewhat extreme sensibility. . . . How do I do it? *Juerga.* Continual orgy. . . . Whisky, women, gypsies, the most indecent whores."

Though Dos Passos found this answer, like the others, insufficient, he did manage to tell Posada that he didn't hold him responsible.

Posada persisted. "I will see to it his wife and children are not molested . . . I promise . . . but from now on . . . silence."

Posada "melodramatically" lifted two fingers to his lips. Then he let them drop. He walked back into the salon, looking for more whisky.

chapter 10

HEMINGSTEIN'S
DYNAMICS OF DYING

The very next day—April 23—Joris Ivens left Spain, never to
return.

He took with him the completed footage of *The Spanish
Earth* and exited the country just in time to sidestep the events
of May. Though he would be editing and finishing the picture
throughout the early summer of 1937, Ivens was, despite lots of
talk, in the process of washing his hands of the Spanish tragedy.
The Comintern was turning its attention elsewhere. In late July,
Japan invaded China: Stalin ordered his apparatus to redirect its
propaganda against the gathering Japanese menace. And so it
was to China that the obedient Ivens's attention now turned in a
minor but meaningful indication of Stalin's changing interest in
the whole march of events in Spain. It is quite true that as the
May provocations approached, the dictator stood poised to so-
lidify his grip on the Valencia government. Yet it would be
wrong to assume Stalin was intruding his power in order to turn
Spain into some sort of Soviet possession. Quite the contrary.
Merely parking the Red Army in Spain would only make Stalin
vulnerable to Hitler on a second, Western, front.

Nyet. Stalin's interest in Spain was *tactical*; his idea was to divert German aggression from his own borders by fomenting trouble between Hitler and the democracies in the West. For Spain to be useful in this tactic, Stalin needed the administration in Valencia to do his bidding. But he never had the slightest intention of going to war with Hitler over Spain. On the contrary, he always intended to abandon Spain. That was why the new Popular Front government must not be too obviously a Soviet surrogate. And why it must not win.

Anyway, by April's end, Ivens was on his way to the exit. Though Hemingway never stopped liking Joris, even he was a little shocked at the moviemaker's cool readiness to walk out of Spain. "So you're going there!" he grumbled, when he realized that Ivens would not be coming back. "It's all over with Spain. The Third International"—that is, the Comintern—"is now turning its attention to China!" It seems Hem understood more about Joris's unseen agenda than either man ever said. Even Martha Gellhorn, always a cheerleader for Joris, was taken aback. "In New York," she remarked in her old age, "we were promoting *The Spanish Earth* as if the whole world depended on it. What always astounded me was that Joris did not return to Spain. Ernest and I went back there, he didn't. I believe he wasn't that emotionally involved after all."[1]

Ivens took the footage of *The Spanish Earth* first to Paris and then New York, there to shape *his* movie in consultation with the Comintern professionals who really mattered. These emphatically did not include John Dos Passos. Unlike Hemingway and Martha, not to mention any number of lesser collaborators, Dos Passos was never allowed to see any part of *The Spanish Earth*. Back in New York by June, Ivens worked nonstop on finishing the picture. The only Hotel Floridian at his side was Martha, who was fully complicit with Ivens's effort to exclude

Dos Passos from any credit whatever in the film. That summer, Martha maintained a steady stream of letters to Hem. One particularly gloating report on Ivens's plans takes special delight in the way Dos Passos has been excluded from the film's forthcoming premiere, at the Comintern-controlled League of American Writers at Carnegie Hall later that month.[2]

(Stalinist propaganda, Tresca had snapped. He spoke with the self-possession of a croupier at Monte Carlo.)

Concerning Dos, Ivens also now dropped his old genial mask and began to level personal attacks. From Valencia, about four days after the Fifteenth Brigade lunch, Ivens wrote to Hemingway that Dos Passos was in town, "running here for the same cause [i.e., Robles] as he did in Madrid—it is difficult. Hope that Dos will see what a man and comrade has to do in this difficult and serious wartime." This remark, though insensitive, seems mild enough. The mild tone did not last. Ivens would soon be writing to Hem calling Robles "the friend-translator-fascist of Dos Passos," and he would continue to spread the lie of Robles's "fascism" for the rest of his life. What made Ivens's distress over Robles swell to outrage was his discovery that Dos met and interviewed Andrés Nin. *That* was beyond fascism. "I still get angry when I think of the fact that Dos after being with us went into the POUM office in Barcelona—it is not only the worst political thing to do—but more: dirty disloyal to all of us." The next day he was forthrightly calling Dos Passos an "enemy."[3] Radek's attack was bearing fruit.

The same morning that Ivens checked out, Dos Passos left Madrid, too. But not before he had yet another unpleasant run-in.

Neither Hem nor Josie were anywhere in sight when Dos Passos came down to breakfast that morning, bags packed, looking for his cup of pallid Hotel Florida tea and his hard little roll. (Strange fare indeed after yesterday's lunch, which had featured a sauce béarnaise "worthy of Foyot's.") When Dos walked into the breakfast room, he was mildly surprised to see his old acquaintance, and Hem's longtime hanger-on, Evan Shipman, slouching at a nearby table. Dos and Shipman were friendly enough—or so Dos thought. Except that when Dos walked in, Shipman did not favor him with a smile.

Dos knew Shipman, who had been driving International Brigadiers around the country, from the Paris days. In one famous incident, Shipman had rolled his ever-ready dice against Hem for the right to buy Joan Miró's early masterpiece *The Farm*. Hem won the throw and (helped out by a loan from Dos) bought the picture as a birthday present for Hadley. Miró, Hemingway claimed, was the "only painter who had ever been able to combine in one picture all that you felt about Spain when you were there and all that you felt when you are away and could not go there."[4] *The Farm*—now in the Guggenheim in New York—would hang above Hemingway's work desk for decades to come.

Primed by Hem, Shipman greeted Dos Passos with a glare of hatred. Are *you* still here? Shipman snapped. That's not smart. These days, Spain wasn't safe for friends of fascist spies. Now that the truth was out, Dos should be watching his own back. Friends of fascists were courting danger. It was time for Dos, if he knew what was good for him, to pack those bags.

Dos Passos's reply is not on record, but when Shipman recounted the story in years to come, he always insisted—falsely—that after hearing this warning, Dos Passos "went right out of that restaurant, took the first conveyance he could get, and went back to Paris."[5]

Thus was the myth of Dos Passos's "cowardice" set in motion. From this moment on, fabrications about Dos Passos's supposed lack of bravery in leaving Spain became a standard item in Hemingway's private mythology, a bit of personal malice soon taken up as a staple of the Stalinist propaganda that now began to be directed more generally against Dos Passos.[6] Hemingway's inventions on this subject eventually became flagrant. "I couldn't believe the change in the man from the last time I had seen him in Paris!" he crowed to an early biographer, A. E. Hotchner, in the late 1950s. "The very first time his hotel was bombed, Dos packed up and hurried back to France. Of course, we were all damned scared during the war. But not over a chicken-shit thing like a few bombs on the hotel. Only a couple of rooms ever got hit, anyway. I finally figured out Dos's problem was that he had come into some money, and for the first time his body had become valuable. Fear of death increases in exact proportion to increase in wealth: Hemingstein's Law on the Dynamics of Dying."[7]

Virtually every syllable of this diatribe is false. Was Dos Passos frightened by the bombardment? Josephine Herbst's notes, made the morning that the hotel was being hit, describe Dos Passos as notably calm under fire. (Her exact words: "Dos very composed and at ease.") Dos? "Come into money?" The will of John Dos Passos, senior, had been probated twenty years before. In 1937, Dos Passos was as broke as ever. Had Dos "hurried back to France"? As Ivens himself had made clear to Hemingway, Dos Passos had left Madrid not for Paris but Valencia, and in order to comfort Márgara and once again confront the Spanish government's lies. After that—as Hemingway surely knew—Dos was scheduled to proceed to Barcelona, there to report on a rapidly deteriorating, and genuinely dangerous, political situation of prime importance that Hemingway was determined to ignore. Dos may have been tangled in "the dynamics of dying," but not in the way Hemingstein defined them.

Now a new obsession began to gnaw at Hemingway. At the end of April, he was losing interest in events at the military front;

the battle scenes he had covered for NANA, often with Ivens at his side, were (for the moment) not quite as compelling as police action, especially secret police action; the treacherous working of covert intelligence. Hemingway was becoming preoccupied with the business of treason, with fifth columnists, with unseen executions.

Not long after Dos left for Valencia, Hem and Josie found themselves escorting the foreign correspondent Virginia Cowles, another Hotel Floridian, to lunch at the Gran Via restaurant. For some reason, Martha Gellhorn wasn't there, though she and Virginia had struck up what became a lifelong friendship at the Florida. The group was having a long Spanish lunch on the terrace outside, when shells—light ones, like the ones that had smacked into the Florida not long before—started pelting down again.

At first the people lunching on the terrace stayed put. Some of the explosions landed near enough to send fragments scattering across the restaurant plaza. A few hit close enough to make the ground under the *terraza* heave a little. Yet people were treating the raid as if it were a thunderstorm, a nuisance. It was as if, since they had forgotten their umbrellas, they would have to stay there under the awning, nursing their coffee, until the cloudburst let up. Certainly Hemingway and his group did not move. Josie was still working hard at controlling her fear. She sat very still.

Not far from Hemingway's table sat a fastidious man wearing a dove-grey uniform. He had long, elegant fingers, and he wore horn-rims that gave him the look of an intellectual. This man was looking at them, but he made no sign of moving.

After taking in this somber but elegant figure, Hemingway leaned confidentially toward Virginia Cowles. "That," he murmured, ticking his glance toward the stranger, "is the executioner of Madrid." After watching a slightly frozen expression of distress harden on Virginia's face, he turned and called out *"Pepe!"*

One *"Pepe!"* was all it took. The "executioner of Madrid" was up in a flash, hurrying over to the fame table to present himself, all smiles over Hem's invitation to join them.

The executioner's name, as Virginia learned during those introductions, was Pepe Quintinilla, though Cowles never knew that the "executioner of Madrid" was the same secret policeman whom Josie had told Hem was lying to Dos about Robles. By now the shells were getting maybe a little nearer. Hem's party dominated the terrace, all the more so now that the executioner was there. The waiters hovered, eager to help the man in dove-grey light his cigarettes. Another shell landed somewhere, and as Josie flinched, Quintinilla, who had begun talking, paused to call out his count of the shells since the attack had begun. *"Six!"* he'd bark, as the sixth shell hit.

Josie was getting a little better with her fear. But just a little. Another shell landed. *"Seven!"*

In her memoir, Josie reports "looking hard" at the man who had lied to Dos, as if a glaring glance across the lunch table could reprimand his mendacity, and on the very last page of the "Spanish Notebook" she wrote out, in a slightly tremulous hand, "Quintinilla: *El Comisario General de Investigación y Vigalencia*" (General Superintendent of Investigation and Security). Meanwhile, Quintinilla ignored Josie entirely and began to lay it on thick with Hem.

Hem basked in it, beaming, spreading the charm, and filling glasses all around. There had been plenty of wine at lunch, and now there was plenty more. Quintinilla's manner with Hemingway was sycophantic to a degree that Virginia Cowles found nauseating. By the time Quintinilla called out *"Ten!"* his face was quite flushed. Buoyed up by the Hemingway bonhomie, the writer

and the secret policeman kept drinking, trading stories about the
artist's life in Paris and then about the wild and wonderful heroism of the November assault. *"Eleven!"* Again and again, they
toasted the antic bravery of those crazy kids, saving Madrid. Now
that was heroism! Virginia Cowles watched Quintinilla's eyes.
They were very lively eyes, very pleased with all they surveyed.
They sparkled. They were also, she thought, mean. In fact, Quintinilla's eyes were worse than mean. Cowles saw them as "filled
with all the sadism of Spain." Josie looked around. She couldn't
see the waiters anymore. And everyone else on the terrace had left.
"Twelve! . . . Thirteen!"

Virginia Cowles was watching Hemingway, too. What struck
her most about Hemingway was how the talk about the "crazy
kids" dying in the battles of the November assault seemed to ex-
cite Hemingway. Arouse him. Meanwhile, the shells kept on
whistling in all too near the *terraza* of the Gran Via. Josie and
Virginia sat tight while Hemingway dug for details, keeping the
wine gushing into the "executioner's" glass. Stories, always
more stories, about crazy kids and their heroic deaths. Quintinilla was delighted to oblige. He had a whole lot of them.

"Fifteen!" By now Quintinilla's face was quite flushed.

Then, rather abruptly, Hemingway changed the subject. The
dead warriors from November were wonderful, of course. But
what about some of the other people who'd died back during
those days? Not the ones who had died in battle. The ones who'd
had to be killed. For other reasons. The ones who'd had to be
shot. Like, say, the fifth columnists that had been rounded up?
Fascist traitors? Spies? Hemingway had heard there had been
kind of a lot of them. It seemed a little hasty, the way some of
them had been executed.

"A revolution is always hasty," Quintinilla answered, seeming
quite delighted with the unarguable truth of his reply. *"Seventeen!"*

Hemingway took up Quintinilla's platitude and pretended to be interested in it. Haste, yes. Yet haste, after all, meant mistakes. "And," he asked, "have there been many mistakes?"

Josephine Herbst sat silent, like stone.

"Mistakes?" The question didn't seem to trouble Quintinilla in the least. His answer was quick. "It is only human to err."

Another truism, impossible to contradict. By now, Virginia noted, though the shells were still whistling in, they did seem a little further away.

Hemingway was not going to let up. "And the mistakes," he persisted. "How did they die?"

This question plunged Quintinilla into a meditative, almost philosophical mood. "On the whole," he mused, "considering they were mistakes, very well indeed. In fact, *magnífico!*" Cowles caught a "note of rapture in his voice." Swept on this little surge of joy, Quintinilla picked up the carafe to refill glasses all around.

"Twenty!"

But Quintinilla was not done with his reflections on the dynamics of dying. A waiter had reappeared and, noticing that Quintinilla was out of cigarettes, rushed over, rolled one for "the executioner," and then helped him light it. "I know how men die, all right," Quintinilla went on. "It's worse if it has to be a woman. . . . One officer shat in his pants, huddled in a corner. He had to be carried out, to be shot like a dog."

Hemingway let that sink in, and then, having what he wanted, muttered something about having to leave.

"Nonsense," Quintinilla snapped. "No one goes."

The "executioner's" manners were slipping a little.

And Hemingway gave him a few minutes more. Quintinilla now turned to Virginia Cowles and made a pass at her. Or more precisely, he embarked on a drunken sexual fantasy about her.

All about how she ought to go home with him, meet his family, and then they would become lovers. They would turn his wife into their cook, and continue to be lovers and everything would be just wonderful. The numbers in the count were mounting. "*Twenty-seven!*"

Cowles made some feeble little joke about all the fun and everyone at the table laughed.

"*Twenty-eight!*"

And then the raid, like a rainstorm, seemed really to subside. Silence, like a kind of sunshine, broke through. Hemingway was fidgety. This time he meant it. He really did have to go. He wanted to get back to work.

Quintinilla's shining hour at the fame table was over.

And this time the "executioner of Madrid" took the hint. He made his way out, leaving Hemingway and his party behind. As he left, it was Hemingway who was eyeing Virginia, catching the way she gaped at Quintinilla's back as he turned a corner and disappeared. Virginia Cowles sat, silenced. She was shaken, appalled. And it showed.

Hemingway moved in on Virginia and once again spoke in that confidential tone of his. "A *chic* type—eh?" Cowles stared back at him. The distress on her face did not go away. Then Hemingway tossed off a remark that Virginia would remember many months later. Looking straight into Virginia Cowles's shock, Hemingway added, with a confidential smirk, writer to writer: "Now remember—he's *mine.*"

Virginia would remember that remark in New York the next year, attending Hemingway's Popular Front propaganda play, *The Fifth Column.* A character based on Quintinilla in *The Fifth Column* is a dark yet much-admired, even heroic figure named Antonio, the "executioner of Madrid," busy with the heavy work of vigilance and security. Antonio rounds up fifth columnists. Antonio rids the world of traitors. It's nasty but necessary work. Luckily, Antonio is being quietly helped by the peerless—flawless—efforts of the play's lead, the Hemingwayesque Philip Rawlings. Philip Rawlings is a boisterous American writer-warrior who happens to be staying at the Hotel Florida and in Room 108, no less. He has come to rescue Spain. Because Philip Rawlings is a past master, internationally celebrated, of just this nasty but necessary work. A pro. Rawlings knows all there is to know about traitors. Rawlings knows exactly how to handle treachery. He is an all-American hero of the dark side of "security." Rawlings is *par excellence* the writer-warrior of this new age, the Hemingway hero turned secret policeman and basement killer. Yes, it's nasty work, and yet Rawlings is a patriot. This dark paragon kills for liberty. He is a slightly bloody champion of *la causa. He* knows what has to be done. How did Ivens put it? "He knows what a man has to do in this difficult and terrible wartime."

Besides, Rawlings never ever makes "mistakes."

Fondling these vile absurdities, Hemingway was trying to claw his way out of the moral pit he'd dug for himself.

"*A chic type—eh? Now remember, he's* **mine!**"

On his way back to Valencia, Dos made one quick stop—it was probably less than a day—at Fuentedueña, finishing up his reportage on that town, and then went on to the Spanish coast. He assumed his first task would be to tell the truth about José to Márgara, but he was wrong. By the time he got back to the apartment on the Calle Fonseca, he was too late.[8]

Dos Passos found her sitting "like a woman of stone" on one of the low beds in that dank little apartment. Márgara barely responded to Dos's presence in the room. She could barely speak. She did not respond to whatever words of comfort Dos tried to find. Dos told her about the efforts he was about to undertake on her behalf. Márgara could barely muster signs of interest. He was, he pointed out, on excellent personal terms with the American ambassador to Spain, Claude Bowers. He was going straight to him. He was going to get the American government to intervene on her behalf.

That made Márgara laugh. It was a harsh, dry little laugh. It hurt to hear it almost as much as it must have hurt to laugh it. So far there was no eye contact.

Once again, Dos was thinking like a lawyer's son. José had held a life insurance policy, issued to him through Johns Hopkins. Márgara and the children would need to have this policy paid in full. That meant they would need proof of José's death from the Spanish government. They would need a death certificate.

It was time for Dos to have another talk with Julio Alvarez del Vayo.

And so Dos made the trek again to Alvarez del Vayo's office. This time at least Alvarez del Vayo did not attempt to sidestep a meeting. He didn't keep Dos Passos stewing for hours in a waiting room. Alvarez del Vayo was prompt. Now that both men fully understood how much each detested the other, the atmosphere was one of "poisonous cordiality." Dos Passos probably didn't even go through the motions of trying to learn the truth from Alvarez del Vayo. Somewhere around this time Dos Passos did somehow learn that it had been a "special section" that shot Robles: that is, by an extralegal (but not necessarily illegal) unit somehow connected to the communists. He also heard from someone that José had made unspecified "powerful enemies" during the November assault. There was unsubstantiated and contradictory talk about how Robles had possibly been framed, maybe even killed by the "uncontrollables." Wherever Dos Passos picked up these things, it is most unlikely that he picked them up from Julio Alvarez del Vayo.

Nor does Dos seem to have grasped, then or ever, that it was Alvarez del Vayo who had engineered the humiliation at the Fifteenth Brigade fiesta; never grasped that it was Alvarez del Vayo who had planted the black propaganda about Robles's "treason" that was now being used to justify his friend's murder *and* to damage his own reputation; never grasped that it was Alvarez del Vayo who had set up and used the obedient Josie Herbst as his pawn in these moves. John Dos Passos seems to have gone to his grave believing that Josephine Herbst really was his friend. Right to the end, Dos Passos insisted he had never heard anything about Robles's "treason" "from any Spaniard." To the end, Dos believed that the smear was "the fabrication of romantic American Communist sympathizers"—that is, Hemingway and his hangers-on. He never twigged on the possibility that the Americans were being used—manipulated—by professionals who had darker purposes than Hem's personal malice.

So in the "poisonous cordiality" of Alvarez del Vayo's office, Dos Passos asked for only one thing. It was a small thing, but crucial. Señora Robles would be needing her husband's death certificate. Dos Passos asked the minister if he would do her the kindness of using his good offices to procure it.

Alvarez del Vayo stared at him. Naïvely—or was it a masterstroke?—Dos Passos had nailed the bastard. He was asking Alvarez del Vayo for the obligatory official documentation of what *had* to be a secret death. A death certificate would have a blank to be filled in with the time and place of Robles's death. Some medical officer of some kind would have had to have examined the body, and would have to provide some statement about the cause of death. Like what? A bullet through the brain?

An honest death certificate for José Robles was out of the question. Of course, it would be quite possible to forge a death certificate with false answers. But even a forgery would open dangerous avenues of inquiry. Here was a famous man, one with access to the media worldwide, obviously dead set on pursuing this matter to the bitter end. The lies in any forgery would have to contradict everything that had been said so far, officially and unofficially. That would only make them more grist for Dos Passos's mill. An honest death certificate would give the game away, but a forged one—in addition to making a total hash out of a phony cover story about "treason" that Alvarez del Vayo himself had just planted with the most famous writer in the English-speaking world—would raise questions that this government could not afford to answer, or even have asked.

Things had gone too far. Alvarez del Vayo could not admit that his government had killed José Robles. Nor could he deny it.

Faced with these options, Alvarez del Vayo did what he usually did, and did so well. He lied. But of course he would get a death certificate for Señora Robles. Promptly. Immediately. Mr. Dos Passos could rest assured.

Of course, no death certificate was produced. Ever.[9]

And Dos could not wait forever. All too soon, there was nothing more that could be done in Valencia.

April was drawing to a close. May Day was very near. The Stalinist apparatus in Spain, after careful preparation, was ready to strike. On May Day, they would provoke the anarchists and non-Stalinist leftists in Catalonia, drawing them into shooting confrontations that would be followed by waves of arrests and killings. The insufficiently pliant government of Prime Minister Francisco Largo Caballero would fall as a result. As the prime minister's old allies and friends were rounded up and mowed down, Largo Caballero would naturally resist and protest. That resistance would be used to force him out, and the fully compliant Stalinist-dominated government of Juan Negrin would replace him. And the Soviet agent who would play a key catalytic role managing this transformation would be Julio Alvarez del Vayo.

Sensing some of this—it was everywhere, in the air of menace—but knowing none of it, and no longer able to help or console, Dos Passos left Márgara and set out. It was time to go on to Catalonia.

Meanwhile, Liston Oak was getting near his breaking point.

The American was sick. He was sick physically. Every morning he woke up sick; every day, all day, he worked feeling sick. His body ached all the time. Something was wrong. He felt he was dying. He'd seen a doctor, and the doctor had told him he should leave Spain. But Liston was also sick spiritually. There was a pestilence of fear and loathing in the depths of his soul. Back in Moscow, Liston had turned down Borodin's offer of a Moscow job because, if he finally admitted it to himself, he was repelled, repelled and *frightened*, by the Terror he saw being unleashed in the Soviet capital. Every party official was terrified. Fear was stamped all over everyone he met. Nobody ventured an opinion. Nobody ventured a thought. Everything was a party slogan. And the *Lie*! The *huge* disparity between the lifestyles of the *nomenklatura* and the masses. The *obvious* repression. The *obvious* fear. And not just among the Russians. There was Liston's own fear. If this sometime schoolteacher from Monterey, California, admitted the truth, he was petrified. He was sick with fear.

Liston had gone to Spain and taken a job working in Alvarez del Vayo's office because he thought it was a way to get away from all that horror and back to the revolution of his dreams. But the horror had followed him to Spain. In Valencia, just like Moscow, the secret police were everywhere. In Valencia, just like Moscow, everyone was frightened. A sinister extralegal system for enforcing terror was being put in place. There were covert prisons—the small secret *checas*—hidden away everywhere in NKVD safe houses. *Checa*—the very word was a play on a Russian word for the Soviet secret police, Cheka. It was in just such a boutique torture chamber, located in the basement of the sumptuous home of a friend of Hemingway's in Alcalá de Henares—Cervantes' town—that Andrés Nin would be held and tortured: it may well have been in just such a place that José Robles Pazos met his end. Guided by operatives like Gustavo Durán, a Spanish branch of the NKVD had been trained and put in place, obedient to Orlov, not the prime minister. People—good people, revolutionaries, people like Robles—were being killed. And more were going to be killed. Soon. In mid-April Liston probably did not know the when or where, but he knew it was coming. Something big, something deep in the dynamics of dying.

Yet he could not make a break. Liston yearned to cut and run, but he couldn't. Though a break would leave his life a shambles, his life was already a shambles. There was another, less noble, factor: that fear of his. Becoming a "renegade" was *dangerous*. "Stalin plays for keeps," a famous high-level American penetration agent once mused. Liston was in deep. Every week, Stalin killed thousands, and killed them for a lot less than what Liston knew. The NKVD maintained an elite squad simply for foreign assassinations, the Bureau of Special Tasks. It was there just to deal with people like Liston. And the Bureau of Special Tasks was good at killing: patient and relentless and skilled at covering its tracks. Methodical. When the bureau opened a file, sooner or later it closed that file. If the apparatus had murdered an important man like Robles—and Liston knew perfectly well that they *had* murdered Robles—for damn sure they wouldn't hesitate to get rid of a nobody like Liston Oak.

We catch a glimpse of Liston around this time through the eyes of an American socialist on his way through Valencia, who had to be interviewed by Liston as part of his job. The visitor walked into the meeting expecting a hard time at the hands of a hard-line communist hatchet man. Instead, he was startled to find himself facing a man in obvious agony. "I could see at once that he was deeply troubled; his intellectual face furrowed by an inner struggle that was most evident in his eyes as he peered through his glasses. . . . This suffering was so obvious a result of his sincerity that I couldn't question his good faith." The visitor sensed he was looking at "despair" and "spiritual agony."[10]

Luckily, Liston's spiritual agony was not yet evident to Alvarez del Vayo. On the contrary. Around this time, Alvarez del Vayo told Liston that the communists wanted to open two new covertly controlled offices of English-language propaganda and offered Liston the job of running the one in Barcelona.

That was some offer. No more running around the suburbs of Madrid, hustling up fancy booze for Ernest Hemingway. This new thing in Catalonia was going to be big.

chapter 11

BARCELONA
ON THE VERGE

"*M**r. Dos Passos!*" A very long, very lanky young Englishman with a very long, very lanky face hoisted himself
from an ample wicker armchair in the lobby of the Hotel Continental in Barcelona and crossed the lobby, smiling, his hand out-
stretched, intent upon catching Dos before the American master
could reach the elevator and disappear.[1] Eric Blair had been in
that wicker chair watching and waiting, determined not to miss
the moment Dos Passos came in through the big revolving front
door. It was almost the end of the morning, and Dos, who had
been in Barcelona since maybe yesterday afternoon, was just
back from a conference with his government hosts, finalizing his
schedule of interviews and itinerary until his return to France a
few days hence. The day of his departure was set for April 30.
The day before May Day.

Hurrying forward to intercept his man, Eric Blair wore a
uniform of the anti-Stalinist POUM militia; the uniform had
been torn to tatters at the front. Perched on his head was a
ragged service cap that might have been run over by a hundred
tanks. One arm was in a sling, and his Spanish boots, which

were too small for his long English feet, looked like they had
been used to stamp out the coals of hell itself. Young Blair—he
was thirty-four—was also a writer, a still rather obscure radical novelist and essayist, who wrote under the pen name
George Orwell. Ever since the electrifying moment that George
Orwell had learned that John Dos Passos was in this very hotel
right here and now, he had decided not to budge until he had
shaken the hand of the man who wrote *Manhattan Transfer*
and *The 42ⁿᵈ Parallel*.

"*Mr. Dos Passos!*"

Greeting this eager Englishman with the gently inquisitive
smile that was among his most typical expressions—his shy but
open "What-have-we-here?" smile—John Dos Passos gave
George Orwell his hand, and two worlds met.

They were two very different worlds, and both of them were
about to change forever.

Dos Passos was American, a high modernist, and a man of
the twenties, who had just crested at the unrecoverable pinnacle
of his fame. His sensibility had been shaped by Verdun and Ver-
laine, by Joyce and Stravinsky, by Picasso and Lenin and the
Café Flore. The great Dos Passos novels are modernist works,
and they ride on waves of rapturous distress. Dos Passos was no
optimist—his critique of society is far too radical for that—but
despite his anger over the human wasteland, Dos Passos wrote
surfing through what the twenties saw as "the new" in almost
Whitmanian intoxication. At its greatest, his prose surges with
all but unmanageable energy and insight. Orwell was an Englishman, a man of the thirties, and a classicist—his very name
would become a byword for the classic literary virtues. Orwell
had looked at the grand modernist dissociations that were so
dear to Dos Passos's generation—the "new"—and turned his

back on them. He was not unduly impressed by the power of language to intoxicate. It was a little too close to the original sin of language: the power to lie. His supreme test for seriousness in any writer was whether she or he knew how to undo a lie. Orwell wrote for precision, not excitement. His career was stuck in that particularly dark hour that comes just before the dawn of recognition, and given his exceptionally clear view of the new totalitarian modernity that was descending over Europe, Orwell saw a lot more reason for horror than hope. Orwell did admire Dos Passos as an artist, no question. He was not going to leave the lobby of the Hotel Continental until he had shaken the master's hand. But George Orwell's anger was going to take him places that were very far from Dos Passos's rapturous reality.

Both men were obsessed with politics. Yet neither quite grasped—at least not yet, not on that morning of April 27—that each stood at a point of no return. The crimes happening then and there in Spain were forcing each into a head-on confrontation with the great totalitarian lie of the twentieth century. When that confrontation was complete, nothing would be the same for either man, ever again. Yet the effect of the confrontation would be very different for each. Orwell's confrontation would leave him made as a writer. Dos's similar confrontation, on the other hand, would leave him, as an artist at least, almost undone. That day in April, Eric Blair stood on the verge of completing a transformation so profound that Dos Passos took it— or mistook it—as a readiness to die.[2]

And in some sense, the old Eric Blair did die that spring in Spain. George Orwell left Catalonia with his destiny defined. After the events of May, Eric Blair definitively became George Orwell; in Catalonia the steel, at long last, entered his soul. As for the inner life of John Dos Passos, he too was going through an equally potent encounter with the lie that needed to be undone, but for him the consequences would be far more dire and destructive. Dos Passos was about to leave Spain with all the essential assumptions of his art and energy shaken, if not shattered. Some faith, some hope—something—was broken inside him, and he would never again quite recover the greatness that once had been so plainly within his grasp.

Dos Passos wrote two versions of his encounter with Orwell. There is a nonfiction account in *The Theme Is Freedom*. This is not as detailed as what appears in the fictional account in *Century's Ebb*, though unfortunately, some of the details in the latter are more fiction than lightly disguised fact. For example, the May provocations are invoked as if they had already begun. Not so. The two men met on April 27. (*Maybe* it was a day later.) That was around six days before the real outbreak of trouble.[3]

When the accounts are combined, a plausible picture of what happened emerges.

"Things I've heard," he has Orwell mutter, seemingly aware of Dos's run-in with the Stalinist establishment, "lead me to believe that you are one of the few who understand what's going on."

Dos Passos liked Eric Blair. "He had a bloody-but-unbowed air that was almost a swagger." Like everyone, Dos was struck by Orwell's narrow ravaged face, with its "sick, drawn look," and by the incongruity of his fluting Etonian accent against his ragged exterior and radical passion. Orwell seemed tattered and battered. His eyes, Dos noticed, tended to drift into the remote distance, their gaze "farsighted . . . like a seaman's eyes." V. S. Pritchett would describe this same face as "lined with pain," with "eyes that stared out of their caves, look[ing] far away over one's head, as if seeking more discomfort and new indignations."[4]

Yet what most seized Dos Passos's sympathy in Orwell was the gentle and unexpected rediscovery of an experience called trust. After weeks of talking to people who were either grieving or lying, Dos Passos suddenly felt an "extraordinary sense of relaxation" realizing "that he was talking to an honest man."

It made Dos want more. They walked over to a corner of the lobby and settled into those wicker armchairs for some ersatz vermouth and an exchange. Listening in his typical, slightly breathless way, Dos heard about the party Orwell was fighting with—the POUM—and about the front. After that, Dos suddenly found himself pouring out the story about José Robles. The whole story just kept coming and coming. Eric Blair sat quietly, soaking up every word.[5]

Dos Passos had expected to find the true Revolution in Barcelona. He was not alone. Everyone agreed that Catalonia was where the Spanish Revolution—not the Civil War itself, but the searing working-class upheavals of late 1935 and early 1936 that provoked it—had originally been most intense. Andrés Nin, who had seen Russia during the twenties with Trotsky, thought Barcelona in the spring of 1936 was even more authentically revolutionary than Saint Petersburg in October 1917.

Orwell thought the same. He had come to Spain as a journalist, but Barcelona in December 1936 looked to him like the genuine article: a place "where the working class was in the saddle." The bourgeoisie in flight, the very language of servility had disappeared; there were no more coats and ties; equality seemed to be everywhere. Orwell was exhilarated. Turning in his press card, he signed up to fight.

The Barcelona that Orwell and Dos Passos saw five months later was a very different place. "Barcelona," Dos wrote of what he saw in April, "had a furtive, gutted look, stores shuttered, people glancing over their shoulders as they walked. In every street there was a smell of burning from the charred ruins of churches."[6]

Returning from the front, Orwell found the intoxicating air of revolution gone. The Barcelona of December "was liker to a workers' city than anything I had conceived possible. Now the tide had rolled back. Once again it was an ordinary city, a little pinched and chipped by war, but with no outward sign of working class predominance.... As we made our way up the street, I noticed that people were staring at our dirty exteriors."[7]

The air of menace had replaced the air of revolution.

"It is pathetic," Orwell said, "the confidence the Russians have in their terror. They are purging Trotskyites in Moscow and Leningrad, so they have to find Trotskyites to purge in Spain. Since there don't happen to be any Trotskyites they pick on the independent working-class parties. It's our hard luck. It has all happened very fast. Besides an infected finger, I got this leave to enlist in the International Brigade. Not enough action on the Aragon front...."[8]

But could Orwell really join the International Brigades? The Stalinists were obviously in charge. Where to turn if you wanted to save this revolution?

"It's this bloody Non-Intervention Committee that is the root of all evil," Orwell added. Note that on this one subject— the evils of the democracies' policy of "nonintervention"—Orwell and Dos were in full accord with even the Popular Front at its most Stalinist. Early in the war, the democracies—England, France, and the United States—had decided not to feed the Spanish flames. The entire left—Stalinist and anti—railed against this policy as craven appeasement, a service to Hitler, and, for anti-Stalinists like Orwell and Dos, as tantamount to handing Spain to Stalin on a silver platter.

"Stalin furnishes the Republic with arms," Dos seethed, "but the Terror goes with them. The Terror alienated the working class parties and the middle class moderates. A perfect recipe for a Fascist victory."

"Isn't 'alienate' rather a euphemism?" Orwell asked.

"I guess 'liquidate' is the proper term," Dos Passos answered, speaking softly.

"A Fascist victory," Orwell said. "And it won't be the last."

Keeping his fear hidden behind a mask of obedience, Liston Oak had arrived in Barcelona maybe a week or ten days earlier, assigned the job of setting up Alvarez del Vayo's new English-language press office. Liston was still trusted. The brass saw him as a reliable member of the *apparat*. And what was pounding in his head?

Defection! Defection! Defection!

A dream of defiance and flight had taken possession of his mind with a force he could no longer control. What had started small in Moscow and come blurting out when he told Coco the forbidden truth about his father, was getting to be too big to handle. Terror and the hatred it breeds were driving Liston toward his breaking point. He loathed all he had seen in Valencia. And now he was also scared. More scared all the time. It was awfully easy to die in Spain.

Going through the motions of his new job, Liston one day in April suddenly took a step. It was a big step, though Liston made it very, *very* discreetly. Nobody knew anything about anything. He put out a feeler to Andrés Nin. With a word planted in the right place, he suggested they meet.

A meeting with Nin? Nothing could have been more dangerous. Yet at this first meeting with the prime anti-Stalinist of the
Spanish left, Liston was probably seeking protection: safe haven,
maybe even an underground escape from the country. He knew
it was suicidal to walk away from Stalin's service without some
sort of protection. The Bureau of Special Tasks was busy in
Spain, looking for "renegades." He needed cover. And it was
after all not so crazy to look for that cover from this man.

For his part, Nin very likely looked upon a defector like Liston
as an intriguing opportunity. A well-plugged-in, well-informed,
mid-level American apparatchik ready to break, talk, and fight?
Such things did not come his way every day.

Andrés Nin had his reckless side, but he was not so wild that
he would let Liston come to his office blind, or talk to him on
the telephone. If there was to be a meeting, security was the
prime issue. Nin settled on a tiny, very obscure café in the depths
of a twisting little back street off the via Durutti, behind the
Ramblas. The place was a hole in the wall, almost unnoticeable
from the street. Its proprietor was an anarchist with eagle eyes, a
build made for crushing bones, and a suspicious nature.

This dour gatekeeper greeted Liston when he stepped out of
the noonday sun into his dark little cave. He led Liston to an
even darker corner in the rear, and there sat the ebullient red-
headed Spaniard who was chief of the POUM. Nin was alone.
He had thick, curly, flamboyant hair and wore goggling intellectual horn-rims—very chic—and had a strong solid body
churning with still-youthful buoyancy and energy. A man
named Molines, the editor of the POUM's newspaper, *La
Batalla*, had set up this meeting, and Oak was slightly surprised that Molines was himself not there. Oak and Nin settled into lunch—snails, with lots of wine and bitter black
coffee—while Nin held forth, railing in his driven way against

the sins of the Stalinists. The Soviet "advisers" were seeking to take over the Spanish government. They were counterrevolutionary. They were blackmailing dissenting parties. Their so-called aid was a devil's bargain, too little help in exchange for too much subservience to Stalin's will. Nin filled the time inveighing, speaking mainly about simple truths that, as it happened, were burning up his soul.

At this point, two men approached the back table and joined them. Molines was one; he was with a "big, stout" German who called himself, simply, Hans. Hans had a "broad, round, florid, jovial face, surmounted by a shock of clipped blond hair." An active Communist since at least 1930, Hans had at last escaped Hitler's persecutions, and like Liston, spent time in Moscow. In 1936, though shaken by the oppressions of Soviet life, Hans joined the German contingent of the International Brigades and came to Spain, where he was surprised to discover that the Brigades were entirely under Stalinist control. Hans didn't like that. Hans had turned against Stalinism. Stalinism was oppressive. Stalinism was counterrevolutionary. Stalinism was a crime.

Liston needed little persuading on that score.

And so Hans had defected from the Brigades and joined the POUM. The POUM was fighting for the real revolution. Besides, the POUM was going to protect him.

Liston leaned back in his chair and took a last sip of that bitter black coffee. About that last bit, the stuff about the POUM protecting Hans?

Liston was not so sure.

Dos Passos's interview with Andrés Nin, held soon after, was public enough to make the news, though it did take place at night, and in the pouring rain. Nin's office was quite close to the

Hotel Continental, but Dos Passos was driven there quietly, in a government-supplied car.

The politics of the POUM need a little special explaining. Though the POUM's stronghold was Catalonia, prior to 1937 the Catalonian left was not at all communist but a center of old-fashioned Mediterranean anarchism—the sort of politics that Carlo Tresca stood for. As such it was the home bailiwick of the Spanish Republic's leftist but noncommunist prime minister, Francisco Largo Caballero. The POUM, on the other hand, really was communist. It was not an anarchist party. Though fervently anti-Stalinist, it was by its own definition Leninist, and therefore, like Lenin himself, at least in principle hostile to anarchism.

The really contested question was whether the POUM was also Trotskist. The Stalinists railed that the case proving Nin's Trotskyism was open and shut. The POUM railed back that the charge was just another Stalinist lie. The truth was not so simple. After May, the *apparat* would flood the press with one gross libel after another about the "fascist POUM." Even in making the Trotskyite charge, they distorted the facts. The POUM did maintain a fairly clear-cut independence from Trotsky's political organization in exile, and by local political osmosis it had soaked up more anarchist attitudes than one would expect from a strictly Leninist party. Yet the Stalinists were not entirely wrong about the essence of the POUM. While he was still a very young man, Nin had served as a private secretary to Trotsky in Moscow. He had worshipped his boss, and his own rebellion against the Soviet status quo coincided exactly with Trotsky's break with Stalin. Nin left Russia when Trotsky left, and he remained in frequent, almost filial contact with his famous mentor. While Nin's sassy independence kept them perpetually quibbling, by 1937 his youthful awe for "the old man" had matured,

but not abated. He moved in Trotsky's shadow. As for Nin's anti-
Stalinism—which was unequivocal—it followed Trotsky's own
anti-Stalinism in its every feint and lunge.

Arriving at POUM headquarters, Dos Passos found his energetic
young subject enthroned behind a grandiose "fake gothic" desk
that had been commandeered, Dos supposed, from some
grandee's library. Nin was, as billed, charismatic, buoyant, and
obsessed. With Dos he laid on the charm. It was only when Nin
snatched up the telephone that Dos glimpsed a different Nin:
hard and unsmiling, speaking low in the kind of hyper-Spanish
that fluttered by so fast that nobody but a native could follow.
Dos tried to catch the drift, but couldn't.

Nin's office was a darkened hodgepodge. Dos sat in a mangy
overstuffed armchair before the regal desk, and a lieutenant hovered nearby, a man who until recently had been an editor in a radical publishing house. (It may have been Molines.) Dos sensed
Nin's daring. He was also "wellbuilt," Dos Passos thought,
"healthy looking," and radiant with the look—was it illusion?—
of absolute certainty about who he was and what he was doing.
And that smile of his! His smile lit up the whole gloomy room.
Everyone loved it. The Catalonians loved it. At the front, the soldiers loved it.

In addition to being a radiant smiler, Nin was a laugher. Dos
was struck by how, for somebody in his very unfunny position, the
man laughed rather a lot: too much, maybe, and too easily, and in
strange places. Another thing: his laugh was like a child's laugh.

At that moment in late April, Andrés Nin's most immediate
political problem—other than staying alive—was how to resist
the Valencia government's reassertion of its police powers over
the streets and villages of what still billed itself as an independent Catalonia. Who would police the cities and villages of Cat-

alonia? The Valencia government? Or the local anarchists and the POUM?

The interview quickly turned to how Barcelona's revolutionary pendulum was swinging away from the radicalism of July, back to its old ways.

"Barcelona was settling down," Nin admitted. "Getting bourgeois again." Then he giggled that kid-like laugh. The rightward swing of the pendulum, which had so disturbed Orwell, seemed almost to amuse Nin. "You can see it in people's dress. Now, we're beginning to wear collars and ties again, but even a couple of months ago everybody was wearing the most extraordinary costumes . . . you'd see people in the street wearing feathers."

Once more, there was that kid's titter.

The phone interrupted them again. Nin instantly snatched up the receiver, hunching over the telephone, talking again in that flutter-tongue Spanish, humorless and very adult, speaking in the inaudible voice of command.

After hanging up, Nin shrugged his shoulders, and turned back to Dos with that smile.

"It's the villages . . . ," he told Dos Passos. "They want to know what to do."

And? What were they going to do?

Not submit. Hold their ground. Fight.

"Take a car," Nin suggested, "and drive through the suburbs. You'll see that the villages are barricaded."

But then Nin tossed a nervous glance toward his lieutenant. Second thoughts: "Maybe you'd better not."

Again, he giggled.

The lieutenant jumped in. Mr. Dos Passos must not get the wrong idea. There would be no physical danger of any sort to someone like himself in the POUM villages. "They have great respect for foreign journalists."

Dos Passos moved on to a question about how the competing Catalonian factions—anarchist, liberal, communist—would coordinate their response to Valencia's challenge.

Nin's response resembled a shrug.

"It's complicated. . . . In Bellver"—a suburb—"our people want to know whether to move against the anarchists. In some other places they are *with* them. . . ."

That night, after this inconclusive interview, Dos Passos paused to wonder whether this very brave young man had grasped how dire his situation really was. Leave aside the villages of Catalonia. Andrés Nin was caught between the fascists and the Stalinists, two of the most fearsome adversaries of the twentieth century. Couldn't he *see* what a very dangerous place that was to be? Couldn't he *see* that it called for something more than laughter and charm and valor?

Later that night, visiting a syndicalist short-wave radio station, a wave of despair—it was really a classic wave of his dark rapture—came sweeping over Dos:

I couldn't help thinking of the rainy night and the workingmen on guard with machineguns and rifles at sandbag posts on the roads into villages, and the hopes of new life and liberty and the political phrases, confused, contradictory pounding in their ears; and then the front, the towns crowded with troops and the advanced posts and trenches and the solitude between. . . . How can they win, I was thinking? How can the new world full of confusion and crosspurposes and illusions and dazzled by the mirage of idealistic phrases win against the iron combination of men accustomed to run things who have only one idea binding them together, to hold on to what they've got.[9]

So, Dos pushed before he left Nin's office, what *would* the villages do?

"*You* know Spain," Nin said to Dos Passos, leading his visitor to his office door. Somehow or other, things would work out.

Yes, Dos Passos *did* know Spain. At least, he used to know a Spain that seemed to be vanishing, and now he was getting to know a Spain that was coming into being. As Dos Passos disappeared into the rain, the young Spaniard once again flashed Dos that husky white-toothed smile of his, the one all his soldiers loved.

Dos loved it too. It was irresistible. He did not yet know—he only guessed——that it was the smile of a dead man.

But Liston Oak knew that fact for sure.

Shortly before, seeing George Mink strolling down the Ramblas made Liston stop in his tracks and hold very still. There were grounds for pure, concentrated fear in that one simple fact: George Mink was in Barcelona.

And there was no way out, Mink had spotted him. George was striding toward him with a great big smirk, his hand ready for backslapping. And why not? Weren't they pals? Liston and George went way, way back to Liston's earliest special party work, back during his days in conspiracy's kindergarten. *Small world!*

Liston had met Mink first in New York. "George Mink" was not his real name, of course. Nor was he a real American, though by now he probably had a stack of passports proving he was as American as apple pie. Liston had been introduced to Mink in a party safe house—really an apartment—on Manhattan's West Side, back in the twenties, when Mink's main job was to be the enforcer, the muscle behind an NKVD agent of espionage named Leon Josephson. At the same time Mink assisted the party with the Maritime Union, seeing to it that longshore-men never forgot what was good for their health. Then and always, Mink was a goon, a gangster: in three words, a hit man, but a hit man for Stalin.

And here he was, right here in Barcelona.

And why would George Mink be in Barcelona?

George Mink was greatly changed from the good old days on the waterfront. On the Ramblas, he was nattily and expensively dressed, installed in Barcelona's best hotel. He was delighted to see an old friend. Why didn't Liston come around later to see him? They could catch up. Have a drink or two. Thinking quickly, Liston jotted down Mink's hotel room number and said he'd be delighted.

Wonderful meeting again. Wouldn't miss it for the world.

Not for the world. Liston knew that if he handled it right, this meeting would reveal something momentous, if for no other reason than that George Mink could only be in Barcelona for something momentous. If Liston remembered rightly, an invitation from Mink for "a couple of drinks" meant "come up and get plastered with me." But Liston had no intention leaving his meeting with Mink drunk. Liston would need to keep his wits about him. Just before he left, he drank down a pint of heavy cream.

Mink's hotel was probably the Colón. That's where the more important communists stayed. When Liston arrived, Mink was in an expansive mood.[10] He was installed in a luxurious suite, and there was lots of luggage arrayed around the rooms, all of it leather and expensive. Just in case Liston didn't notice, Mink was quick to point out how very fine his baggage was. While pouring the Scotch, he added some advice. Travel rich, Liston. Mink had learned that lesson long ago. If you want service, travel rich. Take a joint like this. The first thing the flunkies downstairs look at is your luggage. Not your face, your luggage. You get treated accordingly.

Bottoms up.

Moving on from his luggage, Mink proceeded to his suit. The suit he was wearing, he pointed out, like all his many suits these days, had been hand-tailored for him in London. 150 bucks each. Mink produced a bulging roll of bills. See this? Travel rich, Liston. Travel rich.

Liston was quick to show George how very impressed he was by it all.

Pouring a new drink, George wasted little time wallowing in the warm shoals of memory from the good old days with Leon Josephson. In fact, Mink and Josephson had recently run into difficulties in Copenhagen, and guess what? Josephson—that shyster—had wormed his way out of the rap, and Mink had served time. Now *that* did their friendship no good at *all*.

Mink was pouring himself another drink and sizing Liston up. So, George wanted to know, what was Liston up to? Propaganda still?

Mink was eager to boast about his work in the NKVD. Look around, Liston: the $150 suits, the luggage, this suite. The party knew how to reward the right kind of work. In fact, George had a proposal to make. The service was running a passport racket and a big part of it was right here in Spain. Right now, there were plenty of people in Spain who needed good, solid, high-class documentation. American passports were the best, though getting an authentic American passport away from its original owner and into the right hands sometimes took a little doing. Another thing. The service needed to know which of these Brigade volunteers were really reliable and which weren't. Oak could help out there, too. We need good people for this. Liston should think about it. It would be a step up.

No kidding.

George could fix it. It could take Liston a long way.

Mink was getting nice and high.

Liston explained that his doctor had told him that this Spanish climate was absolutely terrible for his health. It was killing him, he was sick; he was getting out of Spain soon.

"That's all right," Mink said. "You can work in France and England and the United States."

No kidding. Mink kept slugging it down.

Then it was Liston's turn. So what brought Mink to Barcelona?

Well, there was work to do in Spain. Things, Mink said, were about to change in Spain. The party had decided to deal with these problems in Catalonia. The CNT—the main anarchist party—and the Left Republicans and these renegades in the POUM: Trotskyites, all of them. It couldn't go on. This jackal Nin. Others. The service was going to fix them, and fix them good. May Day was coming. During the merry month of May there would be some scores settled in Barcelona. It was all worked out. A little shooting here, a little shooting there, and when these traitors started shooting back, the Assault Guards would move in. Lots and lots of Assault Guards, all set to go, all prepared. And when the last shot was fired, this town would be a very different place.

Liston took it in. He could just imagine. After all, he'd been sent to Barcelona to handle the propaganda.

No doubt about it, Mink slurred on. The party was going to fix things in Barcelona. Fix them real good.

Mink was now fully drunk. After a little more chat about this and that, Liston took his leave.

The meeting had been even more productive than Liston hoped. For one thing, it was clear that Liston was still trusted at the top. He had just been offered an NKVD promotion. Then there was the stuff about policy. The "independents," the POUM and the CNT and the others, were about to be provoked and then crushed. Simple as that.

Finally, some special people had been marked for death, and not just death in street fighting. George Mink was no soldier. He was not going to muss up his Savile Row suit taking potshots at desperate POUM soldiers in the Ramblas. George Mink was an assassin. He was here to kill some special person or persons. Because killing special people was what George Mink did.

For some reason, Liston did not take his next step until several days after this encounter, but when he did take it, the step was a giant one. In form, it was simple. He got up and walked through Barcelona straight to the front door of the POUM offices. He approached it in broad daylight. He could easily be seen from the street. And then he walked straight through the door.

Was he *insane?*

Once inside, he announced that he had to talk, very privately to Andrés Nin. Now. Right now.

Escorted into the same big gloomy office that Dos had sat in in the armchair across from the lordly desk, Liston Oak proceeded to tell Nin every detail of his conversation with George Mink. Sometime very soon—on May Day, or very shortly after May Day—the Soviet apparatus was going to stage a series of provocations against the non-Stalinist militias in Barcelona. They assumed the militias would fire back when fired upon, and when they did, the Stalinists would accuse them of rebellion and treason. Then they would move in with overwhelming numbers of Assault Guards and they would crush every militia of

every "independent" leftist party in the area. No more negotiating. No more talk. After May, the choice would be submit or
be destroyed.

Comrade Nin should understand that what he was hearing
now was not just another rumor. Oak knew perfectly well that
Barcelona was filled with rumors. This information was fact.
This came from an NKVD assassin who was as close to the top
as Nin was likely to get. The scenario he'd just outlined had
been scheduled, and in his experience Stalin did not schedule
such ventures when he was uncertain about the outcome. Nin
had once offered Oak a job. All right, here was service rendered.
Nin's organization was going to be provoked, and then it was
going to be wiped out. The whole Catalonian "independent" left
was going to be destroyed. Nin's personal safety, and that of
every POUM official close to him, was in the gravest possible
danger. Not later. Soon. They were going to try to kill them all.
And they were good at killing. Comrade Nin must understand.
This was not a maybe. This was for sure.

Nin listened. Did he smile? Did he laugh?

He responded, Liston felt, like a man in a dream. He was perfectly aware, he told Liston, that the Stalinists hated the POUM
and wanted to destroy it. He likewise understood that they
hated and wanted to destroy the anarchists and Left Republicans, too. There was no news in that.

But he was not afraid. Stalin's enmity did not trouble him at
all. Provocations? Assault Guards? Nin was not really concerned
about anything the Stalinists might try. Why? Because the *people*—the Catalonian *people*—were on his side. And the *people*
could never be defeated. The *people* supported the POUM.
They supported the Catalonia revolution. Knowing that, Nin
had no fear at all.

Liston took that in.

It may have been at this point that Oak asked about Hans. How was Hans?

Hans? Nin pounced on it, almost eager to tell Liston about Hans's fate. *Another* Stalinist crime!

"The day after you saw him, he walked out of the Hotel Falcon, where our POUM members stay. Comrade Ortega saw him cross the street; he was hailed by someone, evidently an old friend. Hans got in and they drove away. That's the last we have seen on him. . . . His wife got a letter yesterday. It was a queer letter, from Madrid. He wrote that he had made a mistake in leaving the Communist Party to join the POUM. He wrote that if he was killed in action, she should remember that he was loyal to the Comintern to the end. She'll never hear from him again. He was kidnapped by the GPU, and taken to Madrid, where he'll either be shot secretly or sent out to the front into no-man's land, in a special squad composed of soldiers the Stalinists don't like, and if the fascists don't kill him, the Stalinists will. . . . Another hero killed defending democracy."

Nin glowed with his sarcasm. It was almost if he were talking about some kind of triumph.[11]

Early the next day, Liston Oak had a call from a man named Albert Edwards, the Comintern's special representative overseeing Americans in Barcelona. Edwards ordered Liston to come to his hotel immediately.

Liston had been observed entering and leaving the headquarters of the POUM yesterday. The party demanded an immediate explanation.

Liston replied that as a journalist and propagandist, he was here to open a press office, and he naturally had to appear to deal evenhandedly with the various factions. So of course he had made contact with the likes of Nin.

This explanation cut no ice with Albert Edwards. Oak's explanation would have to be better than that.

As he left Albert Edwards's hotel room, Liston saw two things with new and perfect clarity.

The first was that the POUM was incapable of protecting anybody from anything.

The second was that It—*It: The* event he'd been waiting for— had happened. It had happened yesterday afternoon; it happened the moment he walked openly into the POUM headquarters. Liston Oak had reached his breaking point.

And now?

Now it was time to run.

chapter 12

FLIGHT

What was *that*?

It was the middle of the night, and the sleepy hotel room was dark. As Dos Passos listened through the murk of his half-awakening, the darkness seemed silent. Yet something had made him wake up. What *was* it?

It was almost a tapping that woke John Dos Passos in his room at the Hotel Continental after midnight on April 30, a knock so gentle, so tentative and cautious, that it barely got him to open his eyes.

Yet Dos did open his eyes, and lay in the darkness, listening. Maybe it was some meaningless random night noise. But no. There it was again. A deliberate rapping: timid, so quiet it almost could not be heard, but *intentional*. Some *person* was doing it. Somebody was on the other side of the door, trying to wake Dos up.

But quietly. *Very* quietly.

Dos Passos turned on his bedside lamp, got out of bed, put on his robe, opening the door on the frightened face of the last man on earth he expected to see.

Liston Oak?

What have we here?

Dos Passos's whole knowledge of Liston came from various contacts back in the States. If and when Dos thought of Liston at all, he thought of Liston as a Communist propaganda hack. Their contact had been in passing, and the roles involved had invariably been that of courted celebrity to hovering party handler.[1] Back in ever more distant days when the party still was trying to secure Dos Passos as their man, Liston had often been the apparatchik in the background, bringing coffee, arranging tickets, managing details. In the very early thirties, Liston had been the CP chaperon guiding Dos and Theodore Dreiser on a celebrity fact-finding tour of a strike in Harlan Country, Kentucky. In New York, Liston had been an editor at various party publications that were always banging away at Dos, trying to get him to say or do this or that. As for Liston's presence in Spain, Dos seems to have been only vaguely aware of it—"I'd seen him in some office or other in Valencia." He had as yet no clue that the man who'd told Coco the truth about his father's death had been Liston Oak.

And now Liston Oak stood looking at Dos Passos through tortured and terrified eyes, a hard-line Communist Party operative, and an errand boy for that liar Alvarez del Vayo, inexplicably standing in a hallway of the Hotel Continental in the middle of the night.

Could Liston come in? Please?

Liston was let in. The door closed behind them.

It's anyone's guess what Liston and Dos Passos talked about behind that closed door. The conversation probably took place in whispers. Liston had every reason to suppose that the room was bugged.

Did Liston tell Dos what he'd heard from Mink about Nin and May? It's not clear. Dos Passos wrote about this encounter with Oak three times, always sketchily. He does not mention Nin in any version. He never explains how or even that the midnight meeting was linked to the May provocations. Why? Well, one possibility is that when Dos Passos was writing, the danger had not altogether passed. And Liston Oak may have been in no hurry to tell the world that in Spain he'd been on confidential terms with an NKVD assassin. Yet either that night or soon after, Liston told Dos a fair amount. The climactic scene of Dos's next novel, *The Adventures of a Young Man*, shows commissars of an International Brigade murdering a dissident by sending him to certain death in a battlefront no-man's land. The scene sounds a lot like the fate of "Hans."

For sure, either that night or very soon after, Liston told Dos Passos that he had been the one who'd told Coco that his father was dead. That must have come as a jolt. During all the time Dos was banging on doors in Valencia, the insider had been Liston, this yes-man, this clerk, this almost invisible man. *He'd* been the one to tell Coco. *He'd* known the truth all along.

And Liston undoubtedly told Dos Passos that then and there, that very night, he was desperate. Things had reached the point where Liston was in direct physical danger. The party had turned against him. He had nowhere to turn. As of something like yesterday, he had been marked as a "renegade." He'd never *wanted* to be a renegade. He didn't want to break. Not at first. But it had happened, and now somehow he was defecting. Almost despite himself, he was defecting. And he was a marked man. He was in danger. Now. Tonight.

The NKVD was watching him. If they wanted to, they would kill him now. Nobody would ever hear from him again. He'd be shot in some basement, or hustled onto some Soviet ship, and once it was on the high seas, the corpse of a former schoolteacher from Monterey, California, a high-minded guy with radical ideas and artistic interests, would splash down into the churning wake, food for the sharks. That's how it was done.

Liston explained all this, maybe in a whisper. He was pretty sure that if he tried to leave Spain now—leave on his own, that is—he would never reach the border alive. Just now, when he'd come here, they had very likely followed him. They could be watching the hotel right now. They maybe even knew whose room he was in—and that would be further proof, as if they needed it, that he was a traitor and renegade. And now, if Liston were to be so foolish as to walk out of the Continental alone, they could easily seize him off the street before he got home, and that would be that. He would vanish, and vanish forever.

And would anybody care? Most of Liston's friends back in the States didn't even know he was in Spain. He'd purposely kept them in the dark about that detail. Suppose he did vanish. Would anyone even *notice?* Okay, in six months or a year maybe somebody back in New York might ask out loud what had happened to Liston Oak. And if they asked loud enough, maybe, maybe, the party would concoct some lie. Would that lie be challenged? In New York in 1937? Where the Popular Front *defined* sainthood? Where swallowing its line *was* what it *meant* to be an antifascist good guy? Not bloody likely. Maybe, just maybe, many years from now, Liston would end up as a perplexed footnote in some unread book or other.

The party and its killers knew damn well that they *could* get rid of him. Easy as pie. And these days they were confident. Never more so. Take Robles. That April they were pretty sure they could get away with killing José Robles. And Liston was pretty sure they were dead right. Yet just look at Robles. An important man. A professor. From a notable family. Well-connected. Highly placed. A friend of John Dos Passos: all that. Yet they could kill him without paying any really serious price. OK, maybe somebody might ask a few annoying questions. It was nothing serious. They had it in hand.

Then compare Robles to Liston Oak. Liston Oak was . . . nobody. If killing Robles came reasonably cheap, killing Liston Oak came almost for free. That's how they thought, and they were right.

So just by walking into the Hotel Continental in the middle of the night, Liston had made an irrevocable move. He couldn't walk out again. Not from here. Not alone. They were out there waiting for him. He had nothing left. He had nobody left.

Except maybe one man.

And Liston was looking at him.

Dos Passos did understand, didn't he? Maybe they could kill Liston for free, and Robles for a manageable cost. But kill John Dos Passos? Even intimidate him? *That* was not so easy. Not so cheap. An unseen but impenetrable shield protected John Dos Passos. Call it the shield of *visibility*. He was John Dos Passos. He was a famous man. Killing him would cost the party an unpayable price in headlines across the world, in dangerous questions coming at them from every side. They could and would lie to Dos Passos. They'd already done it, and they were going to keep it up. They could and would try to wreck his career and discredit him, for sure. But they couldn't *kill* him. Because if John Dos Passos were to be killed, every newspaper reader in the whole world would read about it the very next day. And the questions would never stop. So John Dos Passos was invulnerable. His face had been on the cover of *Time*.

And Liston happened to know that Dos Passos was leaving Spain tomorrow morning in a special government car.

Liston looked at his man.

Please. Please.

When Dos's response came, it was brisk and decisive. All right. From this moment forward, if anybody asked, Liston Oak the

Communist Party operative had turned into Liston Oak the private secretary of John Dos Passos. And yes, they would go to Barcelona, side by side, at the crack of dawn this morning, exactly as scheduled. And as they moved toward the border, Liston would not leave Dos Passos's side even for a minute. Liston's information was quite correct. Yes, Dos Passos was going to be traveling in a government-supplied car. So that was probably pretty safe.

On the other hand, before they reached the border, Dos's schedule called for an official stop at a cooperative that the Catalonian government was especially proud of in the little coastal village of San Pol de Mer. There would be interviews, lots of local official hooh-ha, a celebratory lunch, doubtless various festivities. There was no way to skip or cancel the thing, and besides, Dos Passos had no wish, no intention of skipping or canceling it. It would take up the late morning and most of the afternoon. It was on the official schedule, and as Dos's new private secretary, Liston would just have to stick as close as possible to his boss's official schedule and make the best of it. The town was probably safe. It was a long way from the front. The communists did not run it. At least not yet.

Then, once the visit was over, the car was scheduled to take Dos to the French border, and out of Spain. They would be crossing the frontier at Perpignan. As for whatever was left of tonight, Liston could sleep on the couch. They'd divvy up the sheets.

Whether either man slept much before dawn broke over Barcelona is not on record.

The Catalan government's limousine—a Hispano-Suiza, and a beauty—was ready at dawn. Everyone involved was friendly and very deferential. When Dos Passos presented Liston as his secretary, nobody asked a single question. After breakfast had been eaten and the car loaded, the two men were driven about thirty kilometers up the coast road to Sant Pol de Mar, a town of "pale blue and yellow and white-washed houses" perched on as ravishing a site on the Spanish Mediterranean coast as can be imagined. There Dos Passos was greeted by virtually the entire town. He emerged from the limo smiling, while his trembling, oddly watchful private secretary stepped out behind him, constantly glancing from right to left. The town council had gathered to greet their visitor. They wanted to tell Dos the whole history of their liberation, and as they did, out came the reporter's notebook. It was a matter of particular pride in Sant Pol de Mar that in *their* town the old regime had been overturned without anyone on either side being killed. There was a "little colony of refugee children from Madrid living in a beautiful house overlooking the sea with a rich garden behind it." They had welcomed some refugee priests to the town. Even the local fascists were adjusting. That very day, the new town council was celebrating its decision to communize San Pol's fishing industry. Would Señor Dos Passos like to see what had been accomplished? He would indeed. While Liston Oak died a thousand deaths, scanning the doorways, flinching at every sudden move, Dos was taken to "a fine building on the waterfront," a sometime beach café and dancehall, now remodeled as an amateur theater, while on the beach blue and green fishing boats had been pulled up in clusters. He was shown every boat and every net.

Dos Passos was affable, appreciative, and curious. He later produced a fine piece about Sant Pol for *Esquire*, making no mention of his "private secretary." After inspecting the beaches and wharves and the little theater and talking to the newly enfranchised fishermen, he was led to a lavish lunch with "various local officials." The meal was exactly to Dos Passos's taste, with broad beans in olive oil followed by a "magnificent" dish of fresh sardines, then roast chicken with new potatoes and lettuce. Lunch went on and on, and all through it Dos sat listening, pleasant and animated and genuinely interested while his tight, jumpy private secretary sat drumming his fingers, doubtless imagining machine-gun fire. Their hosts were at pains to point out that everything on the table before them—except unfortunately for the wine and the coffee—had been either caught or grown in Sant Pol itself. Actually, they added, they *did* make wine in Sant Pol. It was just that this local wine wasn't really *quite* good enough to serve to distinguished foreign guests. They explained how the sardines had been caught, with a technique new to Dos Passos. They went out at night, in boats loaded with "great batteries of acetylene torches to attract the fish to the surface." Torches! Luring the fish! The scene of the new technique suggests Picasso's great painting from around this time: *Night Fishing at Antibes.* Dos took it in, absorbed, while Liston stared at death, hovering at the door.

The meal, in its Spanish way, just would not end. Dos Passos seemed in no hurry to leave. Liston sat and sat, in agony. But of course the festivities did finally end. They did finally leave. There were elaborate farewells. Then, under drizzle, the two men *finally* piled back into the Hispano-Suiza.

What Dos and Liston said during the rest of the ride to the border we will never know. The beautiful limo swept northward from Sant Pol without stopping once. It must have gotten into Perpignan around dusk. As the car pulled up to the frontier inspection station, everyone of course had to show his passport. Dos handed his over. Then Liston handed his, in an agony of anxiety. *Nothing* could go wrong. Nothing, *nothing,* **nothing,** could go wrong.

The French guards, in their trim blue uniforms, flipped through the classic American documents. World travelers, these guys. Take a look: America, Moscow, everywhere. But all was in order. After a couple of perfunctory chops of their official stamps, it was over. The car was waved through. It was the thirtieth of April. José Robles was dead. The Catalonian terror was about to begin. But when that limo swept over the invisible line, they were free.

PART III

THE END OF
THE AFFAIR

chapter 13

SPANISH REALISM,
SPANISH ROMANCE

The time it took Hemingway to end his marriage to Pauline Pfeiffer and make a new beginning with Martha Gellhorn was exactly the time it took for the Spanish Civil War to end.[1] The process did not last *approximately* as long as the war. It lasted *exactly* that long. Hem's tortured triangular drama of "loving two women" began in Madrid during that spring of 1937, just when Robles was murdered. It reached its climax in late March 1939, on the day—the *very* day—that Franco marched in triumph into Madrid. That day Hemingway began writing *For Whom the Bell Tolls*. And the final break with Pauline came at last at the very end of August 1939, virtually on the day that Stalin's long-sought pact with Hitler precipitated the real Second World War.

This cannot be coincidence.

Hemingway had asked Martha Gellhorn to marry him as soon as she arrived in Madrid that March. From that March forward, Martha quite naturally built her dreams on the assumption that someday soon she would become Ernest Hemingway's wife. That someday did not come soon. Or easily. Hemingway proposed to

Martha well before he had fully resolved to leave Pauline. He had proposed while he "loved two women."

The key factor in the melodrama of loving two women is that for Hemingway, it was a process of renewal—the death of an old love, the birth of a new. That process could not be completed or validated unless and until the triangular agony had rewarded him with the birth of a new work. By creating another of his love triangles, Hemingway was looking not just for a new woman. He was after renewal as an artist. For him, artistic renewal invariably involved some sort of imaginative, symbolic embrace of the death that made the new life possible, that "gave it birth," as it were. *A Farewell to Arms* (with its tragedy, a death in childbirth) had emerged from his embrace of Pauline. In the same way, *For Whom the Bell Tolls* (with *its* tragedy, an act of solitary suicidal heroism) would emerge from his commitment to Martha.

But *For Whom the Bell Tolls* was still two years away. Meanwhile, ripping a new love from the womb of the old was exquisite agony, and it wouldn't be over until it was over. During the next two years, Martha's expectations would repeatedly soar, only to crash again, while Pauline would repeatedly stare into what looked like the end, only to be reassured: Ernest was coming home, the nightmare was over, her battered marriage had been saved.

Pauline would later bitterly claim the Spanish Civil War had destroyed her marriage. It was an acute insight. Without the war, the artistic rebirth Hemingway sought through Martha would never have happened. Before the Spanish War concluded, Hem would make three more visits to Spain, invariably with—and as part of his love for—Martha. Spain *was* their romance. And Martha was its heroine.

Yet whenever Hemingway returned to the States, Pauline would be waiting for him, still loving her husband, and still able to kindle the old embers to a warm, if flickering, glow. Even in Spain, only days after secretly proposing to Martha, Hemingway could speak to Josie Herbst, movingly and at length, about Pauline's essential place in his life. Way up until late 1938, there are letters that show Pauline rejoicing, sure that this time, *this* time, her marriage had been saved.

The shootout in the streets of Barcelona started on the morning of May 3, when the Spanish Communists and their Soviet allies made their first overt move: seizing the Barcelona telephone exchange. Within hours, they had taken possession of many other strategic buildings throughout the city. The hit came as no surprise: the Catalonians had been expecting a communist coup for weeks, and when it came, they hit back instantly. Exactly as per Stalinist plan.

The city came to a stop. The emptied streets echoed with rifle and machine-gun fire. Cars were left behind on the sidewalks: trams stood idle on their tracks, sometimes in the middle of intersections, abandoned where their conductors had bolted for cover. Barricades crisscrossed the streets and machine-gunners peeked out from piles of sandbags on the Ramblas. A terrorized population slammed their shutters closed and huddled behind them. The few civilians who ventured into the mêlée dodged from empty doorway to empty doorway, waving frightened little white handkerchiefs at the ends of long poles. Gunfire filled the empty streets. As Orwell would report, "all the while the devilish noise, echoing from thousands of stone buildings, went on and on and on, like a tropical rainstorm. . . . A deafening fusillade . . . it never stopped while daylight lasted, and punctually next dawn it started again."[2]

As a soldier in the POUM militia, Orwell found himself posted across from POUM headquarters, perched on top of a building that housed a movie theater and a museum and was capped by a small domed observatory. "I used to sit on the roof, marveling at the folly of it all. From the little windows in the observatory you could see for miles around—vista after vista of tall slender buildings, glass domes and fantastic curly roofs with brilliant green and copper tiles; over to the eastward the glittering pale blue sea—the first glimpse of the sea I had had since coming to Spain. And the whole huge town of a million people was locked in a sort of violent inertia, a nightmare of noise without movement. The sunlit streets were quite empty. Nothing was happening except the streaming of bullets from barricades and sand-bagged windows."[3]

The POUM and anarchist defense failed, of course. The Stalinist scenario was a complete success. Within a week, the Assault Guards whose arrival George Mink had foretold had come, taken command, and put an end to the Catalonian "treason."

Resolutely ignoring all of this, Hemingway and Martha Gellhorn made their way out of Spain the day after the shooting began, traveling to Paris via Valencia. To the end of her long life, Martha Gellhorn would stick to what her biographer concedes was a "blinkered" view of Stalinism in Spanish Republican politics. She remained faithful to the Popular Front—far more faithful than Hemingway—to the day she died, loyal to its hopes, and, locked in her naïve sophistication, loyal also to belief in its lies. In her nineties, Gellhorn was still brushing off the May coup as an "insignificant incident."[4] For the duration of the war, Hemingway would likewise play good soldier for the Front. But as he did, he could feel himself rationalizing its morality. He was obsessed with thoughts about treachery: treachery personal and treachery political. He couldn't quite shake the Robles thing. He *had* to be right about the Robles affair. It was *essential* that he be right about it. Because if he wasn't right about it . . . what then?

Numerous other celebrities and heavy hitters were also leaving Madrid around this time. The Soviet military presence was fading. It was being replaced by the rising omnipresence of Soviet secret police.

Not incidentally, Hemingway's glamorous prime confidant in the war, Mikhail Koltsov, was likewise recalled to Moscow at this time.

In the middle of 1937, to be recalled to Moscow was to take a first look at the face of death. The stated reason for Koltsov's return—it was a deception—was for him to report in person about the triumph of the Popular Front. Once home, Koltsov really did have an audience with Stalin. The interview (several other high officials were there) seemed at first quite a jolly affair. Greeting Koltsov with laughter and smiles, Stalin kept calling his man in Madrid by his Spanish code name: "Comrade Miguel." Yet as he made his report, watching the listening dictator's eyes, Koltsov felt sure that behind his smile Stalin was sizing him up and thinking: *"Too smart. Too smooth."*

At the end, there were a few questions. Then Stalin thanked Koltsov and wished him good luck. Koltsov saluted the general secretary, averring that he served the Soviet Union. Then he turned to walk the longish distance to the entrance to the chamber. Just as he was about to leave, Koltsov heard Stalin call after him.

"Comrade Miguel!"

Koltsov turned, still smiling. "Yes, Comrade Stalin?"

"Comrade Miguel, do you own a revolver?" Stalin's smile was a little fainter.

Koltsov was perplexed. "Why . . . yes, Comrade Stalin."

"But you're not planning to kill yourself with it?"

Fear drenched the man. "Certainly not," Koltsov stammered. "The idea never went through my head. . . ."

"Well, that's splendid," Stalin said, seemingly relieved. The smile came back. "Splendid! Once again, Comrade Koltsov, thank you. . . . Goodbye, Comrade Miguel."[5]

Stalin's gratitude was lethal. Koltsov didn't commit suicide—not literally, anyway—but even while he stood in Stalin's presence, plans for his demise by other means were well advanced. Just before their meeting in the Kremlin, Stalin had arranged for a file on Koltsov to be opened by the NKVD, purporting to show that while in Spain, Koltsov had betrayed the revolution by signing on as a British agent. If he had wanted to reward Koltsov's service with death then and there, he needed nothing more.

But Stalin was not ready to kill Koltsov. Not quite yet. In June 1937—perhaps two weeks after the Kremlin meeting—a brand-new reign of terror began in Moscow, a third wave of purges and killings, staged under the cover of the Popular Front. This wave was directed against the Red Army, particularly against those generals who were urging that the USSR get ready for an inevitable war with Germany. Stalin didn't like talk about inevitable war, and he feared a move toward real readiness might tempt the Nazis into a preemptive attack. Liquidating those who thought otherwise would consolidate the autocracy and entice Hitler into the all-desired Nazi-Soviet alliance. So the killings began.

Yet even while the June 1937 Terror was being unleashed, Stalin was laying plans for yet another wave, a fifth, that would clinch the Nazi-Soviet alliance by purging the "antifascist" cadres along with their propaganda about humanism and democracy and all that. It would be time to wipe the antifascist "tactic" out of historical memory.

Thousands would be slated for death, but the show trials of antifascist traitors would need some star villains: The most important would be Maxim Litvinov, the Soviet foreign minister who'd orchestrated the Popular Front's diplomacy. Beside him would be Mikhail Koltsov, the smooth-talking toady to the artists of the decadent West—Gide especially (and Hemingway too?)—who had orchestrated the Front in Spain.

This last wave of the Terror was short-circuited by Hitler himself, when he invaded his new "ally" too quickly for it to be put into effect.[6] Koltsov would be shot of course, but secretly, incidentally. The key fact remains. At the very moment that the Popular Front was being secured in Spain, Stalin was laying plans to arrest the "antifascists" who had secured it, and once he was safely allied with Hitler, kill them all.

Dos Passos left Liston Oak at the border and hurried to Antibes— it was nearby—to meet Katy.[7] They spent a little more than a week there before setting out for Paris and the trip home. In Antibes, Dos worked on the journalistic pieces about Spain that he would publish in his collected reportage, *Journeys Between Wars.*

Some biographers have suggested that Dos Passos left Spain in May 1937 after having turned hostile to the Spanish Republican cause. This is a fundamental misunderstanding, and a gross one. Assuming one clearly distinguishes the Spanish *causa* from Stalinist influence on it, Dos Passos never turned against the Spanish Republican cause, even in his later—*much* later, in the 1950s and after—politically conservative phase. In his eyes, Pepe Robles had died for a revolutionary republic in Spain, and Dos Passos never ceased to believe in the fundamental—albeit betrayed and lost— rightness of that republic. His 1937 journalism is filled with unequivocal and enthusiastic support for the radical communes he'd seen in Fuentedueña and San Pol. Even his criticism of the Valencia government's increasingly obvious submission to Soviet power looks, to modern eyes, mild to the point of invisibility. Certainly it was circumspect when compared to what Orwell would soon say in *Homage to Catalonia*, and genteel when put beside the fiery defiance then filling New York's newly anti-Stalinist *Partisan Review*.

No matter. Even mild criticism was treason enough for Hem. Besides, once he got to Paris, Dos seems to have freely expressed, in private, his outrage over what he'd been through. And when Hem got to Paris, he must have heard about it. In any case, on May 11, 1937, the day Katy and Dos were to take the train from Paris to their ship, Hem had somehow discovered the train's exact time and gate.

Katy and Dos got all their luggage to the station a little late that morning. It was raining hard. Struggling with their bags, they suddenly became aware of a stir: Hemingway was in the station. He was alone. Martha Gellhorn once remarked that "Hemingway moved in group formation." Not this time. The entourage had been parked somewhere, and Hem was hurrying down the long train platform alone.

Look! Katy exclaimed. Wemmage! Coming to see them off! They should be flattered, she whispered; the "great man" usually reserved his bon voyage visits "for major agents and Hollywood producers." Dos and Katy kept loading their luggage—they really *were* a little late.

When Hem got close, there was no happy "hello." "His face was a thundercloud," Dos would write. His words seemed to snap from the end of a whip. Hem wanted to know exactly what Dos planned to do about "this business."

"This business?"

The Robles business, of course.

"I'll tell the truth as I see it," Dos Passos replied. "Right now I've got to straighten out my ideas. You people"—notice how a "them" and "us" had already crept into the dialogue—"are trying to believe it is one isolated instance. It isn't."

That was putting it mildly. The date was May 11, 1937.

This remark stirred Hemingway to his old refrain: war is war, people get hurt; old friends can fool you, you have to *accept* . . .

"Ernest," Katy cut in hard and angry. "Dos knows all about that."

By now a porter was piling the Dos Passos's bags into the second-class compartment. Above them, the heavy rain kept battering down on the heavy opaque glass tenting the platform.

"The question I keep putting to myself," said Dos Passos, "is what's the use of fighting a war for civil liberties, if you destroy civil liberties in the process?"

Hemingway's rage burst. "Civil liberties, *shit*. Are you *with* us or are you *against* us?"

Dos Passos simply lifted his hands in a gesture of uncertainty, a kind of Frenchman's shrug. Then he added that he would write what he had to write.

Hemingway was now fully in the grip of his fury. Grinding his jaw, he lifted his clenched fist.

"You do that," he said, holding the fist right before Dos's eyes, "and you will be finished, destroyed. The reviewers in New York will absolutely crucify you. These people"—he was speaking of the communists then so instrumental in the Popular Front culture wars—"know how to turn you into a back number. I've seen them do it. What they did once they can do again."

Katy stared. She had once loved this man. Wemmage had introduced her to Dos. They had spent some of their happiest days with him. And now, this—this fist in the face, this craven careerist *threat*.

"Why Ernest," Katy said, "I have never heard anything so despicably opportunistic in all my life."

The wail of the "all aboard" had to come. *"En voiture, Messieurs'Dames."*

No more time for talk. As Katy and Dos pushed onto the train, Hemingway turned on his heels and burned out of the station without a backward glance. From their compartment window, Katy and Dos caught a last glimpse as he turned off the platform, and vanished.[8]

Two days later, Hemingway sailed by himself. By May 17, as his ship was nearing New York harbor, the communists in Valencia forced Prime Minister Largo Caballero out of office and, as Stanley Payne puts it, "the Communist strategy was crowned with success."[9]

Largo's successor, Juan Negrin, cannot properly be called a Soviet agent, though real Soviet agents surrounded him on every side. Stalin preferred his Popular Front celebrities to keep the patina of independence. What counted was that Negrin saw things—all things—Stalin's way. The day he assumed office, the legal assault on the POUM and the anarchists and their "treasons" began, sweeping through Catalonia with a new totalitarian fury.[10]

Did Hemingway grasp Negrin's real role? Not likely. Until May, Hemingway's insider guide in Spain had been Koltsov. Though Hem would see Koltsov at least one more time—in November 1937—from mid-1937 onward, Hemingway's new inside adviser became Herbert Matthews, the *New York Times*'s correspondent on the ground. Matthews was, and would remain, a relentless proponent of the Popular Front, its most visible apologist in American journalism. From the start, Matthews brushed aside—and attacked—any doubts about Negrin. Negrin was, in his view, one of the most farsighted European statesmen of the twentieth century.

Hemingway seems to have swallowed the Matthews line whole.

And yet, and yet . . .

When Hemingway at last found his way out of the Spanish moral maze, when he began writing *For Whom the Bell Tolls* in 1939, he decided to use this precise moment in May 1937—May 18–May 21—as the time span of his novel. He chose the three days of the Soviet near-coup as the same three days during which his hero, Robert Jordan, makes his choice between failure in his mission and his own death. He makes his choice on the radical peasant mountaintop, high above the corruption of politics in Madrid and Valencia. Robert Jordan does not make his choice—his *suicidal* choice—for the politicians. Nor does he even do it for victory. He is not sure, not in his heart, that the Republic will win. Robert Jordan lays down his life for . . . himself. His is not the "separate peace" of old, but something closer to a separate war, a separate death, a solitary, tragic, purely individual heroism, a stand against his own defeat. And it is made between May 18 and May 21, 1937.

This is not coincidence, either.

The Terror proceeded. Two days before Negrin was put in office—both Hemingway and Dos were still on the high seas—Stalin was handed the documents he intended to use to "prove" that "treason" was rife in the Red Army. An accommodating Gestapo had forged the papers for him; there was good reason why they looked so *very* Nazi. Six days later, Negrin's government was in place, and new totalitarian measures against the Catalonians began. Three days after that, on May 26, Stalin ordered the arrest of Field Marshall Tuchachevsky and a number of his closest colleagues. After five days of brutal torture, Tuchachevsky "confessed" to being a Nazi agent.

On June 11, Tuchachevsky and many other senior officers were herded into the closed granite courtyard of the NKVD's headquarters in Moscow. Black Marias pulled up to block the single exit. This made the courtyard a holding pen. NKVD men stepped out of the vans. Armed with machine-guns, each took his place in line. The cadre of once-proud generals huddled in despair. It was impossible to run. While the Black Marias revved their engines to high-pitched wails, the better to drown the sound, the machine-gunning began, and the bullets kept firing into the shrieking human cluster until everything in it lay still on the pavement, and the clangorous granite space was silent again.

It was probably the day after this event that Stalin, working in his study, reached for a single blank piece of paper and wrote out, in his own hand, a special order for the NKVD in Spain. In the midst of the general slaughter of the Red Army—thousands of officers would be killed in this appeasement of Hitler—it was, to be sure, a mere detail. But Stalin was a stickler for details.

It was an order concerning the Spanish Trotskyite Andrés Nin. The time had come. Shoot him now, without trial, and without delay.

Then he handed the order to his hovering secretary.

chapter 14

THE NECESSARY LIE

Hemingway's return to Pauline that summer was far from painless, but at least it was not the exercise in agony that marked their reunions after Hem's three subsequent visits to Martha and their Spanish romance. Pauline's cool was still firmly in place. Did she even "know the truth"? Not the whole truth. Not that Hemingway had actually proposed marriage to Martha. And even though she knew Martha was in Spain and that she had surely seen Hem, Pauline may not even have grasped how brazen the infidelity had really been. All spring, Pauline had churned out sweet brave letters to her husband, while keeping busy with compensatory dreams. She was going to see to it that when Ernest returned he would walk into a home even more beautiful and perfectly suited to his needs than ever. First, an ingenious little bridge was built between the second floor of the main house to Ernest's separate writing room. Then a serpentine brick wall, both elegant and high, was built around the property to confound the damned tourists. Not least, a salt-water swimming pool was installed. It was tranquil and huge: sixty-five feet long. Did Papa like to swim? Well, Papa would have the grandest swimming pool in Florida.[1]

Above all, Ernest must not be met with reproaches or bickering. Years after her death, her son Patrick mused that his mother saw her role in the marriage as that of the sage older woman offering stability to a wild younger man. (Pauline was all of six years older than Hemingway.) He was the temperamental artist; she was "Poor Old Momma" or "P.O.M." as he called her in *The Green Hills of Africa*.² Was P.O.M.'s spoiled boy occasionally enchanted by some pretty face? Inevitable. Pauline would wait out the sexual storm, sure that her supportive love could survive it. Just look at the passion that had bound them in the great days. Ernest had come home after Jane Mason, hadn't he? Why? Because Pauline offered sanity, seasoned love, help in dark times. Her tactic was calm.

Hemingway himself, sure that he was in love with two women, returned to Key West and then went off to Bimini with Pauline, plunging into one last pass through *To Have and Have Not*. The work consisted mainly in gutting the book: tearing out the most outrageous libels, including most of the offensive passages about Katy and Dos. These excisions left an already fragmented manuscript shattered: "Hemingway in pieces," as Edmund Wilson shrugged. Not that Hem seems to have cared. He had lucked into a vastly better way to clear the crud of his old life. Spain. Martha. Put them together, and it was what he called "the big parade" starting again.

Martha herself was in New York, toiling away with Ivens on *The Spanish Earth*. With his mangled English and his communist history, Joris was not the ideal point man in meetings with the moneymen of the American movie business. But Martha had an imposing presence, grand—even overwhelming—connections, and movie star looks. "I am now Joris' fingerwoman, secretary and etc," she wrote Hemingway, deep in the futile search for a major distributor. It wore her down. "I hate like hell," she wrote Hem, "being treated like a cuckoo idealist up and down the Great White Way."[3]

Yet if it failed as commerce, *The Spanish Earth* was a bonanza as propaganda. In June 1937, the main event of the Popular Front was the Second Annual Congress of the League of American Writers, a broadly based Comintern front filled with leftists connected, often very vaguely, to writing and communications. Its Congress was less a literary event than a propaganda jamboree for Popular Front true believers. It was to be held in Carnegie Hall, and *The Spanish Earth* would be screened, and the keynote speaker was by God going to be Ernest Hemingway.

Ivens arranged it. Part of the spin was to make the most of Hem's presence while conspicuously excluding Dos Passos from everything, and making sure he was the butt of hostile rumor. (In *Century's Ebb*, Dos Passos says that a flow of hate mail and anonymous calls began after the Carnegie Hall event.) An admiring Martha watched Ivens do the job: Joris had had, she wrote Hem, "a dandy meeting with our pals Archie [MacLeish] and Doss, [sic] and it must have been something. These communists are sinister folk and very very canny. The upshot is that [Archie] is president of the affair and Dos is the poison ivy. I have no doubt forgotten all of the more interesting points."[4]

Hemingway hated making his speech. He wrote it, grumbling, in Bimini, and then faced misery over delivering it. Ivens flew to Bimini for three days while Hem fussed with it—Joris may even have advised Hemingway on the text—and then flew back to New York with him to deliver it. Strangely enough, Hemingway seems to have suffered from agonizing stage fright. Yet the speech had to be made. It was a necessary step for what Gertrude Stein noticed he never neglected: "the career . . . the career. . . ."

Yet the whole business made him sick. *Speechmaking?* It was so . . . *political*. So very far from his bohemian independence, very remote from the separate peace. Luckily, when he flew up from Bimini, Martha was there to guide him through every miserable, unwilling step.

The night of June 4, 1937, in New York was suffocating, insufferable, sweltering as only Manhattan swelters on its most miserable summer nights. Earlier in the day, Hem had had a brief reunion with Scott Fitzgerald, who came to his hotel. As the time for delivering the speech approached and arrived, it was Martha's job to propel the reluctant propaganda king from the hotel to the stage door of Carnegie Hall. It took all she had to coax the man from bar to bar. He seized any excuse to delay, and any excuse to drink, just a little more. And there was always another bar, and Hem always needed another sip of liquid courage.

Waiting on stage at Carnegie Hall, MacLeish—the president— was rigid with anxiety. The crowd was huge—thousands filled every seat and every inch of standing room in the place. The stage was jammed with Popular Front celebrities—a "sea of so-called faces," as the New York novelist and wit Dawn Powell quipped. Everyone else was there. But no Hem.

And, oh yes. No Dos.

Archie sat stiff under the lights, faking a smile.

Until at long last, and late, Martha pushed her man into the wings. In 1937, Carnegie Hall was not air-conditioned. For some insane reason, Hemingway had come dressed in tweeds. (But then, Martha herself was in that silver fox.) Drowning as much in sweat as in alcohol, Hem was drunk and miserable, complaining so loudly he could be heard from the wings. But this was it. *Now*. Hemingway stepped into the vast blinding light of the great stage and ground toward the lectern.

The applause was massive, unstopping, and wild. This was a crowd for which the mere sight of Ernest Hemingway was a lifetime event. Working up a faltering smile, he pulled out his speech and began to recite the thing in his surprisingly high-pitched voice, through his surprisingly potent midwestern accent.

The speech itself was a pack of Popular Front platitudes rehashed in Hemingwayese. Spain was the place to stop fascism. Artists had to be committed to the fight. Fascists couldn't be artists. There was even the obligatory swipe at Trotsky, dismissing "marvelous doctrines and lost leaders." Consoling Dos with a "you-didn't-miss-a-thing" letter, Dawn Powell sighed that the speech's "sum total was that war is pretty nice and a lot better than sitting around in a hot hall and that writers all ought to go away and get killed and if they didn't they were a great big sissy."[5] During his seven minutes or so under the lights, Hemingway's reading glasses kept fogging. He'd stop to window-wipe them. He was strangling on his tie. He'd try to yank it loose. Then he'd return to his almost whiny monotone.

When at last it was over, the delirious audience was already on its feet, shouting its approval, whistling and clapping and not letting up. Hem had turned the trick. He was their main man. By the time he left that stage, Ernest Hemingway was the prime spokesman for the Popular Front in the English-speaking world. "These people"—the ones who were going to turn Dos into a "back number"—were backing *him* now. He'd hated doing it, but he meant every word, and besides, there was the career. . . . The job was done.

John Dos Passos? Foremost leftist writer in English?

The tables had been turned.

Five days later, the Red Army's prime generals were machine-gunned to death in the courtyard of the Lubyanka, and Andrés Nin, along with all his senior colleagues, was seized and imprisoned in the Atocha prison in Madrid. The Negrin government announced that it would try them all in a trial forthrightly modeled on the Moscow Terror Trials. Soon after, in obedience to Stalin's order, Orlov had Nin transferred out of Atocha to a "private" *checa* in the nearby suburb of Alcalá de Henares, a boutique torture chamber located in the basement of the home of the communist commander of the Republic's air force, Hidalgo de Cisneros, whose wife, Constancia de la Mora, was a propagandist in the service of Alvarez del Vayo and much involved with Hemingway. Before moving him out of Atocha, Orlov's men planted evidence purporting to show that "his friends in the Gestapo" had rescued Nin. These falsehoods became the cover story. Hemingway not only bought them but even perpetuated them in *For Whom the Bell Tolls*.

Nin was tortured in the basement of "Connie's" home. The torture was, according to Stanley Payne, "savage."

This done, the NKVD carried out Stalin's kill order. On the night of June 21, 1937, a car with a driver in front and two men in the back—one of them Orlov—pulled up outside the Hidalgo de Cisneros house. It was after curfew, but the driver, who was also an interpreter, carried a badge identifying him—perhaps falsely, perhaps not—as a member of the Madrid police, just in case some too-inquisitive Spanish policeman happened to pull them over. The car stopped at the locked gate of the courtyard.

The driver doused his lights. A waiting collaborator stepped from the house into the courtyard, swung the gate open, and stepped aside. The car crawled forward, lights out. When it stopped, the gatekeeper opened the trunk. Then everyone waited.

Waited until three other men emerged from the house lugging a large, crumpled, human-sized sack. Orlov called it "the cargo." "The cargo" was carried down the steps to the waiting car. The man inside "the cargo" seems to have been still alive—unconscious, probably drugged. The bag was dumped into the trunk, and the trunk door shut. Then the three men climbed in, and the car backed into the street, headlights still doused. The gatekeeper stepped out again, pulled the gate shut, and locked it.

The car went due south out of Alcalá de Henares, toward a place called Perales de Tajuña, driving until it reached a particularly isolated spot and pulling over at the edge of a large open field. Except for the moon and stars, the darkness was complete. There was not a house in sight. The trunk was opened. The body bag was lifted out and carried into the obscurity about a hundred meters into the field.

The driver had to sit waiting in the car a rather long time. What's known as a shallow grave was being dug. Maybe this one was a little less shallow than most. Then the silence was split by the crack of just one pistol shot.

The next stop for *The Spanish Earth* was the White House. Martha had persuaded Eleanor Roosevelt to arrange a presidential dinner, followed by a screening in the White House theater. After spending most of June in Bimini with Pauline, Hemingway once again flew up to Newark and joined Ivens and Martha for the quick hop to Washington.

It was still summer. Washington was, if possible, even hotter than New York, prostrate under one of its interminable heat waves. In those days, only a few rooms of the White House were air-conditioned and "the food," as Hemingway wrote to Pauline's Republican parents, "was the worst I've ever eaten. (This is between us. As a guest cannot criticize.) We had a rainwater soup followed by rubber squab, a nice wilted salad and a cake some ad-mirer had sent in. An enthusiastic but unskilled admirer."[6]

Martha loved and even revered the Roosevelts, despite a cer-tain incongruity: "nonintervention" *was*, after all, FDR's Span-ish policy. Hemingway despised the New Deal. At first, he'd despised it from its right. ("Starry-eyed bastards," he'd sneered in *The Green Hills of Africa*, "spending money that somebody will have to pay.") He now despised it from its left. His account of meeting the Roosevelts is insolent about FDR and condescending toward Eleanor, describing her as "enormously tall, enormously charming, and almost stone deaf. She hears practically nothing that is said to her, but she is so charming that most people do not notice it." (Eleanor Roosevelt was deaf in her left ear; hearing in her right was normal.) He fixed on FDR's paralysis—still care-fully kept from the public—calling the president "Harvard charming and sexless and womanly." In general, any reference to Harvard—Dos's alma mater—coming from Hem was an epithet.

Ivens was also paying close attention to his White House hosts, and we may be sure he passed on his mental notes to his Comintern superiors. At the dinner before the screening were the Roosevelts, their son James, and (Ivens noted it well) two senior military people, along with "a couple of people" the Dutchman could not place. Joris made no comment on the meal—though he did think the wine was not what he'd expect at the table of a head of state. The conversation, he said, was about the "folklore of war." Hemingway must have been in high form.

After dinner, everyone adjourned to the White House theater, where about thirty other guests joined them. In case either had questions, Ivens was seated between the Roosevelts. They did have questions. The couple's personal sympathies—hers pub-licly, his implicitly—were clearly with the Republic. At first, they watched in silence. During the second reel, FDR spoke up.

"That's very interesting. It holds up even without a story." Eleanor chimed in. "This fascinates me as if it were fiction." Ivens noted that FDR responded to every scrap of military information on the screen, peppering the filmmaker with questions about troop numbers, guns, planes, and tanks. He was well informed. Yet near the end, a tank he couldn't identify rumbled across the screen.

"What kind of tank is that?" he asked Ivens.

"A French tank, a Renault."

France was the leading noninterventionist state. Ivens noticed that his information produced not even a faint flicker of surprise on the president's face.

"Were they any good?"

"No," Ivens told him. "They didn't stand up against the anti-tank fire of the Franco troops."

Another phalanx of tanks rolled across the screen.

"Those are not Renault tanks," Roosevelt observed.

"No, Mr. President. Those are Russian."

Russian? Again, not one blink.

"Were there many of them?"

When the lights were turned up, both Roosevelts were gracious, though both thought the film should be much more forthrightly propagandistic. "Why don't you give more stress," Roosevelt asked, "to the fact that the Spaniards are fighting, not merely for the right to their own government, but also for the right to bring under cultivation those great tracts of land that the old system forcibly left barren?"

At which point the president's wheelchair was "skillfully maneuvered" out of the room, and so the other guests could leave. Ivens, Hem, and Martha were left alone in the screening room with FDR's closest personal adviser, Harry Hopkins, and Mrs. Roosevelt.

Ivens spoke up, worrying aloud that "the Spanish people" might lose.

Eleanor—who had privately lobbied for aid to Spain while publicly maintaining an ambiguous silence over her husband's policy—firmly interrupted. "We in the White House think the Spanish people are not going to lose."

Note that "we."

Hemingway and Ivens promptly chimed in, assuring her that they too had unshakable confidence in a Republican victory—*provided* the Loyalists got help, *provided* the democracies' arms embargo was lifted.

Eleanor finessed this pitch. "Do *you* think the Loyalists will win?"

Hemingway and Ivens said they thought the Loyalists were sure to win because the embargo was *sure* to be lifted in time. It *had* to be.

This both was and was not an answer, and Eleanor did not reply. Harry Hopkins said nothing, and in the ambiguous silence, the audience came to an end.

Then came Hollywood. Otto Katz himself set up the first West Coast screening of *The Spanish Earth*, yanking the chain of his Comintern front and cash cow, the Hollywood Anti-Nazi League. The event was held in the home of Fredric and Florence March. (Later screenings, all with Ivens but not Hem present, took place in the homes of John Ford, Darryl Zanuck, and Joan Crawford.) Seventeen heavy hitters from the ranks of Hollywood Stalinism—mainly members of the League—gathered at the Marches' and ponied up an average of a thousand dollars apiece for the privilege. (Miriam Hopkins paid with one of the thousand dollar bills she used to gamble.) Hemingway made a speech he'd scribbled out on hotel stationery, and

Ivens gave one, too. Ivens's speech—a remarkably good one—has survived, and is so very like Hemingway that you can wonder if maybe Hem had scribbled out that one, too. The event left Dorothy Parker—who regularly cried over Popular Front propaganda—dissolved in tears. F. Scott Fitzgerald, no League member, but present as an invited "non-political" guest, sent Hemingway this telegram: "THE PICTURE WAS BEYOND PRAISE AND SO WAS YOUR ATTITUDE."

The next day, the Committee of Film Artists for Spanish Democracy—another Comintern front—screened the film in the auditorium of the Los Angeles Philharmonic. Some 3,500 people crowded into the aisles and onto the stairs—with, it's claimed, another 2,500 turned away. Hemingway and Ivens briefly appeared on the stage: each said a few words; then the committee milked the 3,500 people for donations. The effort produced all of two thousand dollars.

And the rest of the country? In the end, neither Hemingway's name, nor Martha's charm, nor the anti-Nazi League's glamour could secure a major distributor for *The Spanish Earth*. Shown to the converted—in film societies, on college and university campuses, or in large centers of Popular Front opinion—the picture flourished. It never made it to Main Street.

Was it therefore a failure? If the goal was to induce the United States to enter a war over Spain, or even to risk fomenting a wider European war by arming the Spanish Republic, the answer must be that it failed. Franklin Roosevelt had made up his mind about both those options.

On the other hand, if the purpose was to galvanize the Popular Front in America and clinch its position in elite opinion, *The Spanish Earth* was a shining success, one of the Comintern's most stellar.

Back in New York, Hemingway was courted by the then publisher of *Esquire*, a man named David Smart, who'd decided to launch a cutting-edge men's magazine—the now-forgotten *Ken*—using Hemingway as its doyen and Popular Front chic as its motif.

This fatuous effort to use Stalinism to sell high-end gin, brandy, and men's cologne guttered out of existence after about a year. *Ken* is remembered today—if at all—because a few of the better pieces Hemingway wrote for it can still be read in his collected journalism. The uncollected pieces were mainly hasty propagandistic diatribes that sometimes read like uncorrected, and none too sober, first drafts. *Ken* would not be of much interest to us, except for one fact. Within a year, Hemingway would use *Ken* to add his own voice to the swelling Stalinist smear of Dos Passos.

But the main job was done. The career turnaround was complete. After L.A., Hemingway flew back to New York, and then on to Key West. From there he set out with Pauline to cross back to Bimini on the *Pilar*, where they were going to celebrate his thirty-eighth birthday. As the *Pilar* jounced through the Caribbean waves, the duplicitous husband and menaced wife were back together, just like the old days. Did it feel anything like the old days? As the *Pilar* cut through the aquamarine, there was lots of time for talk. The talk may even have been loving. If it was, Pauline would have done her level best to believe every word. Maybe it wasn't even that hard.

When Dos Passos and Katy got back home to Cape Cod that summer of 1937, Dos was in deeper trouble than he seems to have grasped. Very understandably, his experience in Spain had left him shocked, shaken, and angry. How not? His Spanish

Eden was being Stalinized; one of the great political and social ideals of his youth was turning to squalor before his eyes. Yet the Robles murder seems to have reached more deeply into Dos Passos's inner life than the mere shock of grief and anger. He was, without knowing quite how, losing his grip on his art.

He still was up and at work every morning at dawn, focused and productive. He still signed political petitions and made public statements, though now they were for the anti-Stalinist left. He plunged into a new novel. He was in fact facing the gravest threat he had ever known as an artist—one every bit as grave as the one Hemingway had sensed menacing him in 1936. The difference between the two men was that back then Hemingway recognized the threat for exactly what it was, while in 1937 Dos somehow did not seem to grasp what was happening.

The workability of Dos Passos's genius was in peril. Faced with similar danger, Hemingway had at first tried to shout it down. That was *To Have and Have Not*. When that effort failed—and fail it did—he made a more intelligent, more deliberate move. Not kinder, but smarter: he turned to Martha. To Spain. Somehow, *somehow*, he needed new inspiration, new force, and new material. He *had* to crawl up out of the pit of 1936 and get himself onto the heights of *For Whom the Bell Tolls*. Through all the bullying and bullshitting, he never lost track of that make-or-break need. That is what "The Snows of Kilimanjaro" is about. Some rot within was killing him. The old inspiration of *A Farewell to Arms* was moribund, succumbing to some vile gangrenous thing. He knew it. He could see it. The hyena kept nuzzling into his tent. He was sure he needed to be saved. To save himself. And he was not wrong.

Thus alarmed, Hemingway set out to save himself with Martha and Spain. He would do it for better or worse, "by pride and by prejudice," as he wrote in "The Snows," "by hook and by crook." Every minute he spent in Spain, soaking up a new vision, was guided by this deepest agenda of all. It was not going to be easy. And it was certainly not going to be pretty. So what? Whatever it took.

With the triumph of *The Big Money* behind him, Dos Passos faced equivalent danger, and somehow failed to grasp the fact. Despite his acute political and personal distress that summer, Dos seemed, in a way, almost complacent about his art. He showed none of the agitation—the almost desperate panic—that Hem had felt facing a similar menace the year before. Yes, this last book in the *U.S.A.* trilogy was maybe not as strong as the first two. But Dos's trouble went way deeper than that. The force that drove *his* genius, *the* thing that enabled his talent, was dying inside him. He does not seem to have seen it. But even if he did see it, he did not know what to do about it.

The true art of John Dos Passos—the *great* art of John Dos Passos—flies on the wings of a movement. That movement is modernism: the modernism that sprang from the shattering impact of the First World War. From *Three Soldiers* to *The Big Money*, almost all the genuinely great writing in Dos Passos—and there's a lot of it—rides on the surge of an esthetic and social radicalism that in the early twentieth century became a movement as momentous as the Romantic Movement had been a hundred years before.

And Dos Passos knew it. He explicitly identified with what he himself called

the relative tidal wave that spread over the world from the Paris of before the last European war. Under various tags: futurism, cubism, vorticism, modernism, most of the best work in the arts of our time has been the direct product of this explosion, that had an influence in its sphere comparable with that of the Octo-

ber revolution in social organization and politics and the Ein-
stein formula in physics. . . . The group that included Picasso,
Modigliani, Marinetti, Chagall; that profoundly influenced Ma-
iakovsky, Meyerhold, Eisenstein; whose ideas carom through
Joyce, Gertrude Stein, T. S. Eliot. . . . The music of Stravinsky
and Prokofieff and Diageleff's Ballet hail from this same Paris already in the disintegration of victory, as do the windows of Saks
Fifth Avenue, skyscraper furniture, the Lenin memorial in
Moscow, the paintings of Diego Rivera in Mexico City and the
newritz style of advertising in American magazines.[7]

Dos had seized on this European movement and made it American, distilling from it something uniquely his own. It was exactly
what he needed to make his genius work. It is the key to his friendships, not only with Hemingway but also with Léger, Blaise Cendrars, and the Murphys. It is the key to the tremendous artistic
energy he tapped through his encounters with the early Soviet
avant-garde. It is the vehicle he found for his uncanny ear for the
sounds and cadences of American speech—the best since Mark
Twain. Using that vehicle, Dos Passos could capture that sound in
a Whitman-derived prose that aspired to the condition of poetry,
prose that was like nobody else's, and filled with wonders.

Problem: in 1937, the force behind it all was dying. It was
maybe dead.

It can be argued that the great first wave of modernism, the
great life-giving liberation of the imagination mobilized by the
First World War, was terminated by the totalitarianism that
emerged from that same war. Born from the same beast, the one
may have killed the other. Maybe the triumphant rise of Hitler
and Stalin put that movement—the one behind Dos Passos's art—
at risk. At the very least, it ceased to function with the energy,
confidence, and visionary éclat that drove it through the twenties

and early thirties. By 1941, Joyce and Virginia Woolf were dead. Picasso did go on making pictures. Stravinsky and Prokofiev continued to compose. Thomas Mann (but was he *really* a "modernist?") would produce *Doctor Faustus*. Yet by 1937, as an all-too-new barbarism defined an all-too-new world, the grand twenties phenomenon of "the new," which once had lit the imagination with the hopes of a pure tradition-shattering futurity, was receding into a wistful, glamorous past, toned sepia with history.

Maybe that modernism was not dying from mere inanition. Maybe it was murdered. Murdered in the Terror. Murdered in the camps. Murdered on the dictators' desks.

Killing it was already official policy. Hitler assailed "degenerate arts." When Karl Radek made "socialist realism" the obligatory artistic ideology in 1935, he had forthrightly aimed the executioner's pistol at precisely this modernism, using as his prime targets James Joyce and John Dos Passos.

But now something subtler and more personal, something unofficial but intrinsic to a terrible time had begun to eat away at what had so recently been an exalted and irresistible sense of possibility. Dos Passos did continue to write. He was at work on important political novel—*The Adventures of a Young Man*—by midsummer. Yet Dos Passos never found his way to *his For Whom the Bell Tolls*. The driving force behind his life as an artist, the dazzling medium that had once lifted his talent into genius and inspired a generation of radical artists around the world, had been maybe fatally wounded. He had taken it with him to Spain, but he did not come home with it. Somehow the great modernism of *Manhattan Transfer* and *U.S.A.* had died in Valencia. The bullet that murdered José Robles had also shot down the soul of his art.

chapter 15

THE NECESSARY
MURDERER

Hemingway was now fixated—small wonder!—on betrayal. An obsession with treachery had turned into a very large stone in the road of his imagination's climb to its magic mountain, the high heroic setting of *For Whom the Bell Tolls*.[1]

There was no lack of treachery to trouble him, beginning with his own. On the personal level, Hemingway had to rationalize his manipulation of Martha, his unfaithful mendacity with Pauline, and his assault on Dos. But Spain too was treacherous, and it had a way of making the personal political. There Hem had to square the Robles killing and the emergence in Valencia of what looked rather like a Stalinist state, rationalizing a new secret police that was increasingly active not just in Barcelona but throughout the Republic. Meanwhile André Marty, the French Stalinist who was commissar of the International Brigades, was spreading terror through the Comintern's foreign legions. On the world scene, motivated partly by delusion, and partly by opportunism, Hemingway had made himself a spokesman for a political movement that behind its wash of sententious rhetoric was clearly in service to Stalin and his state-sponsored terror. Locally, the new Negrin government was obsessed with treason. Almost its first official act had been to set up new tribunals for Soviet-style show trials. A culture of denunciation was emerging, not just denunciation of "fascists" and "fifth columnists." It turned out that the "enemies of the people" could also be old friends.

Finally, there was the betrayal of the Republic itself. Largo Caballero had been forced from office, and the Republic's government had sold itself to Stalin, in the name of securing the Soviet aid needed to win the war. Hemingway had no way of knowing it—though someone more politically acute than he might have guessed—but Stalin had no intention of giving Spain what it took to make victory possible. If more fighting served his cat and mouse with Hitler, Stalin didn't mind protracting the country's agony for a year or two. But eventually the Spanish Republic was going to lose. Stalin was going to let it lose. He was going to *make* it lose. That couldn't be said quite yet. Very few people could even see it. But if you peered carefully enough through the murk of all that betrayal, the one clear fact emerging from it was the hard cold face of defeat.

Hemingway and Martha Gellhorn's second trip to Spain was much less exciting than the first, composed of longish flats of boredom spiked here and there with flare-ups of all too much excitement. Life at the Hotel Florida was in every way less amusing than it had been that spring. The visiting celebrities had mainly moved on; the world press crops had thinned. The hotel was packed with International Brigadiers, many wounded, and most on leave, and the prostitutes they attracted.

The lovers' reunion was less than rhapsodic. Martha soon grasped that during his summer with Pauline, Ernest had not taken even one small step toward a formal end to his marriage.

Martha and Hemingway began to argue, and both began to discern trouble ahead. "Things thought or spoken in anger," Martha worried in her Spanish diary, "must have had their beginnings somewhere, when the mind was calm. . . . If the beginnings can come, what is the end?" Martha still wanted Hemingway—all too much. But was she still confident? "Oh God," she told the diary, "either make it work or make it end now."

The clash between Hemingway's egocentricity and Gellhorn's ambition was inevitable and blindingly obvious. To be sure, Martha's consuming wish to be the wife of Ernest Hemingway mingled ambition with love so thoroughly that the two seemed fused. But such a mix could not survive. Hemingway expected the woman in his life to do as Pauline had always done, and focus exclusively on him and his needs. *Exclusively.* The man was just that selfish; and the truth was just that simple. Yet in 1937, Martha Gellhorn could not see that her situation was impossible; that she was set on marrying a man with whom she could never live happily; that she had bound her future to a man who, whatever else he may have been, was just plain wrong for her.

As soon as the couple got to Madrid, Hem learned that Martha had taken advantage of her new visibility as *Collier's* Spanish correspondent to set up a high-visibility, high-fee lecture tour advancing *la causa* across the United States. It was a big career break. Martha Gellhorn was no longer just some talented pretty girl hanging out with a famous man. She had turned herself into an important independent journalist, and she was acting like one.

It enraged Hemingway. What was "his girl" doing setting up speaking tours without even *consulting* him first? Pauline never did *anything* without consulting him first. Over dinner at the Gran Via, Hemingway lit into her. Martha, he sneered, was a cheap money-grubber. A sellout. An opportunist. Cashing in on Spain's suffering. "Dinner," Martha confided to her diary, "was a meal like scratching your fingernail over the blackboard. . . . For an hour perhaps he put on, without opposition, a really excellent show but the kind of show usually reserved for enemies." They trudged back to the Florida in seething silence, and with "plenty of sidewalk" between them. Hem was in room number 108, Martha in 109. Once the door to whichever room they shared closed, the violence, verbal and physical, began. "Someday," Martha wrote, a little shaken, "I must learn to describe E. as hyena because I know it is a marvelous thing. . . . It was very hyena indeed, with everything called out and spat on, and the first round ended with a side swipe at the electric light which crashed beautifully all over the room."

There were other obvious problems. Martha drank plenty, but Hemingway was obviously a flat-out alcoholic, and getting worse. She was fastidious; his physical uncleanliness was stomach-turning. Beneath his charm was a mile-wide mean streak. He was arrogant to an insufferable degree.

And then there was the sex. Martha—who, despite her seductive manner and unfailing attention to her great good looks, was not generally all that turned on by sex—found their sex lousy. Hemingway talked it up all the time. He was forever playing Chopin and spinning stories about their beautiful life together. Yet Martha later confessed that even in Spain she went to bed with Hemingway "as little as she could manage." "My whole memory of sex with Ernest is the invention of excuses and failing that, the hope it would soon be over."

They did have fun together, if not in bed. They partied. They shopped. They toured the war. They hung out with Hemingway-worshipping International Brigadiers in the hotel. They drew steadily closer to Herbert Matthews, the *New York Times* correspondent, a mainly uncritical apologist for the Popular Front who now replaced Koltsov as their inside guide to events.

Even so, they had time on their hands. In November, Hemingway filled that time by writing a play—a very odd choice for a writer who had previously never expressed any sort of even perfunctory interest in the theater. The play set out on the impossible task of squaring the circles of treachery surrounding him. Impossibility did not stop Hem. He wrote the play quickly and skillfully and called the result *The Fifth Column*.

The Fifth Column is an exceptionally nasty piece of work and the moral nadir of Hemingway's entire career. Its mission—*the task of all Popular Front propaganda*—was to dissolve the facts of the Spanish terror in a heroic antifascist glow. To do this, Hemingway mixed vulgar bravado with a kind of brutal sentimentalism so as to promote what W. H. Auden, in a famous and anguished phrase, called "complicity in the necessary murder." Parallel to this effort, *The Fifth Column* sets out to make Hem's manipulation of Martha and his betrayal of Pauline look like saintly acts.

The play's hero, Philip Rawlings,[2] is concocted out of crude egomania. Rawlings is, naturally, a writer. He lives in the Hotel Florida, room number 108. His beautiful girlfriend lives in 109. He unendingly plays Chopin on the gramophone. He drinks—drinks a whole lot—at Chicote's Bar. Yet all this is mere façade. Beneath it, Philip Rawlings is an undercover agent, James Bond in Spain, a kind of secret policeman outsourced from America, a George Mink who's read Proust. He is a wonderful, if gruff, Popular Front assassin who, motivated by antifascism, kills not for money but for goodness; a real man who, in contrast to the lily-livered liberals around him, understands the necessity for complicity in the necessary murder.

In fact, complicity in the necessary murder is Philip's specialty. As a committed revolutionary—or is it antifascist? they *do* blur—Rawlings has come to Madrid to show the Spanish how to root out all the spies and traitors who inevitably sap the good guys' strength in any civil war. Lucky, lucky Spain. When it comes to fingering, interrogating, and, ah yes, liquidating traitors and fifth columnists, nobody nails them better than our Phil. At the climax of the play, Madrid is purged of no less than three hundred fifth columnists—plotters, saboteurs, and spies all—rounded up thanks to the ruthless but necessary work of Rawlings. The man can generate a Madrid-based Days of May all on his own.

Assisting Rawlings in this bloody but necessary work is his Spanish ally, Antonio, a character modeled in every detail on Pepe Quintinilla—Hem's mendacious guide during the Robles affair. In 1938, seeing the play in New York, Virginia Cowles would recall that lunch under bombardment at the Gran Via with Hem and the man in the dove-grey uniform, recalling their drunken talk about how magnificently the "mistakes" had died.

(*"A chic type, eh? Now remember—he's **mine!**"*)

Cowles had never imagined that "chic type" would become the hero she saw on a Broadway stage.

A third character, also a heroic assassin, is Max, a Comintern agent sent to Spain to fight the antifascist fight. Max is also killer, but instead of being a cruel Spanish killer like Antonio, or a two-fisted he-man of a killer like our Philip, Max is a sad, saturnine Middle European killer. Max kills with a breaking heart. His greatness of spirit while blowing out the brains of fascists and enemies of the people is almost too much to bear. Philip, Antonio, Max—they each pull the trigger in a different mood, but only because they must. They serve the People. To question the justice of their mission is almost treason in itself. Do they murder? Yes, but these are *necessary* murders. And they—Hemingway heroes all—are necessary murderers.[3]

More interesting is the commentary on Hem's love life woven through all this. For *The Fifth Column* is also about Martha and Pauline. Its trick is to use each woman against the other, and it does so with a nastiness that almost defies belief. Pauline is insulted in her absence, while Martha Gellhorn as the character Dorothy Bridges is depicted with a contempt so stinging and insolent that one has to wonder why Gellhorn did not walk out on Hem on the basis of her walk-ons alone.

The device is very ingenious: Martha's political commitments and talent are invoked to sneer at the apolitical worldliness of the absent Pauline. This done, Pauline's strengths—her aristocratic manner, her social self-possession, and her wealth—are rolled out to make Martha look like an opportunist and a buffoon. While assailing the old rich life he is renouncing in the name of revolution, Philip "very bitterly" waves its many luxuries in front of the wide-eyed Dorothy: his safaris in Kenya, his trips to Egypt, his breakfasts in bed at the Crillon and the Ritz, his steeplechasing at Auteuil followed by pheasant shooting in the Solange, his nights in the Mathaiga Club in Nairobi and then back to Europe where his weeks in Kitzbühel were so much better than those in Saint Moritz. Vulgar Saint Moritz. "You meet people like Michael Arlen in Saint Moritz." Dorothy slavers on hearing it. *"Oh darling, think how it would be!"* It is too wonderful for her to handle. *"Have you that much money?"*

This is what Hemingway called "loving two women."

But every characterization of Martha is insulting. "A bored Vassar bitch" (Act II, Scene 1). Or: "She's lazy and spoiled and rather stupid, and enormously on the make. Still she's very beautiful, very friendly, and very charming and rather innocent—and quite brave" (Act II, Scene 2). Again: "She has the same background all American girls have that come to Europe with a certain amount of money. They're all the same. Camps, college, money in family, now more or less than it was, usually less now, men, affairs, abortion, ambitions, and finally marry and settle down or don't marry and settle down. . . . This one writes. Quite well too, when she's not too lazy. Ask her about it if you like. It's very dull though, I tell you" (Act III Scene 1).

Sometimes Philip loves Dorothy. Sometimes he doesn't. Sometimes he wants to marry her. Sometimes he doesn't. When a prostitute in Chicote's Bar warns Rawlings against making a mistake with "that big blond," Philip replies, "You know Anita . . . I'm afraid that's the whole trouble. I want to make an absolutely colossal mistake." In the end, he tells Dorothy that she is a "commodity" that a self-sacrificing revolutionary hero like himself cannot afford.

The miracle is that, after one glance through the manuscript, neither woman walked out on him for good.

Hemingway finished *The Fifth Column* in Madrid in early December 1937. He and Martha were just preparing to leave Spain for the second time when, after two mainly empty months, something big finally happened: a military event with real significance.

Franco's position was getting stronger and stronger. He controlled almost the entire western half of the country, and the eastern half, still held by the Republic, was very much on the defensive. In late 1937, Franco decided the time had come to split the Republic in two, and he set out to drive a wedge between Barcelona in the northeast and Valencia to the south by taking possession of all the real estate between the two cities, seizing the valley of the Ebro River and thereby cutting through to the Mediterranean coast. This came to be called the Aragón offensive, and Franco proposed to use as its base and point of entry a poor but pretty little hillside town, his easternmost stronghold, called Teruel.

Rather than let this happen, the Republic decided to launch a preemptive offensive that would drive the rebels out of Teruel, thus nipping the Aragón offensive in the bud. During the very cold pre-Christmas of 1937, just as Hemingway and Martha were getting ready to leave the country, the Republican forces decided to seize the town and its environs. This battle and its aftermath would be *the* decisive event in Hemingway's war, *the* pivot of his thinking about victory and defeat.

Then came unexpected news. Hem heard that Pauline had come to Europe and was in Paris and was arranging for a visa to come to Madrid herself. A journalist friend who'd seen Pauline in Paris brought Hem the news at the Florida, and a delighted Hemingway grilled the visitor for "hours," teasing out every nuance to Pauline's talk about her reasons for coming. Pauline was coming because, Hem was told, she now saw that Spain had become the new center of her husband's life, and Pauline had to understand why and how. She *had* to be with him, *had* to be at his side, sharing this great new experience. His center was her center. Whither thou goest, and so on. She didn't care about the danger. She was coming, she was going to be with him, and that was that.

Hemingway made the messenger repeat this perfectly true, though partial, tale over and over, savoring its every nuance, touched, enchanted. Pauline! Joining him in Madrid! Coming for Christmas. To be with and understand him. Brave, good, loving Pauline . . .

The war got there first. On December 20, 1937, the Spanish Republic launched its offensive on Teruel. Pauline was stalled in Paris. Martha and Hemingway left for Barcelona with Herbert Matthews and the British journalist Sefton Delmer, and Hemingway proceeded to Teruel with Matthews and Delmer to see it firsthand.

It was winter, but worse. A vast, violent winter storm was sweeping over all of Europe: from London to Tarragona, the snow was blizzard-driven and everywhere falling without stop. Around Teruel, snow-blasted air sliced into the flesh of everyone on the battlefield, which was a winter wonderland turned into hell through the *terribilità* of war, the fields burying their corpses under the unending fall of whiteness. Accompanied by Matthews and Delmer, Hemingway saw the first battle of Teruel from beginning to end, embedded so deeply in the action that he was able to help one crouching soldier use a rock to smack open the jammed bolt of his rifle while enemy fire swished overhead; close enough, while the snow caked on his face and glasses, to see the Falangist soldiers in the front lines break into "the leaping plunging gait that is not panic but a retreat."

For retreat they did. At the end of the day, the soldiers of the Republic swept into the Teruel town square, and it was theirs. No "Aragón offensive" was going to be launched from this place. Not now, anyway. Franco's troops were running, and for the moment their freezing adversaries were flushed with victory. Here at last was the real thing: a victory, and a big one. Maybe even big enough to change the course of the war and end the drift toward defeat.

For the first and last time in his Spanish romance, Hemingway could savor the full joy of winning. He entered the town with Matthews and Delmer. "In town, the population all embraced us, gave us wine, asked us if we didn't know their brother, uncle, or cousin in Barcelona, and it was all very fine. We had never received the surrender of a town before and we were the only civilians in the place. I wonder who they thought we were."[4]

It was right around the time of Teruel that Vladimir Gorev, Robles's general and the mastermind of the defense of Madrid, was suddenly summoned home to Moscow. He went, and his reception perfectly captures the duplicity of the Popular Front. Publicly, Gorev was celebrated as a worldwide hero of the antifascist movement. There were banquets and medals. Stalin's deal with Hitler was not yet in hand. He was not quite ready to drop his "antifascism" yet. So the "Hero of Madrid" got a lavish, high-profile welcome.

At the same time, Stalin didn't want the Nazis to get the wrong idea about the true nature of Soviet "antifascism." Like all of Stalin's antifascist generals, Robles's general had been marked for liquidation for at least a year. Two days after being decorated in the Kremlin, the hero of Madrid, the living embodiment of Spanish antifascism, was arrested and summarily shot.

Buoyed by the victory at Teruel, and carrying *The Fifth Column* in his suitcase, Hemingway left Spain for the second time the day before Christmas, making his way through the huge European snowstorm to a reunion with Pauline in a white and silent Paris.

There he was surprised to walk into the unleashed ferocity of Pauline's fully aroused rage and despair.

chapter 16

SINGING "GIOVINEZZA" FOR FREE

In Paris, Pauline had not yet reached her breaking point. She may not have not have known everything about the scene in Madrid by Christmas, but she knew enough. Hem had been pleased to learn she wanted to join him in Madrid. It was true. She did want to join him. But she was also bewildered and enraged.[1]

Earlier that year, as she began to piece together the truth about Martha, Pauline had turned for advice to her beloved sister Jinny. This was a self-protective move, and a sure sign that part of Pauline at least wanted to get tough. She was turning for advice to someone she knew would put her interests far ahead of his. She knew full well what her son Gregory would later explain in six words: "Aunt Jinny," he wrote, "hated my father's guts."

Jinny did not counsel patience and love. Virginia Pfeiffer saw her brother-in-law as a callous brute who, after exploiting her sister for years, was now humiliating Pauline in front of the whole world. She advised Pauline to prepare for the worst. Above all, she should prepare to hit back hard. Main force was the only language the man understood. Pauline had given him two sons, a home, and years of adoring support. She had put up

247

with his infidelities, flattered his egomania, served his success, endured his insults, dodged his drunkenness, edited his manuscripts, sustained his moods, paid for his pleasures, and created ideal conditions for his work. Enough. End it now. And whatever else, do not let the man walk away from his latest outrage the way he had walked away from Hadley. Cost free.

Pauline had turned to Jinny for exactly this kind of advice, and she listened to it well. But she was still far from ready to accept that her marriage was at an end. During the next eighteen months of suffering, her shifting moods confounded hope and confidence and desperation, making each look like the other. But there was plenty of rage in the mix, too. Clutching at straws did not leave her blind. When Pauline did at last reach her breaking point, she would astound and enrage Hemingway by following Jinny's advice to the letter, and implacably.

It seemed the snow in Paris would never stop. After Teruel, Paris lay frozen in that magical silence that descends on any great city under snow. The silent whiteness swallows the metropolitan roar. Sound, like sight, is cleansed. Inside is a cocoon. Outside, all you hear is the crunch of your own footsteps, the distant scrape of shovels, children's voices. The snow stops for a while. Then it begins again. Whatever else, it's not over.

Stalled in Paris by visa problems, Pauline was waiting for her husband in the very grand Elysée Park hotel, in a top-floor suite with a perfect view of the Bois de Boulogne. And she couldn't help it: the moment she saw him, the confrontation burst from her. She raged. She wept. Of *course* she knew about Martha Gellhorn. Who didn't? How could he possibly imagine she didn't know the obvious truth? *Everyone* knew it. It was all over every goddamned newspaper in the country. How *could* he? How *could* he? Did he have any idea what kind of pain he was

causing? And for what? Martha *Gellhorn?* The woman was de-
spicable: "egoistic, selfish, stupid, childish, phony, and 'almost
without talent.'"[2] Her rage grew on itself. At one point, Pauline
flung open the windows overlooking the wintry Bois, and
shouted that if their life together had finally sunk to this, she
was ready to end it here and now: one good jump and this whole
unspeakable misery would be over.

Hemingway coldly waited it out. In public, they bickered. In
private, they raged. After two weeks of this sort of marital misery, the battling couple left Paris, sailing straight for Nassau—
skipping New York—from which they flew on to Miami and
Key West. There, a kind of sullen calm descended on them both.

Something beyond mere misery was in play. Confronted,
Hemingway was eaten by silent remorse, and more: by signs of
the mental instability that had haunted him from his early
youth, very possibly symptoms of the same disease that eventually killed him. Most biographers agree that "his rejection of
Pauline in favor of Martha stirred up the remorse that had remained quiescent ever since his rejection of Hadley in favor of
Pauline. Without being precisely beside himself, he continued to
be petulant, quarrelsome, and almost pathologically suspicious
all through the early months of 1938."[3]

Almost pathological? Of course he was under pressure.
Hemingway admitted to his Scribner's editor, Max Perkins, that
he was in "such an unchristly gigantic jam of a bloody kind that
it is practically comic." But his agitation and petulance were
not mild. Suicidal thoughts began to recur. Writing to Hadley,
as he often did when depressed, he wondered if *The Fifth Column* would ever be produced. "Don't really give a good god-
damn about that nor about anything else but on acct setting
bad example am going to stick around and make somebody else
shoot me."[4]

Besides, he couldn't write.

He was able to churn out pieces for *Ken*. None were especially good, and some were shockingly bad. But serious work? He'd come home with a couple of story ideas in mind: one eventually became the suave, ugly little piece called "The Denunciation," very much in the vein of *The Fifth Column*. But that winter, he couldn't make them come. He tried in Key West. He tried in Havana. No good. Mired in his Stalinoid commitment, his imagination was locking down.

Even so, the agents of the Popular Front remained enchanted with him. In late January, Ivens sent him a letter that amounts to an invitation to take the next step into covertly controlled Soviet propaganda operations in the United States. Ivens explicitly welcomes Hemingway into the Stalinist inner circle, speaking forthrightly of the Comintern's declining propaganda interest in Spain and its new focus on China. Contemporary Historians is to be replaced with a new front: History Today. The old front must be "cleansed"; above all, Dos Passos must be kept from using its shell for his own purposes. Ivens will be going to go to China on orders coming direct from "M."—surely the Comintern's propaganda czar, Willi Münzenberg—whom Ivens assumes Hem either knows or knows about. Ivens assures Hemingway that he has passed his test: he now has access to senior Soviet agents in America. "If there is something you would like to talk over with one of our leading people, do it, Helene von Dongen will fix the rendezvous for you. . . . Once and for all, know that we are not impatient—we trust you."[5]

What did Hemingway think? Ivens told him to destroy the letter. He did not obey. Around this time, he began to carp—strictly in private—about the Comintern's, and therefore Ivens's, decision to dump Spain.

He and Pauline could no longer fake happiness. They bickered. They sulked. They drank. The ghastly backbiting that fills "The Snows of Kilimanjaro" filled their days. They inflicted on one another the kinds of large and small wounds that do not heal.

In Spain, despair was hitting hope hard. On February 21, 1938, about a month after the Hemingways got home, Franco retook Teruel. By March 7, the Generalissimo had begun his Aragón offensive; by April 15, he had split the Republic and opened a wide corridor to the Mediterranean. It was no longer possible for even the most optimistic observer to suppose that the Spanish Republic could possibly win the war. Though Hemingway would later write from the front that seen close up, the situation did not look as desperate as the papers made it seem, he was wrong. In fact, the situation was more desperate than it looked.

A few days before Teruel was recaptured, Hemingway and Martha had met in Miami. When the disaster came, they decided to return to Spain as soon as possible, keeping it secret that they would be together. Was Pauline deceived? Around March 15, Hem and Pauline left Key West together, flying from Miami to New York.

And in New York, in what amounted to a fluke, he ran into Dos. It was just a well-intentioned accident. Since both Hem and Dos happened to be in town at the same time, the Murphys, who knew nothing about the tensions in Spain and were giving a party, invited them both.

Archibald MacLeish, who had earlier played the futile role of go-between between the two men, was also there that night. MacLeish now grasped that "Ernest and Dos had not met since their respective returns from Spain. It also seemed to me that they met by accident, and with some surprise. . . ." "What I re-member," MacLeish wrote, "was a terrible icy coldness, mostly of Dos standing with his back to an unlit fire and then walking out of the room onto the balcony"—an elegant Manhattan ter-race near Saint Patrick's Cathedral and within sight of Rocke-feller Center, then being built.

Dos did not walk out onto that penthouse terrace alone. Hemingway went with him. A mid-March night in New York can be very nippy, but the two men were out alone for a rather long time. When they came back, they brought the chill in with them.

When Dos Passos left that night, he said to Gerald Murphy. "You think for a long time you have a friend," he said, "and then you haven't."

The next day, Hemingway sailed on the *Île de France*. As usual, Martha followed shortly afterward, on another ship.

On the high seas, the meeting rankled, and Hemingway fired off an abusive telegram to Dos Passos. When he got to Paris, he sat down to write what started out as a letter of apology. "Sorry I sent you that cable from the boat. It seemed funny when I sent it. Afterwards it seemed only snotty."[6] But by the middle of the third paragraph, his voice starts to rise. By the fourth paragraph, he is shouting onto the page.

One focus of his rage was Nin. They may have talked about what was now a worldwide scandal while they were on the ter-race. In a collection of his Spanish journalism, just published, *Journeys Between Wars*, Dos had ended a three-page account of meeting Nin with the remark that "since then Nin has been killed and his party suppressed."

Not exactly reckless rhetoric. Hemingway's answer about Nin—even as late as *For Whom the Bell Tolls*—was Koltsov's an-swer: Nin's "fascist friends" had kidnapped him; he was safe in

Paris. Dos's belief that Nin was dead infuriated Hemingway. "Then there is Nin," he snarled. "Do you know where Nin is now? You ought to find that out before you write about his death."

But the letter's main paranoid fury focuses on an article by Dos Passos in *Redbook* about the Fifteenth Brigade lunch, precisely the event where they had their confrontation over Robles. Dos's piece is anything but critical of the Republic. It does, however, mention the presence of the Soviet advisers, and singles out "a Russian staff officer who goes under the name of Walter."

Hem found this unbearable. "I think you should at least try to get your facts right. In an article just read in Red Book you do not mention Duran's name when it would have been correct and fair to do so. But you do feel you should mention Walter's and you call him a Russian general. You give the impression that it is a communist run war and you name a Russian general you met."

Except that the *Redbook* piece does not "give the impression that the war was Communist run," and the reference to Walter—who gave a speech at a public event—was merely accurate reporting.

"The only trouble with this, Dos," Hemingway goes on, "Walter is a Pole." He then reels off a list of four more foreign generals in Spain. Not one, he seems to shout onto the page, is a Russian. "I'm sorry Dos," he triumphantly concludes, "but you didn't meet any Russian generals, and this hasn't been a communist-run war for a long time."

We now know that Stalin explicitly insisted that the senior Red Army officers publicly sent to Spain maintain deniability by being foreign-born non-Russians. Walter, like all the other "generals" on Hemingway's list, was indeed a Pole. He was also, like the others, a longtime senior officer in the Red Army and fully under its discipline.[7]

Not a "communist-run war"? By March 1938, the growing
Soviet influence over the Valencia government was obvious
and explicit. Hemingway was, through Koltsov, even better informed than Dos Passos on that fact. Yet Hemingway's splut-
ter of outrage contains one scrap of truth. There *were* fewer
Russian generals in Spain. Stalin *was* choking off military aid
to the Republic. Many generals, like Gorev, had been summoned home—there to be shot for their "antifascist" suc-
cesses. In Spain itself, Stalin was replacing the military men
with secret police.

The letter gets drunker and angrier. "You know," it an-
nounces, "all people are not cowards." Then comes paranoia:
"Now I am very easy to attack and if you want, instead of trying to get straight on Spain you can simply attack me too. But
that won't help you on the road you're going."

Then Hemingway pauses in mid-rant.

Should he send this letter? After all, they are old friends.

And the mere word "friends" sends him into a paranoid per-
oration. He will send the letter because his friend Dos has
"knifed him in the back."

"Good old friends, you know. Knife you in the back for a
quarter. Anybody else fifty cents. . . . Good old friends. Always
happy with the good old friends. Got them that will knife you in
the back for a dime. Regular price two for a quarter. Two for a
quarter, hell. Honest Jack Passos'll knife you three times in the
back for fifteen cents and sing Giovinezza for free. Thanks pal.
Gee that feels good."

"Giovinezza" was the anthem of Mussolini's black shirts. The
implication? Not only was Dos a traitor to his friend Hem. He
was a *fascist* traitor.

Then the letter was sent.

The next day, Hemingway and Martha left Paris with Herbert Matthews and headed for Barcelona, now sheered off from the rest of the shrinking Spanish Republic. Barcelona was being subjected to massive civilian bombing. The city, overflowing with refugees, was filled with scenes of horror. Martha visited a local hospital and its ward for the children injured in the bombing, and her account of what she saw is searing, one of her best pieces. The city huddled, as if waiting. Ending a sketch of refugees streaming toward Barcelona, Hemingway wrote: "People looked up at the sky as they retreated. But they were very weary now. The planes had not yet come, but there was still time for them and they were overdue."

Matthews was their guide to the front, located mainly in the valley of the Ebro River, which was now de facto frontier between Republican and Falangist forces. There, witnessing scenes of the Republic's defeat, Hemingway began to recover some of his balance as an artist.

While they were in Barcelona, morale was given a boost by an air show, in which squadron after squadron of fighter planes—virtually the Republic's entire air force, truth be told—flew over the besieged city. If the government could not get its troops to Barcelona by crossing the Ebro, its planes could at least fly over. The show of force may have felt wonderful, but it was quite deceptive, and so was the skirmishing along the Ebro. Barcelona was virtually undefended.

Was the war over? Hemingway assured his readers that the smart money was wrong: Spain wasn't going to be over yet. Matthews echoed that view: "It all seemed so gloomy and hopeless in those days," Matthews would later write, "and yet we knew the war would go on." [8]

But why?

It would have been easy to move to a quick ending. As President Manuel Azaña noted in his diary, "between the two cities"—Lérida and Barcelona—"there were no forces at all."[9] It turns out that Franco was holding back at Hitler's behest: the German dictator wanted to keep his ally Mussolini preoccupied in Spain and out of his hair in Eastern Europe while the Nazis moved into Austria and prepared to make his move on Czechoslovakia six months later. Mussolini saw Austria as part of *his* sphere of influence; Hitler was in no mood to share any of his new spoils with the Italians. Stalin meanwhile was quite prepared to see the war go on and on because he hoped Hitler's new aggressions might provoke the general European war both he and the Führer, each in their different way, were hoping to create. So Barcelona, and Spain, were left dangling.

In truth, Spain was being written off, abandoned. The journalists, like the generals, were leaving, too, and not just journalists from the perfidious democracies. Ivens and Koltsov and Katz were also gone. When Martha Gellhorn proposed a story on Barcelona's agony for *Collier's*, the editors shrugged it off, and offered her $1,000 per article—then a huge fee—for dispatches from *the* new places to be: Austria and Czechoslovakia. Martha accepted, and headed for the Danube.

Then one small, but very good thing happened. Outside Barcelona on Easter Sunday, watching a stream of refugees stumbling by, Hemingway had a conversation with an exhausted old man on a road along the Ebro, somebody who had fallen out of the stream of refugees, exhausted. Something in the exchange, some stoic peasant defeat, gave Hemingway something he badly needed. Hemingway immediately wrote a short story about this conversation, filing it as a dispatch. He called it "Old Man at the Bridge." It is a good story, though not one of Hemingway's greatest. It is rather sentimental, a little sententious. In *The Complete Short Stories* it takes up exactly two pages.

Yet this little story stands apart from Hemingway's other work at the time by being agitprop free, and because of its tone of compassion and a recovered authenticity.

"What politics have you?" I asked.

"I am without politics. I am seventy-six years old. I have come twelve kilometers now and I think now I can go no further."[10]

"I can go no further." In this one phrase, mingling defeat with stoic truth, Hemingway heard something that would find fruition in *For Whom the Bell Tolls*. With "Old Man at the Bridge," something was coming back for him. Not much. Just: *"I am without politics. I am seventy-six years old. I have come twelve kilometers now and I think now I can go no further."*

The healing fountain was starting to flow. It wasn't much: just two little pages of dampness seeping back into the drained well of Hemingway's imagination. It was practically nothing. But it was the real thing.

In the New York culture wars, the problems between Hemingway and Dos Passos had begun to be noticed. In the April issue of *Partisan Review*, a hard-fighting culture warrior named Herbert Solow wrote a piece about Dos's move away from Stalinism and Hemingway's move toward it called "Substitution at Left Tackle." And back in Key West, Hemingway was still enraged and still paranoid. On his return he worked more on "The Denunciation," and then settled on his next piece for *Ken*. He decided to call it "Treachery in Aragon" and make it a frontal attack on Dos.

The piece begins with an inflammatory claim: Franco's Aragón offensive had succeeded only because traitors within the

Spanish government, working with the Gestapo, had betrayed the Republic. "The Spanish government is not ready to have the story published," he adds cryptically, "nor to list the traitors yet."

From this claim—it has no known basis in fact—Hemingway moves to an attack on Dos. Mere American liberals ("liberal" was a favorite dirty word in the Popular Front) cannot understand real treachery in real war. Consider, for example, a "very good friend of mine" whose friend and translator had been arrested. "I absolutely guarantee him," he quotes Dos as saying. "I know he is absolutely loyal to the government and I guarantee him personally. Absolutely and without reservations."

"This all made me feel rather badly," Hemingway sighs, "because I happened to know this man had been shot two weeks before as a spy after a long and careful trial in which all charges against him had been proven."

Of course, Hem knew nothing of the kind. And saying it didn't make him feel badly.

After submitting his treatise on the "good hearted naiveté of a typical American liberal attitude" to *Ken*, Hemingway—increasingly hyper—suddenly announced to Pauline that he was going out for a couple of weeks of marlin fishing on a boat called the *Anita* belonging to Josie Russell, the proprietor of "Sloppy Joe's." Given the now unremitting misery of their marriage, Pauline was almost too ready to have Hem leave for a while—and the moment he was gone, she set out to throw a party, a costume party held at a nightclub on Front Street called the Havana-Madrid. All of Key West would be there.

The trip fishing for marlin went weirdly wrong. Out on the open seas, Hemingway was restive, difficult, complaining. Joining Hemingway and Josie was Russell's son, who was known as "little Joe," and a Cuban crew member, an elderly man. A few days out Hemingway made the strike of a "gigantic" marlin and began the struggle to reel in the fish. It was a hard struggle. Sometimes Hem was winning. Sometimes the fish. At some point in the battle, the old Cuban crew member made a mistake and accidentally cut the line. "With one gigantic surge, the marlin rose and dived free."

Hemingway's annoyance instantly flared far beyond anything understandable. He reeled on the offending old man and wrestled the fatal knife out of his hand, screaming that he would "kill him"—and screamed it so convincingly that both Russells thought it just might not be a figure of speech. They grappled with the writhing Hemingway, trying to calm him. Nothing calmed him. He continued to shout and struggle, totally out of control. "Little Joe" kept repeating, "Papa, let's have a drink . . . Papa, let's have a drink . . . "

"I didn't know what was going to happen," the elder Russell later told a friend. "The old man had blood in his eye. Finally we got him settled down. But the trip was busted."

Russell insisted they immediately head back to Key West, bearing the sullen Hemingway home.

They got him home early enough for Pauline's party, and he walked in, still seething, just as Pauline was preparing to leave, dressed as a Hawaiian hula dancer, wearing a grass skirt. She was surprised but seemingly pleased. She told him all about the party and urged him to come.

Oh no. Hemingway glumly announced that he was going to stay home and work. He then marched off to his writing room, which was set apart from the main house, out at the side of the swimming pool. The writing room was a sacred space in the Whitehead Street house. It was kept locked.

Hemingway couldn't find the key. His frustration once again abruptly surged entirely out of control. Within minutes he was in a screaming rage.

Shouting at the top of his voice, charging through the house, rushing up to the second-floor bedroom where—in a bedside table—he kept a .32 "special police revolver." This may or may not have been the .32 Smith and Wesson his father had used to kill himself, the gun that plays a major role in *For Whom the Bell Tolls* and his own gathering obsessions. It was loaded.

Waving the gun he came charging out of the bedroom, shouting that nobody and nothing was going to keep him from getting into his room to write. He was going to "shoot the bloody lock off."

At exactly this moment, Charles and Lorine Thompson, Pauline's closest friends in Key West, arrived to escort Pauline to the party and found themselves confronted by a screaming Hemingway, brandishing a pistol.

"He was like a crazy man," Lorine said, "waving the pistol around." Then she added exactly the same ominous words Josie Russell had used about the scene on the *Anita*: *"I didn't know what was going to happen."*

Pauline was pleading with Hemingway, trying to calm him. It seemed every word she spoke only made him more completely beside himself. At last she made the mistake of reaching, or seeming to reach, to take the gun from him. Hemingway instantly jolted back—"balked like a bull"—and lifting the gun above his head, fired a shot into the ceiling.

It echoed through the house, and it took a few moments for anyone to quite grasp what had really happened. Hemingway spun on his heel and charged out of the living room to poolside, then up to the second floor of the pool house. Still shouting, he fired more shots as he blew the lock on his writing room door to smithereens.

At this point Pauline and Hemingway's two sons, young Patrick and Gregory, came walking into the house with their nanny, Ada. Pauline and the Thompsons, all three in costume, stood frozen with shock and fear. Pauline's thought now was to get the children out of the house: after a quick conference, it was decided that both boys and Ada should immediately be taken to the Thompsons' house. Charles took them, then hurried back as dusk fell. With half of Key West about to show up in costume at the Madrid-Havana club, Pauline decided that she should go through with the party.

Almost as soon as they arrived at the club, Pauline had second thoughts. It was dangerous for Ernest to be left alone. She asked Charlie Thompson to go back to Whitehead Street and persuade Ernest to come to the club, at least for a while.

Thompson drove back to the house and let himself in. He walked out to the pool, then quietly climbed the stairs up to Ernest's second-floor writing room.

The splintered door was gaping open. Ernest sat alone in the gloom, the gun on his desk. He was silent. Thompson stood in the doorway. Ernest was slow to look up at him.

Hemingway once had described the aftermath of his rages as like the dead and empty feeling that comes after having sex with a woman who is not loved. He began to apologize. Thompson was quick to convey Pauline's hope that he might still come to the party.

Sure. Why not?

Charlie drove him. At the club, Hemingway took Pauline aside to apologize. The room was filled with Key West's "social" types, people Hemingway liked to sneer at as "pimps." There was a band. There was dancing. Nobody except the Thompsons had the faintest idea of what had happened.

Hemingway talked. He joked. He even danced, at one point, with a pretty local girl. After that dance was over, a drunken guest came and asked the young woman for the next dance. She declined. The drunk persisted, and got loud. Hemingway told him, firmly, to back off. The drunk threw a punch. By the time the mêlée was over, the drunken guest was unconscious and Hemingway had fled to Sloppy Joe's, where he drank steadily until dawn. Pauline was taken home, close to despair.

Two days later, *Ken*, featuring "Treachery in Aragon," lay on half of the choicest coffee tables in America.

chapter 17

THE SPOILS OF DEFEAT

By late 1938, Europe itself was moving toward the breaking point.[1] As the two dictators drew closer to the alliance they needed to start the Second World War, Hitler and Stalin were inclined to drop the Spanish sideshow. The catalytic event was the Munich crisis in September. After Hitler consolidated major gains in Eastern Europe without meeting even slight resistance from Stalin, he stood poised for his assault on the democracies. Accordingly, Stalin now began publicly to rid himself of his "antifascist tactic." By late 1938, Stalin was clearly, as Edmund Wilson put it, "washing his hands of Spain." By early 1939, the Soviet dictator had begun actively excoriating the democracies for trying to foment a war between the Soviets and Germany—a war for which, he said, there were "no visible grounds."

Antifascism, farewell.

It was no longer possible to pretend that anything could save the Spanish Republic. "The only thing to do with a war is to win it." Hemingway kept repeating this slogan as if to beat back his mounting recognition that the Spanish Civil War not only was lost, but was no longer being fought in order to be won. Immediately after Hitler's triumph in the Munich agreement, Stalin set out to remove the last Soviet military personnel from Spain. He was prepared to see Spain chewed up in the coming war, so long as there was no Soviet involvement. Thus, virtually on the day the Munich agreement was signed, Negrin appeared before the League of Nations to announce that he was withdrawing the International Brigades from Spain not if, but in the mere *hope* that, Franco might do the same with his Italian allies. This grand gesture was absurd on its face; needless to say, Franco did not withdraw even one Italian soldier from his now triumphant forward march. But the concealed motive was perfectly coherent. Stalin was dropping Spain into defeat.

These events ground away at Hem and Dos. On the afternoon of January 27, 1939, Dos Passos completed *The Adventures of a Young Man*, a fictionalized chronicle of his own journey through the left. It ends with the murder of the hero, now a volunteer in the International Brigades. In a final scene, the Brigades' secret policemen set up the hero to be killed, sent (like "Hans") into a no-man's land at the front, knowing he won't come back.

Four months earlier, Hemingway had been sent back to Europe by NANA, not so much to cover the Spanish defeat—NANA was weary of Hem's Spanish dispatches—but in case Munich caused the immediate outbreak of a general European war. When it didn't, Hem and Martha made one last trip to Spain. They were in Barcelona for the formal withdrawal of the Brigades, and Hemingway's response was something like anguish. In their hotel after an emotional farewell parade, watching men marching past "dirty and weary and young, many of them with no country to go back to," Martha witnessed a new scene: Hemingway leaned against a wall and wept. "They can't do it," he sobbed, "they can't do it!" In later years, wondering if she had ever really loved him, Martha would remain sure that she had loved him at that moment.

Not long afterwards Hemingway was invited—presumably with Martha—to what amounted to a farewell party in the hotel suite of *Pravda*'s Barcelona correspondent. André Malraux—a rival Hemingway detested—was present. There was a lot of drinking, and a little dancing. When the hour grew late, somebody suggested a moment of silence for the people who had died defending Madrid. Greatly moved, Hemingway bowed his head, glass in hand, and stood with it bowed for a long time. As Carlos Baker puts it, "like others in the room, he had lost many friends in the Spanish Civil War, including many like Dos Passos who were not killed."[2]

Others would be lost soon. Hemingway could not know that two weeks later, Mikhail Koltsov, his friend and guide to Soviet antifascism, would be arrested in Moscow, and held to be tried for the treasons of what he'd done in Spain.

Pauline's love was hard to break. After her husband's frantic outbursts that midsummer, they had both traveled in now abject marital misery once again to the Nordquist Ranch. Yet when they left Montana in August 1938, Pauline's spirits were somehow soaring again. She was sure that the marriage was saved; somehow all would be well. Before sailing from New York in September, Hemingway was sending Pauline loving letters and gifts. When he got to Paris glowing letters greeted him with the news that she had leased a pied-à-terre in the Murphys' elegant apartment building in New York. She yearned to greet him and press into his hands the "golden key."

A few days later, Hemingway would be in Paris assuring Martha that that *their* new life together would begin in Havana as soon as the Spanish War was over. Both of them understood, of course, that with the end of the Spanish War, the Spanish phase of their romance would also come to an end. The moment of truth was coming for Hem. With the defeat, he would have to act, choose. And so in ways that were both symbolic and very practical, the defeat of the Republic signaled the end of "loving two women." Hem would have to choose one woman or the other. By a kind of paradox, the fall of Madrid would force him into his new life.

And so the Republic's despair offered him hope. Just before leaving Spain for that last time, he wrote to his *Esquire* editor, Arnold Gingrich, "Christ it is fine to write again and not have to write pieces. I was really going nuts with that." He added, "Things here are so foul, now, that if you think about them you go nuts. So am just writing now. You have to climb up in that old tower to do your work every so often even if the flood keeps right on rising until the seat of your pants is wet. A writer has to write and beyond all other things it can make you feel good when it comes out right."[3]

In the same letter, he says he's sketched a couple of chapters of a novel—they may or may not have been some sort of first stab at *For Whom the Bell Tolls*—and mentions beginning a story, wondering aloud if maybe it is one of his best. That story is called "Under the Ridge," and, like "Old Man at the Bridge," it is a breakthrough work. Hem took it back to Key West and finished it, very excited, in Havana.

"Under the Ridge" may or may not be one of Hemingway's greatest stories, but it is certainly very fine: complex, nuanced, and bitter, a marvel of layered economy. Told by a filmmaker attached to the International Brigades, it is set among Republican and International Brigade soldiers after yet another defeat. "We had been all that morning . . . in the dust, the smoke, the noise, the receiving of wounds, the death, the fear of death, the bravery, the cowardice, the insanity and failure of an unsuccessful attack." Gossiping with some bitter Spanish infantrymen, the narrator hears how the Republic's secret police have executed a malingering boy, a scared kid named (like the dead waiter in "The Capital of the World") Paco. Yet as they talk about Paco's fate, another execution unrolls before their eyes. The Brigades' leather-jacketed secret police shoot down a French brigadier who, grasping the futility of the battle, has decided in a moment of suicidal lucidity simply to leave the battle, leave the war. Breaking ranks, he stands up and starts to walk away. Hemingway describes the tall Frenchman's walk, the erect way he holds his head, the awkward resolve in his step. He walks away, not into a separate peace but a separate death. It's not that the man is afraid: he leaves "not from cowardice, but simply from seeing too clearly; knowing suddenly that he had to leave it; knowing there was no other thing to do."

Secret police retribution is swift: the men in leather jackets, armed with Mausers, sprint after him "like hunting dogs . . . and the death he had walked away from," Hemingway writes, "had found him, when he was just over the ridge, clear of the bullets and the shelling, and walking toward the river."

By a curious coincidence, writing a couple of weeks before "Under the Ridge" was finished, Dos Passos ended *The Adventures of a Young Man* with virtually the same scene. After all, his hero is also sent to his death by the secret police, his head held high. There are some differences. Hemingway's tall Frenchman dies in a kind of suicide. Dos's American walks into a kind of murder.

Finishing "Under the Ridge" in late February, Hemingway showed the story, as he always did with the writing that mattered most to him, to Pauline. Not Martha. Pauline. Pauline read and not only approved but thought the story was maybe among the best he'd ever written. Hemingway was elated. He knew it, he *knew* it. The well was filling. What had begun with a little moisture seeping in with "Old Man at the Bridge" was now a slow, steady flow.

The Popular Front ideology that had been silencing him was dying or dead, but it had left him with his romance. Hemingway was ready. On March 30, 1939, the day that Franco entered Madrid, he sat down and in one stroke wrote the first pages of *For Whom the Bell Tolls*. The voice, the sound, the confidence, and the truth of the book—all, suddenly, were flowing for him. He had them from the first sentence: placing his hero, Robert Jordan, alone on the floor of the mountain forest, locked into an all-but-suicidal mission, he knew that what had been gathering in his unconscious for the past two years was ready to be used, to move. *"He lay flat on the brown, pine-needled floor of the forest, his chin on his folded arms, and high overhead the wind blew in the tops of the pine trees."* The images and story came easily. The concept clicked, and clicked right away. Every revision was right. And every morning when he went back to it, the damn thing just got better and better.

Five days later, all need for discretion dead, Hemingway wrote to Max Perkins, exulting that he'd finished a short story that Pauline thought was his best ever, and that he had 12,000 words of a novel about Spain. Not only that, he was sure he had hit on an idea for yet *another* book, beyond this one about Spain. It shone in his mind. It was going to be about an old man, a fight over a giant marlin, and the sea.

The flow that had been almost imperceptible with "Old Man at the Bridge" had become some sort of torrent.

A week later Martha Gellhorn arrived in Havana, ready to begin the long-promised new life. After one nauseated glance at the squalid room in the Ambos Mundos where he was working, she decided that her next move should be to look for a house. Martha's taste, like Pauline's, was at once adventurous and excellent. After some looking, Gellhorn pursued a want ad to a house that could not have been bettered: a run-down but magnificent hacienda (there was a wonderful library, a fifty-foot living room, and a guest house) built on a spacious tract of land on a little hill, with views of the sea. It was in a tiny town outside Havana called San Francisco de Paula and was called the Finca Vigía—Lookout Farm. Hemingway would live there the rest of his life, though not with Martha. By the early summer, Hem and Martha had moved in, though Hemingway kept his Ambos Mundos address, the better to keep lying to Pauline.

Shortly after, that July, Dos Passos's *The Adventures of a Young Man* was published. It was Dos's weakest and most critically vulnerable novel to date, and exactly as Hem had foreseen, the reviewer's knives were out and at the ready, just as they had been earlier that year when the very critics who had once been in ecstasies over the three superb novels that make up the trilogy had set out to stab and smear them when Dos published them together as *U.S.A.*

By far the most important hatchet job done on *Adventures of a Young Man* was by Malcolm Cowley in *The New Republic*. The review, entitled "Disillusionment," opens with a systematically misinformed account of the Robles murder and a personal attack on Dos. Dos Passos, Cowley claims, is a man who has lost his way, and what has made him go astray was a morally disorienting event in Spain. Sadly, though a radical, Dos had arrived in Spain prone to moral confusion. He had, for example, sunk so low as to express public "skepticism" about the Moscow Trials! Such a man could only stumble in the wartime world of Madrid. Cowley then gives, and endorses, the standard Stalinist version of the Robles murder. José Robles had been "arrested as a Fascist spy," adding that "people who ought to know tell me the evidence was absolutely damning." Moved by his long-standing friendship for Dos Passos, Hemingway had "interceded for [Robles] at the highest levels of the Spanish government"—but while performing this good deed,

Hemingway had himself become convinced of Robles's guilt. More in sorrow than in anger, Hemingway had tried to show Dos Passos that in war good men could go wrong. He had somberly explained that sometimes justice must be cruel. All in vain. The deluded Dos Passos had turned his petulant, naïve back on Hemingway's wisdom and, with it, turned against the very workings of justice itself. His reward was to have written a lousy book.

Appearing about ten weeks before the Nazi-Soviet Pact was announced, the review sparked a rousing mini-round in the culture wars.

First, Dos Passos decided to send a letter to the editors of *The New Republic*.

Dear Sirs:

I did not intend to publish any account of the death of my old friend José Robles Pazos (the fact that he had once translated a book of mine, and well, was merely incidental; we had been friends since my first trip to Spain in 1916) until I had collected more information and possible documentary evidence from survivors of the Spanish Civil War, but the reference to him in Mr. Malcolm Cowley's review of my last book makes it necessary for me to request you print the following as yet incomplete outline of the events that led up to his death. As I do not possess the grounds of certitude of your reviewer and his informants, I can only offer my facts tentatively and say that to the best of my belief they are accurate.

José Robles was a member of a family of monarchical and generally reactionary sympathies in politics; his brother was an army officer in the entourage of Alfonso of Bourbon when he was king; one of the reasons why he preferred to live in America (he taught Spanish Literature at Johns Hopkins University in Baltimore) was his disagreement on social and political questions with his family.

He was in Spain on vacation when Franco's revolt broke out, and stayed there, although he had ample opportunity to leave, because he felt it was his duty to work for the Republican cause. As he knew some Russian he was given a job in the Ministry of War and soon found himself in close contact with the Russian advisors and experts who arrived at the same time as the first shipment of munitions. He became a figure of some importance, ranked as a lieutenant colonel, although he refused to wear a uniform saying that he was a mere civilian. In the fall of '36 friends warned him that he had made powerful enemies and had better leave the country. He decided to stay. He was arrested soon after in Valencia and held by the extralegal police under conditions of great secrecy and executed in February or March of the following year.

It must have been about the time of his death that I arrived in Spain to do some work in connection with the film The Spanish Earth, *in which we were trying to tell the story of the civil war. His wife, whom I saw in Valencia, asked me to make inquiries to relieve her terrible uncertainty. Her idea was that as I was known to have gone to some trouble to get the cause of the Spanish Republic fairly presented in the United States, government officials would tell me frankly why Robles was being held and what the charges were against him. It might have been the same day that Liston Oak, a onetime member of the American Communist Party who held a job [in] the propaganda department in Valencia, broke the news to José Robles' son, Francisco Robles Villegas, a seventeen-year-old boy working as a translator in the censorship office, that his father was dead. At the same time officials were telling me that the charges against José Robles were not serious and that he was in no danger. Mr. Del Vayo, then foreign minister, professed ignorance and chagrin when I talked to him about the case, and promised to find out the details. The general impression that the higher-ups in Valencia tried to give was that if*

Robles was dead he had been kidnapped and shot by anarchist "uncontrollables." They gave the same impression to members of the U.S. Embassy staff who inquired about his fate.

It was not until I reached Madrid that I got definite information from the then chief of the republican counterespionage service that Robles had been executed by a "special section" (which I gathered was under the control of the Communist Party). He added that in his opinion the execution had been a mistake and that it was too bad. Spaniards I talked to closer to the Communist Party took the attitude that Robles had been shot as an example to other officials because he had been overheard indiscreetly discussing military plans in a café. The "fascist spy" theory seems to be the fabrication of romantic American Communist sympathizers. I certainly did not hear it from any Spaniard.

Anybody who knew Spaniards of any stripe before the civil war will remember that they tended to carry personal independence in talk and manners to the extreme. It is only too likely that Robles, like many others who were conscious of their own sincerity of purpose, laid himself open to a frameup. For one thing, he had several interviews with his brother, who was held prisoner in Madrid, to try to induce him to join the loyalist army. My impression is that the frameup in his case was pushed to the point of execution because Russian secret agents felt that Robles knew too much about the relations between the Spanish war ministry and the Kremlin and was not, from their very special point of view, politically reliable. As always in such cases, personal enmities and social feuds probably contributed.

On my way back through Valencia, as his wife was penniless, I tried to get documentary evidence of his death from republican officials so that she could collect his American life insurance. In spite of M. Del Vayo's repeated assurances that he would have a death certificate sent her, it never appeared. Nor was it possible to get hold of any record of the indictment or trials before the "special section."

As the insurance has not yet been paid I am sure that Mr. Cowley will understand that any evidence he may have in his possession as to how José Robles met his death that he or his informants may have will be of great use to his wife and daughter, and I hope he will be good enough to communicate it to me. His son was captured fighting in the Republican militia in the last months of the war and, as there has been no news of him for some time, we are very much afraid that he died or was killed in one of Franco's concentration camps.

Of course this is only one story among thousands in the vast butchery that was the Spanish Civil War, but it gives us a glimpse into the bloody tangle of ruined lives that underlay the hurray for our side aspects. Understanding the personal histories of a few of the men, women and children really involved would I think free our minds somewhat from the black is black and white is white obsessions of partisanship.

Sincerely yours,

John Dos Passos

Cowley's review stirred other culture-war skirmishes, mainly behind the scenes. Edmund Wilson, by now married to Mary McCarthy (and so allied with *Partisan Review*), fired a fine volley at Cowley in a private letter, assailing him for his lack of knowledge of Robles's life and politics, his ignorance of Dos Passos's real actions in Spain, his vacuous claims to inside knowledge, and his base credulity over "whatever the Stalinists are pouring into your ear."

At *Partisan Review*, Dwight Macdonald sniffed the sweet smell of a high-profile literary feud. He instantly wrote Dos asking for details. Dos Passos sent him an advance copy of his letter to *The*

New Republic, adding that if "some American wellwishers hadn't started raising a yammer about the matter in Madrid, I should have been able to get at the facts at the time." But in every statement, Dos Passos carefully avoided using Hem's name. Dos was not going to feed that fire. The "intended effect of the Robles killing," he told Macdonald, had been to "make people very chary of talking about the 'Mexicans,' as the Russians were familiarly known." He amplified a little on the *New Republic* letter: he'd "rather underplayed the stupid way in which Del Vayo lied to me about the manner of Robles's death," adding that Ivens's disinformation about Dos's role in *Spain in Flames* and *The Spanish Earth* had made it "appear as if all I'd done in connection with the two movies was sabotage them." That, he said, was "a masterpiece of the peculiar mass formation tactics of our friends the comrats." In any case, his name was now Spanish poison. In a recent raid on the rooms of Arturo Barea in Madrid, the NKVD had seized some books he had autographed for Barea as proof of the Spaniard's "crimes."[4] Macdonald wanted more—a big-time literary feud, a battle of the books: Hem versus Dos; the Stalinist *New Republic* versus the Trotskyist *Partisan Review*. When Macdonald wrote asking for more, Dos put the kibosh on that. "All I wanted to straighten out was Robles' case. I don't think anything could be gained by arguing with Malcolm Cowley about my mental processes or what influenced them. He has a right to make what deductions he cares to. . . ."

The scandal was brief. A month later, the Nazi-Soviet Pact was signed, and the culture warriors had bigger things to shout about. In any case, the lies and misrepresentations in Cowley's attack were light from an extinguished star.

Meanwhile, Hemingway was in Havana, and writing like a man set free. He went striding into that marred but magnificent performance, *For Whom the Bell Tolls*, radiant, strong, and liberated by defeat. His confidence had been restored. Depression, hesitation, confusion; the snide agenda of *To Have and Have Not*; the puerile fraudulence of *The Fifth Column*—all were behind him. The result is a wonderful book, maybe his greatest novel. It may not be as impeccably written, or as moving, as *A Farewell to Arms*, but it is peerless in its fusion of realism and romance, in the way it sweeps its truly shattering accounts of the war—there are many scenes so terrible that you wonder if you can get through them—into the exalted romantic fable of Robert Jordan with a peasant guerrilla band concealed behind enemy lines high in a mountain cave.

There is also of course a love story: the weakest part of the book. Hemingway now felt free to balance Robert Jordan between two idealized women: the nubile, adoring Maria, who joins him in his sleeping bag and with whom "the earth moves," as against the strong, shrewd, wise, older earth mother in the cave, Pilar. Maria is endowed with Martha Gellhorn's physical traits (and very few of her psychological ones), while Pilar bears Hemingway's love name for Pauline. Joined by fate, angel and earth mother can't help but love and respect one another. And of course they adore—just *adore*—our hero.

Yet by isolating his otherwise highly cosmopolitan hero among the *guerrilleros* on that mountaintop, Hemingway was able to mobilize his entire Spanish experience and weave the war story through the love story with awesome skill. The synthetic force of *For Whom the Bell Tolls*, the masterful way it subdues unto itself everything that Hem had learned in Spain, is fully worthy of his genius. True, in a romance that is both erotic and heroic, the heroic part is much stronger than the erotic. Not many twenty-first-century readers will be able to keep from scowling or laughing over the maudlin and insufferable male chauvinism poured over Maria. Yet Hemingway does make his love and war work together: even the fulsome depiction of Maria has its occasional Joycean virtues. Meanwhile the story of Robert Jordan's doomed mission and his saturnine isolated struggle with it remain compelling in a book crawling with horrors of war at least as convincing as Goya's. As a romance, the book's truth is not strictly literal, so that even when its accuracy falters (and it quite often does), Hemingway keeps his grip on authenticity. In contrast to *The Fifth Column*, which is really nothing but a pack of lies, *For Whom the Bell Tolls* does manage to establish a truth of its own. Pilar and Maria and those peasants in their cave were what Hemingway needed to show what was, for all its delusion, an intimate, observed, and passionate view of the Spanish tragedy. Above all the book works because of its hero. In Robert Jordan, he found exactly the sacrificial hero that tragedy required: *his* man, *his* paladin of defeat, *his* persuasive heroic model, *his* way of redeeming his own suicidal melancholia, the imagined character who could bear *his* being, and *his* burning despair.

Speaking of lies, Hem was not a little liberated from them, too. He had entered a Faustian bargain with the Popular Front. Yet this time, and for once, Faust got off lucky. When Stalin pulled the plug on the Popular Front, it was Mephistopheles who was first to back out of the deal. With the fall of Madrid—and the approach of the Pact—Hemingway was perfectly prepared to show treachery in Madrid mingling and merging with the romantic heroism of Jordan and the men and women on his mountain. If the novel is not fully detoxified from Hemingway's trafficking in Popular Front propaganda—and it is far from that—it is nonetheless forthrightly defiant about his sometime Stalinist friends, and the book left most of them gagging with outrage.

Writing steadily at the Finca Vigía, by midsummer Hemingway decided to rejoin his sons for one more August at the

Nordquist Ranch. There, using the Wyoming-Montana Sierras as his model for the mountains, he let his imagination climb. The thematic stream that now came pouring into the book was that of suicide. At last, more fully and more powerfully than anywhere else in his work, Hemingway was able to enter his angry imagination of his father's death. The icon at the center of this mediation is the .38 U.S. Army Colt—his grandfather's service revolver—that Clarence Hemingway had used, about which Robert Jordan obsesses as he confronts what looks like his own approaching end. In a strong, ghostly scene, he has Jordan—a professor of Spanish in Montana—row out into the middle of a "bottomless lake" near the ranch, there ceremonially to deep-six the fatal gun. Suicide: it was the demon Hemingway could not banish or drink away, his oldest adversary, the beast in his jungle, the hyena nuzzling into his tent, his stalker, his fear. Sometimes it got so close that he could see nothing else. Sometimes for a while he almost forgot it. Sometimes it crept up on him from behind. Sometimes it faced him, near enough he could smell its breath. But now at last, high on his mountain, Hemingway had invented a man through whose eyes and destiny he could look at the dark demon straight on, and contemplate the savage god almost unafraid.

Meanwhile, hope, which returns to us all, kept returning to Pauline. Hemingway was with the boys in Wyoming on August 23, 1939, when Pauline arrived at the ranch for yet another try. She knew little or nothing about Hemingway's new life with Martha in Havana: she was being told that he was working in monkish solitude at the Ambos Mundos. She flew to the ranch from New York, leaving the New Weston apartment, where Hemingway had never picked up his "golden key."

On the day she arrived, August 23, the Nazi-Soviet pact was announced.

Hemingway was now prepared to be completely ruthless with Pauline. Not that it took all that much to deliver what her son Patrick later called the "knockout punch," the last cruelty that made Pauline reach her breaking point.

His blunt instrument was that smasher of hearts, silence. On the trip, Pauline had picked up a nasty cold and flu. She had to spend the first week at the ranch in bed. Hemingway dutifully nursed her, and the dutiful nursing was cruel. He did not even feign real concern. He wouldn't even speak to her. Three times a day, without a word, he would bring her a tray. Forty minutes later, he would come back into her room and, still absolutely silent, he would take the tray away. Between times, he left her alone.

By September 1, 1939—the very day that England declared war on Germany and the Second World War began—Pauline at last felt well enough to get up and unpack. Still weak, she opened a suitcase, and found that one of her favorite dresses had been damaged on the flight. For some reason, the buttons had melted into the fabric. She'd loved that dress, and it was ruined. Just completely ruined. Hopeless. Hopeless. It didn't matter what she did. Nothing anybody could do would ever fix it.

Staring at the ruined garment, Pauline began to weep. Then, once she had begun weeping, she dropped the dress and found she couldn't stop weeping. Little Patrick—he was then eleven—hovered by his mom and tried to comfort her. She'd been sick, and of course he wanted her to feel better. Pauline struggled to stop. It was a terrible thing to cry this way in front of the boy. She knew it; she *had* to stop. She tried; she tried hard; but she couldn't. The sobs kept surging up through her body, and they just would not quit. Nothing could hold them back. They came, torn from inside her as though they were being ripped from the earth itself, and they went on, and on, and on.

Epilogue

The doomed marriage of Martha Gellhorn and Ernest Hemingway managed to survive through most of the Second World War, five increasingly angry and confrontational years. From its Spanish romance, their union moved through doubt, avoidance, mounting anger, serious violence, implacable rage, and finally lifelong mutual loathing. The marriage's one real success was Martha's bond to Hemingway's three sons, Jack, Patrick, and Gregory—*les jeunes messieurs*, as she used to call them—each of whom found her an irresistible stepmother and remained attached to her for life.

Pauline recovered her equilibrium, if not her happiness. She died in 1951, and to the end insisted that it had been the Spanish Civil War that destroyed her marriage.

John Dos Passos continued to write novels, historical chronicles, and journalism. He and Hemingway had a few public run-ins, and a few tentative moments of reconciliation. Though it's doubtful that Dos Passos ever understood Hemingway's exact role in his humiliation in 1937, Dos never publicly discussed even what little he knew until well after Hemingway's death.

As an artist, drifting to the right, Dos Passos never quite got free of his debilitating entanglement with that enemy of art, mere political opinion—and he never quite recovered what he had lost in Spain. His superb talent never left him. There is wonderful writing throughout his later books: his memoir *The Best Times* is especially fine. Yet by the time he died in 1970, John Dos Passos was in some sense tending an extinguished fire. He had outlived his genius, rather as his beloved Emily Dickinson, to whose work he had once introduced José Robles, outlived hers.

As a young man, one of Hemingway's many impressive gifts had been an ability to seek out and enter compelling friendships with some of the most distinguished people of his era. After the end of his friendship with Dos, though he later came to regret "my self-righteous period in Spain" and the loss of his old friends, Hemingway was never again close with a real peer: he increasingly surrounded himself with second raters and hangers-on. Meanwhile, his mental instability, marked by its life-threatening suicidal obsessions, became steadily, though intermittently, more dire. By the end of their marriage, Martha Gellhorn was rightly convinced that Hemingway was showing psychotic symptoms. Throughout the fifties, despite periods of lucidity, Hemingway's condition grew worse, and by the end of that decade, by which time he was probably the most famous writer alive, his fourth wife, Mary Welsh, was reduced to service as a kind of psychiatric nurse.

In a bizarre conversation during the Spanish War, Hemingway had told Joris Ivens that his father's method of killing himself—a pistol shot to the temple—was a poor technique. A far better way to do it, Hem said, would be a shotgun blast, from both barrels, through the brain.

By 1960 Hemingway's paranoia and psychotic depression exceeded Mary Hemingway's capacity to cope. He was by then dangerously and thoroughly suicidal. Under conditions of great secrecy, he was admitted to the Mayo Clinic for treatment. Against medical advice, in June 1961, he left the hospital and traveled with Mary to his house in Ketchum, Idaho. Soon after arriving, cursed with the cleverness of the mad, he found the means to do the job at last, and do it his way, with both barrels.

Among Hem's papers at the end were found a very few get-well notes that had managed to pierce the wall of secrecy of those last horrible weeks. One was especially warm, playful, and concerned. It was a voice from the good times.

It was from Dos.

Notes

Chapter 1

1. Throughout *The Breaking Point*, I rely on the several major biographies of John Dos Passos and Ernest Hemingway, and will not cite them individually when discussing generally established facts. In the case of Dos Passos, the relevant works are Townsend Ludington's *John Dos Passos: A Twentieth-Century Odyssey* (New York: Carroll & Graf, 1998 [1980]) and Virginia Spencer Carr, *Dos Passos: A Life* (Garden City, NY: Doubleday and Company, 1984). Ludington is, to date, the definitive biography; Spencer Carr, while here and there inaccurate, is the more richly detailed. For Hemingway, Carlos Baker's *Ernest Hemingway: A Life Story* (New York: Charles Scribner's Sons, 1969) remains even now, as Martha Gellhorn called it, "The King James Version" of Hemingway's life. Though Baker has been superseded in many ways, notably in its treatment of Hemingway's relationship with Martha Gellhorn, the book is the foundation on which all other biographies rest. Jeffrey Meyers's, *Hemingway: A Biography* (New York: Da Capo Press, 1999 [1985]) is up-to-date and contains invaluable new material. I also found useful information in Michael Reynolds's *Hemingway: The 1930s* (New York, London: W. W. Norton, 1997). Kenneth Lynn's controversial *Hemingway* (New York: Simon and Schuster, 1987), despite its relentlessly argumentative tone, does contain useful information, though for some reason I found myself using it less than other texts. John Dos Passos describes his early friendship with José Robles Pazos and the ambience of his graduate school days in Madrid in numerous texts, notably *The Best Times: An Informal Memoir* (New York: New American Library, 1966) and *The Theme Is Freedom* (New York: Dodd, Mead and Co., 1956). Though it does not specifically name Robles, the crucial text for Dos Passos's impressions from this phase

of his life is his first travel book, *Rosinante to the Road Again* (1922), collected in *John Dos Passos, Travel Books and Other Writings, 1916–1941*, edited and annotated by Townsend Ludington (New York: Library of America, 2003). For Dos's relation to his father, I rely mainly on *The Best Times*. The complex tale of Dos Passos's relation to his father's estate can be followed in Ludington. The earliest meetings of Hemingway and Dos Passos were described by Dos Passos in his correspondence with Carlos Baker, now in the Baker archives in the Special Collections of the Firestone Library at Princeton. I have used (and recommend) the detailed discussion of both Hemingway and Dos Passos's relations with Gerald and Sara Murphy in Amanda Vaill, *Everybody Was So Young* (New York: Broadway Books, 1998). The peremptory execution of José Robles Pazos is cited in virtually every history of the Spanish Civil War, usually in conjunction with other killings and executions associated with the work of the NKVD, or Soviet secret police. Though the murder was almost certainly the work of this agency in one of its several guises, precise responsibility has never been fixed. The complete absence of any government record whatsoever concerning the death of José Robles is the most striking, and in a way the most revealing, element in the Spanish Republic's relation to his demise.

2. Dos Passos, *Rosinante to the Road Again*, in *John Dos Passos: Travel Books and Other Writings*, 42.

3. Ibid., 37.

4. Ibid., 31.

5. Ibid., 6.

6. Dos Passos describes this evening in *Travel Books and Other Writings*, 3–9. See also Spencer Carr, *John Dos Passos*, 107.

7. Dos Passos, *The Best Times*, 30–40.

8. Letter from John Dos Passos to Rumsey Martin, June 20, 1917. John Dos Passos Archive, University of Virginia.

9. Letter from John Dos Passos to Carlos Baker, January 13, 1965. Ernest Hemingway Archives, Firestone Library, Princeton University.

10. The meal at the Lipp is described in Dos Passos, *The Best Times*, 141. Hemingway's political wisecracks appear in Baker, *Hemingway*, 88.

11. David Sanders, "Interview with John Dos Passos," *Writers at Work: The Paris Review Interviews*, edited by George Plimpton, Fourth Series (New York: Viking, 1976).

12. Dos Passos, *The Best Times*, 142.

13. See Hemingway's blurb for the European translations of *Manhattan Transfer*: "He alone of American writers has been able to show Europeans the America they really find when they come here." Cited in Spencer Carr, *John Dos Passos*, 215.

14. Ernest Hemingway, *A Moveable Feast* (New York: Charles Scribner's Sons, [1964] 2003), 207.

15. Dos Passos, *The Best Times*, 143.

16. Hemingway, *A Moveable Feast*, 209–210.

17. I rely here on Hemingway's published letters to Pauline Pfeiffer, written prior to their marriage.

18. Dos Passos, *The Best Times*, 198–199.

19. Letter of JDP to EH, cited in Spencer Carr, *John Dos Passos*, 231.

20. For Fitzgerald's response, and for hostile reactions, see Ludington, *John Dos Passos*, 241–242. Hemingway and Lawrence are cited in Spencer Carr, *John Dos Passos*, 215.

21. Ernest Hemingway, *Selected Letters 1917–1961*, edited by Carlos Baker (New York: Charles Scribner's Sons, 1981).

22. Ibid., 354.

23. Baker, *Hemingway*, 199.

24. See *Paris Review* interview, 77; also Baker, *Hemingway*, 199.

25. Dos Passos, *The Best Times*, 219–220.

Chapter 2

1. I have summarized José Robles's relation to the emergence of the Spanish Republic from various sources, including my interview with his daughter-in-law, Sra. Dolores B. de Robles, and various references in Dos Passos's prose. My source for Robles's time spent on Cape Cod is Edmund Wilson's letter to Malcolm Cowley of October 20, 1939. See Edmund Wilson, *Letters on Literature and Politics, 1912–1972*, edited by Elena Wilson (New York: Farrar, Straus and Giroux, 1977). Some biographers, including Carlos Baker and Michael Reynolds, hesitate to assert that the affair between Jane Mason and Hemingway was overtly sexual. Jeffrey Meyers does not doubt that it was, and cites Gregory Hemingway's assertion, presumably based on what he'd been told by his mother: "during the late 1930s, he used to cuckold mother unmercifully in Havana." Kert, whose account is the most detailed in print, likewise makes it clear that the affair was sexual, but does so in a rather circumspect manner. All biographies agree that while Hemingway was never a faithful husband, he was probably not, despite his sexual bravado, highly promiscuous. It is clear to all that Jane Mason was the model for Helene Bradley in *To Have and Have Not*. Dos Passos describes Hemingway's struggle with the tuna in *The Best Times*, 212–214. The anecdote about the bust of Hemingway in the foyer is also from that book, 220. My views of the Popular Front are derived from many historians, as well as an immersion in the contemporary literature needed to write my

own *Double Lives: Stalin, Willi Münzenberg, and the Seduction of the Intellectuals* (New York: Enigma Books, 2003). A good summary of Stalin's relation to fascism can be found in Robert C. Tucker, *Stalin in Power: The Revolution from Above, 1928–1941* (New York, London: W. W. Norton, 1990 [1992]), Chapter 14, and elsewhere. I can also commend François Furet, *The Passing of an Illusion: The Idea of Communism in the Twentieth Century*, translated from the French by Deborah Furet (Chicago: University of Chicago Press, 1999), especially chapters 6, 7, and 8.The classic histories of the Spanish Civil War, notably Hugh Thomas, *The Spanish Civil War*, revised edition (New York: Modern Library, 2001), should be supplemented by Burnett Bolloten, *The Spanish Civil War: Revolution and Counterrevoltuion* (Chapel Hill and London: University of North Carolina Press, 1991); Ronald Radosh and Mary R. Habeck, *Spain Betrayed: The Soviet Union and the Spanish Civil War* (New Haven and London: Yale University Press, 2001); and Stanley G. Payne, *The Spanish Civil War, the Soviet Union, and Communism* (New Haven and London: Yale University Press, 2004).

2. Hemingway to Dos Passos, April 12, 1936, Hemingway, *Selected Letters*, 445.

3. Vaill, *Everybody Was So Young*, 258.

4. Ibid., 256.

5. Ludington, *John Dos Passos*, 349.

6. Katy Dos Passos to Gerald Murphy, as cited in ibid., 349.

7. Vaill, *Everybody Was So Young*, 273–274.

8. Ibid., 274.

9. Hemingway, "The Snows of Kilimanjaro," *The Complete Short Stories of Ernest Hemingway* (The Finca Vigía Edition), edited by John, Patrick, and Gregory Hemingway (New York: Charles Scribner's Sons, 1987), 54.

10. Michael Reynolds, *Hemingway: The Thirties* (New York: W. W. Norton, 1997), 230.

11. Letters to Marjorie Kinnan Rawlings, August 16, 1936, and Archibald MacLeish, September 26, 1936. Ernest Hemingway, *Selected Letters 1917–1961*, edited by Carlos Baker (New York: Charles Scribner's Sons, 1981), 449–450; 453.

12. Letter from Hemingway to Arnold Gingrich, August 25, 1936. Hemingway Archives, Firestone Library, Princeton, New Jersey.

13. Ernest Hemingway, letter to Maxwell Perkins, September 26, 1936, *Selected Letters*, 454.

Chapter 3

1. My discussion of Joris Ivens relies chiefly on Hans Schoots's indispensable biography, *Living Dangerously: A Biography of Joris Ivens*, translated from the

Dutch by David Colmer (Amsterdam: Amsterdam University Press, 2000). Ivens's role in the biographies of both Hemingway and Dos Passos must be entirely re-assessed in the light of Mr. Schoots's remarkable research, which for the first time offers precise and copiously documented information about Ivens's work as a Comintern agent. Thanks to it, we have a completely new understanding of Ivens's role in the making of *Spain in Flames* and *The Spanish Earth*; of his pre-liminary courtship of Dos Passos in the spring of 1936; of his place in founding and managing Contemporary Historians; of his role in Hemingway's subsequent fellow-traveling and the disinformation used to discredit Dos Passos after the Robles murder. (I should perhaps add that in 1985, I interviewed Joris Ivens in Paris, and during this interview he reasserted his claim that Robles—referring to Robles not by name but as "Dos Passos's friend"—had been a fascist, adding the novel fiction, seen nowhere else, that Robles had been caught using a concealed light to flash signals to the fascist lines.) Dos Passos's own naïveté about the ac-tivities of the Comintern, and Ivens's role in particular, is asserted in *The Theme Is Freedom* and in his fictionalized autobiographical account, *Century's Ebb: The Thirteenth Chronicle* (Boston: Gambit, 1975). Dos Passos's involvement with the Soviet artistic vanguard has been treated in both major biographies, and he him-self discusses it in *The Best Times*. My sense is that the entire subject would profit from a full post-Soviet critical analysis. Surely some formative part of the con-nection lies in Dos Passos's 1926 collaboration with John Howard Lawson at the New Playwrights Theater in New York. In any case, during his 1928 visit to the USSR, Dos Passos met and enthusiastically admired Vsevolod Meyerhold, Sergei Eisenstein, and Vsevolod Pudovkin, among many others. The corresponding ad-miration felt *for* Dos Passos by figures in the Soviet vanguard is reflected in many sources: Victor Serge wrote about the influence often, and such Serge works as *The Case of Comrade Tulayev* manifest it quite unmistakably. Dos Passos's influ-ence on Pil'nyak is widely acknowledged. Dziga Vertov wrote of the impression made on him by Dos Passos on numerous occasions: see *Kino-Eye: Writings of Dziga Vertov*, edited by Annette Michelson, translated from the Russian by Kevin O'Brien (Berkeley: University of California Press, 1984), 129. An account of the events surrounding the First All-Union Congress of Soviet Writers of August 1934, at which Radek's speech was delivered, and the various notable Euro-peans—André Malraux, Klaus Mann—who were present, can be found in Gus-tav Regler, *The Owl of Minerva: The Autobiography of Gustav Regler*, translated from the German by Norman Denny (New York: Farrar, Straus, and Cudahy, 1960), 200–216. Regler was a German Münzenberg-man who both personally and within the political apparatus was very close to Ivens. Regler's account is notable for recounting Radek's behavior, especially a drunken rhetorical attack on André Malraux, very much along the lines of his speech, which Radek unleashed at a

288 Notes

banquet held at the home of Maxim Gorky while the Congress proceeded. It is a mark of the importance the regime granted both to the foreign writers involved and to Münzenberg's men, that Regler and his girlfriend were allowed to be present at this select party, which was attended not only by Radek and Malraux, but also by Nikolai Bukharin, Lazar Kagonovich, and Vsaslav Molotov: a senior Soviet Who's Who, in fact. Regler's interpreter at the event was Koltsov himself, with whom both Regler and Ivens were intimately associated. Radek's speech to the Congress was entitled "*Die moderne Weltliteratur und die Aufgaben der proletarischen Kunst*" and was reprinted in H. J. Schmitt and G. Schramm, eds., *Sozialistische Realismuskonzeptionene. Dukumente zum 1. Allunionskongress de Sowletschriftsteller* (Frankfurt/Main, 1974), 140–213. It should be mentioned that another speech delivered at the Congress was by Andrei Zhdanov, the cultural bureaucrat later most associated with the brutalities of the Socialist Realism ideology. Gorev's service in Spain is mentioned in all competent histories of the war. The most detailed and revealing source for his activities and motives is Radosh and Habeck, *Spain Betrayed*. I have also made use, as always, of Bolloten, and Robert Conquest, *The Great Terror: A Reassessment* (New York: Oxford University Press, 1990), on which I rely generally for my entire discussion of the Terror of the thirties. I have also used Stephane Courtois et al., *The Black Book of Communism: Crimes, Terror, and Repression,* translated from the French by Jonathan Murphy and Mark Kramer (Cambridge, MA, and London: Harvard University Press, 1999), notably Part II. The most compelling description known to me of Madrid under Franco's November assault is found in Arturo Barea, *The Forging of a Rebel,* translated from the Spanish by Ilsa Barea (New York: Walker and Company, 2001 [translation originally published, New York: Reynal and Hitchcock, 1946]). In fact, I join many in viewing Barea's book as one of the finest eyewitness accounts extant of the Spanish Civil War. Hemingway was not wrong: Koltsov was surely among the most intelligent and interesting Soviets of his era. Now that his story can be researched and told, a full-scale biography is overdue. His *Spanish Diary* is an important, if manifestly propagandistic, source. My entire discussion of Koltsov and his fate has been shaped by the revelations in Arkadi Vaksberg, *Hotel Lux, Les partis frères au service de l'Internationale communiste,* translated from the Russian by Olivier Simon (Paris: Fayard, 1993). I have read a number of contemporary press reports about *Spain in Flames*. All make prominent reference to Dos Passos's role in the film. None mention Hemingway, even in passing.

2. Dos Passos, *Century's Ebb,* 41.

3. Archibald MacLeish, *Reflections,* edited by Bernard A. Drabeck and Helen E. Ellis (Amherst: University of Massachusetts Press, 1986), 112, 119.

4. Schoots, *Living Dangerously,* 107–109.

5. Ibid., 109.

6. Ibid., 110.

7. Schoots cites Radek's speech, ibid., 96.

8. Ibid.

9. Walter Krivitsky, *In Stalin's Secret Service* (New York: Enigma Books, 2000 [originally published New York, 1939]), 163.

10. Edmund Wilson, letter to John Dos Passos, February 12, 1937, *Letters on Literature and Politics.*

11. Barea, *Forging of a Rebel,* 581–582.

12. Radosh and Habeck, *Spain Betrayed,* 103.

13. Louis Fischer, *Men and Politics* (New York: Duell Sloan, and Pearce, 1941), 395.

14. P. Adams Sitney, in correspondence with the author, May 12, 2004.

15. Schoots, *Living Dangerously,* 116–117.

Chapter 4

1. My account of the meeting between Hemingway and Martha Gellhorn, as well as their entire relationship, is primarily indebted to Bernice Kert, *The Hemingway Women* (New York: W. W. Norton, 1983). Parallel to Kert, and as importantly, I have used Caroline Moorehead's biography, *Gellhorn: A Twentieth-Century Life* (New York: Henry Holt, 2003). The source for Hemingway's fantasy about the Gellhorn family that day is Gellhorn's own interview with Kert. Archibald MacLeish's view of Martha Gellhorn at this juncture is evident in his entire correspondence with Carlos Baker, now in the Princeton Archive, notably a letter to Baker of August 9, 1962. The many inconsistencies in Martha Gellhorn's account of the Christmas visit to Key West can be identified by balancing her account in Kert with the facts established in the archives, in Moorehead, and in the memories of Key West friends published in numerous biographies. Memories of many Key West witnesses, including the Thompsons and Miriam Williams, are found in James McClendon, *Papa: Hemingway in Key West* (Miami: E. A. Seeman Publishing Co., 1972), 164–165. A number of details—such as Gellhorn's response to reading the original manuscript of *To Have and Have Not*—are culled from Gellhorn's copious correspondence with Eleanor Roosevelt, now in the Roosevelt Library in Hyde Park, New York, and cited in many biographies. In her correspondence with Carlos Baker over the manuscript of his Hemingway biography, Gellhorn vehemently denied that infatuation existed in January, despite abundant evidence indicating it. There was, she wrote Baker, "no love affair, *not* lovers, never spoke of love; not even a courting. Not even a kiss! Interest of great author

for a young one, shared interest in Spain. I was much more anti-fascist, polit-ically aware, etc. Get this right." Caroline Moorehead, who as the authorized biographer has had access to the restricted files and who generally tries to stay as close as possible to Gellhorn's version of events, supplies information that suggests Gellhorn's claims to Baker about the early stages of the affair were dubious, and she is the first writer to assert unequivocally that Gellhorn was indeed with Hemingway in New York during February, contrary to Gellhorn's own lifelong claim. See Moorehead, *Gellhorn,* 106–107. Gellhorn's comments about Baker's manuscript are on deposit in the Special Collections of the Princeton University Library. I am grateful to Mr. Sandy Gellhorn for meeting with me and providing me with a photocopy of one of Hemingway's letters to Martha, a gift to him from his mother, dating from circa late January/ early February 1937, through which it can be established that Hemingway and Gellhorn were toying with a "permanent" relationship at this early date. It was during this interview that Mr. Gellhorn made the remark, cited here, about his mother's truly remarkable skills as a letter-writer. Dos Passos's descriptions of what he witnessed in New York in February 1937, as Hemingway was joining Contemporary Historians, can be found in his autobiographical novel, *Century's Ebb,* which was posthumously published in 1975. Though fiction-alized, this novel contains Dos Passos's most complete account of the Robles affair. I have cited it where the fictionalized account is consistent with known facts, with his own nonfiction accounts in *The Theme Is Freedom, Journeys Between Wars,* and his letter to *The New Republic* of July 1939. There are points where *Century's Ebb* departs from the known facts, but most of the account is highly persuasive and entirely consistent with material known from other sources. The creation of Farrell's American Committee for the Defense of Leon Trotsky was an important event in the culture wars of 1937: the misuse of Dos Passos's name on its roster was important to our story here in ways that are hard to measure. We may be sure, however, that even the possibility of Dos Passos being a Trotskyite would have been a matter of intense concern to the Comintern agents dealing with him in both America and Spain. Because of Mary McCarthy's essay—which I recommend—the incident plays a notable role in her biographies, as it does in Farrell's biography. Dos Passos describes the dinner with Tresca in both *Century's Ebb* and *The Theme Is Freedom.*

2. See Kert, *The Hemingway Women,* 282.

3. Archibald MacLeish, letter to Carlos Baker, August 9, 1962, Princeton University Library, special collections.

4. Martha Gellhorn, letter to Pauline Pfeiffer Hemingway, January 14, 1937.

5. Pauline's wisecrack is quoted in Matthew Josephson, *Infidel in the Tem-ple: A Memoir of the Nineteen-Thirties* (New York: Knopf, 1967), 428.

6. Lorine Thompson is quoted in McClendon and in Denis Brian, *True Gen: An Intimate Portrait of Ernest Hemingway by Those Who Knew Him* (New York: Grove/Atlantic, 1987), 101–102.

7. Miriam Williams is quoted in McClendon, *Papa*, 164–165.

8. The account of the weekend with Frederick Vanderbilt Field comes from Jeffrey Meyers, interview with Joseph Losey, August 23, 1983. It is cited in Meyers, *Hemingway*, 302.

9. Hemingway uses this word in a letter responding to an analysis of the novel sent to Hemingway by Martha in January 1937. Gellhorn herself uses the same word—"very smart"—to describe her reading of the novel in a letter to Eleanor Roosevelt dated January 5, 1937. The January 5 date indicates how rapidly Gellhorn's intimacy with Hemingway had progressed since Christmas.

10. Baker, *Ernest Hemingway*, 298–299. Baker relies on a memoir by Gingrich, "Scott, Ernest, and Whoever," *Esquire*, Vol. 66 (December 1966), 189; 322–324.

11. Baker, *Hemingway*, 299.

12. Moorehead, *Gellhorn*, 106.

13. Ernest Hemingway to Martha Gellhorn, undated letter from January 1937, written on the stationery of the Barclay Hotel.

14. Martha Gellhorn to Ernest Hemingway, letter dated February 15, 1937, from a transcription made by Bernice Kert on deposit in the Firestone Library Special Collections, Princeton University.

15. Archibald MacLeish to Ernest Hemingway, letter dated February 8, 1937, in *Letters of Archibald MacLeish: 1907–1982*, edited by R. H. Winnick (Boston: Houghton Mifflin, 1983).

16. Dos Passos, *Century's Ebb*, 37.

17. Kert, *The Hemingway Women*, 294.

18. Vaill, *Everybody Was So Young*, 280.

19. Dos Passos, *Century's Ebb*, 37.

20. Martha Gellhorn, undated letter to David Gurewitsch, cited in Moorehead, *Gellhorn*, 107.

Chapter 5

1. Since there is no written record, the precise dating of Robles's arrest and execution must be a matter of informed guesswork. An important source is Dos Passos's letter to *The New Republic* of July 1939, summarizing the then-known facts of the case. Yet that letter is not strictly consistent about dates, which Dos Passos admits are uncertain. Dos Passos's best source for the time of Robles's arrest would have been Márgara. Dos Passos himself met Márgara in Valencia in the first days of April 1937, proceeding to Madrid on April 4. At that point, Már-

gara still believed (and was being told) that her husband was alive. Yet at least five days earlier, Alvarez del Vayo informed Josephine Herbst that Robles had been shot. While Dos Passos says that he thinks Robles was executed "in February or March," the February date is likely too early: in *Century's Ebb,* Dos Passos quotes the Márgara character as saying that her husband had been arrested five days before Dos's arrival. That is fiction of course, and the time frame is too short. Since the real Márgara made one and perhaps two visits to Robles in prison before secrecy covered the entire matter, it is more likely Robles was arrested at least a week or ten days before he was killed, and since we know from Herbst that he was dead at least by March 28, and probably earlier, the more probable date of his arrest would fall somewhere between the first and third week of March, and of his execution somewhere between the second and fourth weeks of March. Hemingway arrived in Valencia on March 17. I have taken my account of Dos Passos on the *Berengaria* from the biographies and *Century's Ebb.* There are many descriptions of Madrid under siege: Barea is particularly impressive. The ambience of the Hotel Florida and the Gran Via has been described in many memoirs: I am grateful to Mrs. Margaret Regler for having given to me photocopies of Gustav Regler's battlefield notes from the Spanish War, which include not-for-publication descriptions of the more squalid side of life at the Florida. Virginia Cowles's admirable book of reportage on Europe before the war, *Looking for Trouble,* is an excellent source. For Carlos Baker's account of Martha Gellhorn's arrival in Madrid, see Baker, *Ernest Hemingway,* 304, and the related note, 620. For Gellhorn's accusations against Baker and Franklin, see Moorehead, *Gellhorn,* 382. For Franklin's counterclaims, see Kert, *The Hemingway Women,* 295. Note that Kert accepts Gellhorn's dismissal of Franklin's claims on grounds that we now know to be false: Martha's false claim that Hemingway had had no idea when or how she would get to France. But the Moorehead biography has now shown that Gellhorn was (again, despite her lifelong claim to the contrary) in New York with Hemingway before he sailed. There is every reason to suppose they shared their travel plans in detail. One of the best sources in English for Koltsov's Soviet career is Gustav Regler's *The Owl of Minerva* (New York: Farrar, Straus, and Cudahy, 1960). Regler is also a fine source for the ambience of the war in the spring of 1937. There are three sources for Josephine Herbst's relation to these events. The first is her own account in her memoir, *The Starched Blue Sky of Spain* (New York: HarperCollins, 1991). The second is Elinor Langer, *Josephine Herbst: The Story She Could Never Tell* (Boston: Atlantic Monthly Press, 1984). The third is the Herbst papers in the special collections of the Beinecke Library at Yale, most notably her "Spanish Journal" and the correspondence with Ilse Katz and the Agence Espagne cited here. The letter of introduction provided by the Agence

Espagne to Herbst is addressed to Julio Alvarez del Vayo and was to be hand-
delivered to him. There can therefore be no doubt that Alvarez del Vayo was the
"Important Official" whose identity Herbst was ordered to keep secret, and that
conclusion is sustained by all other known facts.
2. Cited in Meyers, *Hemingway*, 311.
3. Cited in Regler, *The Owl of Minerva*, 264–265.
4. Moorehead, *Gellhorn*, 113.
5. Ibid., 126–127.
6. Ernest Hemingway, *For Whom the Bell Tolls* (New York: Scribner's,
1940), Chapter 18, 231.
7. Ibid., 265.
8. The story of Koltsov's remarkable rise and fall is very complex. Though
Hemingway's portrayal is by far the most famous, numerous other portraits of
Koltsov have been available for many years: Claud Cockburn describes him in *A
Discord of Trumpet* (New York: Simon and Schuster, 1956), and a more interesting account can be found in Gustav Regler's *The Owl of Minerva*. (Regler offers
perhaps the best account extant of events around the 1934 Writers' Congress. His
description of Radek's behavior during it is especially absorbing.) Koltsov's role in
the black propaganda used to justify the murder of Andrés Nin is documented in
Courtois, *The Black Book of Communism*, 337. For Koltsov's complex role in Soviet cultural politics, and Stalin's plans for his liquidation in a final round of purge
trials, see Vaksberg, *Hotel Lux*. Though now forgotten (and almost impossible to
find) see Koltsov's published account of his time in Madrid, *Spanish Diary*.

Chapter 6

1. For my account of Dos Passos's reception in Madrid and his meetings
with Márgara Robles, I have relied on his fictionalized version of these events in
Century's Ebb, buttressed by his nonfiction account of some aspects of his experiences in *Journey Between Wars*. In these passages I have substituted real names
for Dos Passos's fictitious ones, tempering my use of the fictionalized material always in the light of other known facts. Sources on Liston Oak's history and
movement toward his breaking point are multiple. Upon his return from Spain,
Oak wrote a series of articles about Stalinist abuses in that country for *The Socialist Call* and other socialist publications. He became an active journalist in the
years to come—eventually a senior editor at *The New Leader*—though so far as
I know he never wrote in detail about the psychological process through which
he came to make his break with the *apparat*. There is a substantial dossier on
Oak from the FBI, obtained by me through the Freedom of Information Act,

which also includes his testimony to the House Unamerican Activities Committee of the Eightieth Congress, First Session, March 5 and 21, 1947. From it I was able to reconstruct the story of his services to the American party and his time in Moscow, and Louis Fischer's role promoting him both with Borodin and with Alvarez del Vayo. I am also indebted to conversations with Oak's children, Ms. Joan Withingon and Mr. Allan Oak, about their father. It is clear from several sources—notably Herbst—that Dos Passos met with Quintinilla at some point between his arrival in Valencia and learning definitively that Robles was dead. Whether this was early in Valencia or later in Madrid is not so clear. My description of Dos Passos's ride into Madrid and his arrival at the Hotel Florida is composed from both *Journeys Between Wars* and *Century's Ebb*.

2. Bolloten, *The Spanish Civil War*, 139.

Chapter 7

1. I continue to rely on *Century's Ebb* for the account of direct exchange between Hemingway and Dos Passos. I concede the need for some caveat over the use of dialogue. What is "quoted" here, consisting of Dos Passos's (lightly) fictionalized memory of what was said, cannot possibly be accurate word for word, or even exchange by exchange. Nonetheless, I am citing a reconstruction based on the vivid memory of a prime participant; it is surely as close to the nature and tenor of real exchanges as would be a more neutral account. A number of points made in the fictional *Century's Ebb*—such as Martha Gellhorn's overt hostility in Madrid—have since been sustained from primary sources. Accounts of visits to the Valencia-Madrid road and the "Old Homestead" are common to most of the biographies, as are discussions of how Dos and Hem disagreed over the proper direction for *The Spanish Earth,* though it is not always pointed out that their difference was also over a major point of Comintern propaganda policy, being upheld by Ivens. (It is perhaps noteworthy that after seeing a screening, President Franklin Roosevelt suggested more emphasis on social change, a revision in line with the view promoted by Dos Passos.) The Soviet effort to soft-pedal talk of social revolution in Spain is a well-known staple of Comintern propaganda policy, noted in all the histories. In her memoir *The Starched Blue Sky of Spain,* Herbst explicitly notes that Dos Passos had suggested she look up José Robles when she got to Spain. My description of the hostility shown to Dos Passos by American communists in Madrid, while it does not appear in the standard biographies, is based on recollections in *Century's Ebb* of encounters with people well known to Dos Passos and in Madrid at the time. Otto Katz's presence in the Hotel Florida in the second and third weeks of April 1937 is established by his role as the Comintern guide, under the pseudonym André Simone, for the visiting delegation of

British fellow travelers headed by the Duchess of Atholl, a group whose conspicuous presence in the hotel is mentioned in all memoirs, both published and unpublished. Simone's work as their guide is mentioned by members of the delegation and by commentators who worked with them—notably Arturo Barea, who provides a vivid if unsympathetic image of "Simone" the propagandist at work in *The Forging of a Rebel*. That Herbst and Ivens, given their intimate association with Katz, should omit any reference to him, once the time came to write their own memoirs, is of course a conspicuous omission.

2. Liston Oak, *Socialist Review*, September 1937. Cited by Burnett Bolloten, *Spanish Civil War*, 139.

3. Barea, *Forging of a Rebel*, 665.

4. Dos Passos, *The Theme Is Freedom*, 137. In referring to this village, I have retained Dos Passos's spelling of its name, Fuentedueña. Most modern Spanish maps refer to it as Fuentidueña de Tajo. It is located a little less than thirty kilometers east of Madrid, just off highway 88, which runs between Madrid and Valencia. The village Dos Passos visited should not be confused with another town, likewise called Fuentidueña, which is north of Madrid, not far from Valladolid.

5. Herbst's "Spanish Journal" (holograph in the Beinecke Library, Yale) records Hemingway in a confidential conversation with Josie, expanding on Pauline's merits, how "Pauline had good sense. When he got inflated, she took him down." Herbst also notes, uniquely among memoirists of the Florida, that in such conversations Hemingway would come close to being quite critical of Martha Gellhorn, and then back away. (Most writers cast an idyllic glow around the couple, something that passages in Martha's own journal, and Hemingway's quite nasty portrait of her in *The Fifth Column*, tend to belie. Theirs was not an untroubled relationship, even during this first phase.) It should be added that under the best of circumstances, Josephine Herbst had much to be bitter about, and the situation at the Florida did little to soothe her irritability. As a non-celebrity embedded in the Florida's Hirschfeld cartoon, she was particularly annoyed by "this quality prevalent here, catering to somebodies. Complete provincial quality and lack of judgment." In the "Journal," her annoyance crests in an attack on a woman in the Florida whom she calls "M." "M." could easily be Gellhorn, and probably was. In any case, the attack on "M" is rough stuff. "Pushing whore like M. gets pretty much around on what she's got. Don't mean in the head. The pants. Plays all. Takes all. Never speaks of anyone not a name. Glib stupid tongue." It should be added that in the approaching rupture between Hemingway and Pauline, Herbst was among Pauline's confidantes, and that she remained steadfastly attached to Pauline, transferring none of her affection to Martha. She was, unequivocally, a "Pauline person." The two women remained lifelong friends.

6. Herbst, *Starched Blue Sky of Spain*, 150–151.

Chapter 8

1. I rely primarily on Dos Passos's own account of the morning of April 22, 1937, published in *Journeys Between Wars,* along with Herbst, *The Starched Blue Sky of Spain,* and Martha Gellhorn's unpublished Madrid diary, quoted and cited in Moorehead. Gellhorn recorded seeing Dos Passos in a "tartan dressing gown," while Herbst reports seeing him in the suit and tie that he himself reports putting on in his own memoir. I infer a likely sequence of Dos Passos in pajamas and robe, stepping into the hall early in the raid; then going back to his room to try for more sleep; when this proved impossible, getting up to bathe and dress, returning to the atrium in jacket and tie. By far the most detailed account of the morning is in Herbst's "Spanish Journal" in the Beinecke library. It is at variance with the memoir in occasional details, and it does not provide any substantive information about Herbst's conversation with Hemingway apart from noting that it took place. I should mention, however, that Herbst's "Spanish Journal" does say that at some point that morning, Dos Passos told Herbst that *he* thought Robles was dead—a detail she does not mention in the memoir, though it is clear that she wrote the memoir (in 1960) with the "Diary" in front of her. Dos Passos making this statement must have been a matter of suspicion becoming conviction rather than new information. New information, both bogus and reliable, reached him later that day, first through his confrontation with Hemingway at the Fifteenth Brigade Fiesta, and then with the final "official" word from Posada, probably at a party that evening. Dos had already heard the statement conveyed to Coco by Liston Oak that Robles was dead: even though he may have discounted that claim, there was by April 22nd plenty of reason to fear the worst. It is possible that Dos Passos's mounting conviction that Robles was dead induced Josie to choose this moment to play her card, which otherwise was about to lose its value as a means of publicly discrediting Dos Passos.

2. Herbst, *Starched Blue Sky of Spain,* 152. Gellhorn's recollection is reported in Moorehead, *Gellhorn,* 118.

3. Herbst, *Starched Blue Sky of Spain,* 153.

4. Ibid., 154.

5. Ibid., 155.

6. Ibid.

Chapter 9

1. Enrique Lister, cited by Bolloten, *Spanish Civil War,* p. 293.

2. The nominal transfer of the command of the International Brigades to the Spanish Republic during the spring of 1937, using the smoke and mirrors of

the "unified command," was the occasion for the Fiesta of April 22. The event is described by both Herbst in her memoir and Dos Passos in *Journeys Between Wars*, though in a conspicuous omission, Dos Passos does not even mention Hemingway's presence at this event. Josie's description of Duran appears in the "Spanish Diary" entry for April 22. Duran's activity as a covert communist, including and especially his work with Orlov, is explored in Bolloten, *Spanish Civil War*, 547–549, and 601. Duran's later life is of some interest. Always falsely denying his Stalinist affiliations, Duran came to the United States and eventually became the brother-in-law of Michael Straight, who himself had accepted recruitment as an agent of Soviet espionage with the original Cambridge group of spies in Great Britain. Duran wanted a senior position in the United States State Department: when doubts about his loyalty prevented this assignment, he proceeded to the United Nations, where he filled various responsible posts. Another Straight brother-in-law was Louis Dolivet, who was likewise a Soviet agent: Dolivet had been a major lieutenant to Willi Münzenberg; postwar, he worked for the Soviets as a close collaborator in America with none other than Julio Alvarez del Vayo. An interesting, although not entirely forthcoming, discussion of Duran's life in the States can be found in Straight's version of his experience in espionage, *After Long Silence* (New York: W. W. Norton, 1983). In the 1950s Duran became the object of attack by Senator Joseph McCarthy, and he seems to have been one of the crypto-communists McCarthy correctly identified. Even a stopped clock is right twice a day. In her memoir, Herbst does not speak of the "German correspondent" but only of "someone from Valencia who was passing through but whose name he must withhold" (155). That she and Hemingway identified this person to Dos Passos as a "German correspondent" is learned in Langer, *Josephine Herbst* (222), whose information, I gather, comes from an unpublished interview with Herbst. My inference that this "German correspondent" may in turn have been Katz rests on the following facts: (1) Discrediting Dos Passos, exactly as Herbst was now arranging to discredit him, was a Comintern priority. Katz was the senior Comintern agent most responsible for Herbst's presence in Spain and a specialist in cultural politics. (2) Katz was physically on the scene, both in the hotel and, since his British charges were at the Fiesta, presumably at the Fiesta, too. (3) Katz would have been a discreet and reliable collaborator in Josie's exercise in disinformation. The event had been put in motion three weeks earlier by Alvarez del Vayo, who was Katz's closest Comintern collaborator in Spain, a man with whom he was in almost daily contact. Finally, the entire event has about it the earmarks of the sort of black cultural propaganda that was Otto Katz's specialty. No memoir I know speaks of Martha Gellhorn's presence at this event, though it seems very likely that she did attend. She would not, however, have ridden to the fiesta in the same car with Hemingway, and she even would have avoided being too conspicuously at his side as it proceeded. She was very friendly with Virginia Cowles, who was certainly among the guests. My account of Josie and Dos's walk to the Plaza Mayor relies upon her memoir. The account of the evening party where Posada broke the "definitive" news to Dos Passos is from *Century's Ebb.*

3. Herbst, *Starched Blue Sky of Spain,* 155.

4. Dos Passos, *Journeys Between Wars,* 376.

Chapter 10

1. The remarks of both Hemingway and Gellhorn are quoted and cited in Schoots, *Living Dangerously,* 136.

2. Martha Gellhorn to Ernest Hemingway, June 1937. Hemingway Archives, Firestone Library, Princeton University.

3. Joris Ivens, letter to Ernest Hemingway, April 26, 1937. Quoted and cited in Schoots, *Living Dangerously,* 126–127. Ivens's later remarks about Robles and Dos Passos, made in letters to Hemingway, are quoted and cited on the same pages. The letters to Hemingway about Dos's "disloyalty over Nin" were written January 27 and 28, 1938. See Schoots, 386.

4. Baker, *Ernest Hemingway,* 158.

5. Shipman made this claim to Matthew Josephson, among many others, who repeated it in his memoir, *Infidel in the Temple.* The entire incident is reported and cited in Carr, *John Dos Passos,* 370.

6. See Constancia de la Mora, *In a Place of Splendor: The Autobiography of a Spanish Woman* (New York: Harcourt Brace, 1939). Josephson retells the Shipman anecdote without any challenge to its credibility.

7. Hemingway's attack on Dos appears in A. E. Hotchner's *Papa Hemingway* (New York: Random House, 1966), and is quoted and cited in Ludington, *John Dos Passos,* 369.

8. There is some possibility that Ivens was with Dos Passos in Fuentedueña, or joined him there, despite what by April 23 would have been tensions between them. In any case, Ivens, who really was on his way out of Spain that day, seems to have made a last stop in Fuentedueña before proceeding to Valencia. Still, the tensions would have been real. We know that Hemingway was fully apprised of Dos Passos's movements through Ivens's letter to Hemingway of April 26, 1937, expressing outrage that Dos Passos was in Valencia, and still making trouble over Robles. Despite their identical itineraries, neither man speaks of being with the other in Fuentedueña on April 23rd. Meanwhile, Ivens really was on his way out of Spain, while Dos Passos still had much in his Spanish agenda ahead of him. See Schoots, 126–127.

9. Curiously, in *Century's Ebb,* Dos Passos portrays the Alvarez del Vayo character, Hernández, producing an obviously phony death certificate asserting that Robles had died "by misadventure." This is fiction. In real life, no certificate was ever produced. Dos Passos continued to seek such a certificate for years, all the while assisting Márgara in the legal complications caused by the Spanish government's failure to provide it. It was not until the 1940s that a court in Maryland, not Spain, at last declared José Robles legally dead. Dos Passos assisted the family in the suit seeking this decision.

10. Sam Baron, Testimony before the House Committee on Unamerican Activities, November 22, 1938, as cited in a Memorandum of the Federal Bureau of Investigation, December 6, 1948. From a dossier released by the FBI in accordance with the author's request under the Freedom of Information Act.

Chapter 11

1. The meeting of Dos Passos and Orwell appears briefly in all relevant biographies and is discussed by Dos Passos in *The Theme Is Freedom* and *Century's Ebb.* The change Orwell went through in Spain is discussed most persuasively in Peter Stansky and William Abrahams, *Orwell: The Transformation* (New York: Alfred A. Knopf, 1980). The changes happening in Barcelona as May approached are discussed in Orwell, *Homage to Catalonia* (San Diego, New York, London: Harvest/HBJ Books, [1938], 1952, 1980). Liston Oak describes his first meetings with Andrés Nin in "A Spanish Incident," *The Socialist Call,* September 11, 1937. To this report, I have added other bits of information from his FOIA dossier. Oak described his growing disaffection in numerous places, including his articles for the *Socialist Call* in 1937. His early relations with Leon Josephson and George Mink are described in his testimony before the hearing before the Committee on Un-American Activities, The House of Representatives, Eightieth Congress, First Session, March 5 and 21, 1947. The best source for George Mink's career as a Soviet agent can be found in a highly reliable account of the working of the Soviet underground apparatus, Jan Valtin [pseudonym for Richard A. Krebs], *Out of the Night* (New York: Allied Book Corporation, 1940). Dos Passos's description of his interview with Nin appears in *Journeys Between Wars.* Oak's description of warning Nin and the threat then delivered to him by Albert Edwards appears in his testimony before HUAC, which, it is perhaps worth noting, was made unwillingly, and under subpoena.

2. Dos Passos, *The Theme Is Freedom,* 146.

3. The relevant passages appear in ibid., 145–146, and *Century's Ebb,* 94–96.

4. Pritchett is quoted in Stansky and Abrahams, *The Transformation,* 284.

5. It is an irony here that in histories of the Spanish War, there is almost always an inventory of notable victims of the NKVD. In these lists, the name of José Robles invariably appears alongside that of Bob Smillie, the son of a noted Scottish Labour MP and a volunteer in the POUM militia, a pal of Orwell's on the Huesca front. As a POUM volunteer who was also the son of a well-known anti-Stalinist leftist, young Smillie was later murdered in Valencia, like Robles under conditions of great secrecy. Such an inventory is found in Payne, *The Spanish Civil War*, 229.

6. Dos Passos, *The Theme Is Freedom*, 241.

7. Orwell, *Homage to Catalonia*, 109–110.

8. Dos Passos, *Century's Ebb*, 94–96.

9. Dos Passos, *Journeys Between Wars*, 393.

10. Oak provided two accounts of his conversation with Mink. The first was in *The Socialist Call* ("I Am Exposed as a Spy," September 17, 1937); the second was his testimony (as an unfriendly witness, under subpoena) before the House Unamerican Activities Committee, Proceedings of the Eightieth Congress, First Session, March 5 and 21, 1947.

11. Liston Oak, "A Spanish Incident."

Chapter 12

1. Dos Passos's most significant prior relation with Liston Oak took place during his "fact-finding tour," made with Theodore Dreiser, of the Harlan County Coal Strike in Kentucky. The party's man on the scene during this propaganda tour was Oak. All the Dos Passos biographies discuss Dos Passos's visit to Harlan County. An interesting addition to these accounts is Edmund Wilson's discussion of his own visit to Harlan County in his *The Thirties: From Notebooks and Diaries of the Period* (New York: Farrar, Straus, and Giroux, 1980). Wilson speaks of Oak's role in some detail, and the *Notebooks* include a photograph of Oak with Wilson's group. Oak appears as a fictional character in *Century's Ebb*, given the name "Don Carp." The novel's account does not stick very close to the truth. It depicts "Don Carp" as present at a meeting with Dos Passos and Hemingway in New York Communist Party headquarters prior to their departure in February 1937, where "Carp" is introduced to "the celebrities" as just back from recruiting new members for the International Brigades in the Middle West. He is also described as on his way to Spain to volunteer for the Brigades himself (p. 39). All this is fiction. By February 1937, Oak was already in Spain, working as a propagandist for Alvarez del Vayo. He met Hemingway for the first time in Spain. He did not come to Valencia from New York, but from Moscow, via

Paris. Oak was never a member of the International Brigades, nor have I seen any evidence that he ever recruited anyone into their ranks. In *Century's Ebb,* "Don Carp" is presented as coming to the Hotel Continental with a fellow defector from the Brigades. This too is fiction. All biographers agree with the passage in *The Theme Is Freedom*, which is nonfiction and which depicts Oak approaching Dos Passos alone. The three occasions on which Dos Passos wrote about Oak are (1) reference in *The Theme Is Freedom*, 146; (2) Dos Passos's letter to the *New Republic* of July 1939; and (3) the relevant passages in *Century's Ebb*. The small variants in these three accounts are too numerous to analyze here. It is in the brief passage in *The Theme Is Freedom* that Dos Passos speaks of having "seen him [Oak] in some office or other in Valencia." Without naming Oak, Dos Passos calls him an "American socialist" and seeks to explain away Oak's service at a desk rather than at the front. But there was never any question of Oak being in Spain to fight. He came to Valencia as a professional propaganda operative, put in position by Fischer's recommendation to Alvarez del Vayo. It is possible that the peculiarities of the 1956 passage can be attributed to an effort to blur Oak's actual role in the Soviet apparatus, which even at this late date, Oak himself was still at pains to conceal. I base my supposition that Dos Passos did not know that Liston was Coco's source on the death of his father on my assumption that Dos Passos would have focused on Liston's whereabouts and actively sought him out before leaving for Madrid on April 11 had he known, or even suspected, that Liston knew the truth about the killing. But Dos Passos did not seek him out. Meanwhile, Liston was very much on the scene with the Hotel Floridians prior to Dos Passos's arrival there on April 11. (I am grateful to Oak's daughter, Mrs. Joan Withington, for supplying me with a photograph of her father in Madrid in April 1937, escorting Hemingway and Virginia Cowles through a bombed-out urban site.) That Dos Passos mentions seeing Oak in Valencia and not Madrid suggests that by April 11, del Vayo had already sent Liston on from Valencia and Madrid to his new job in Barcelona. This would be consistent with the time frame suggested by Oak's own various accounts. Certainly, Liston was in Barcelona by at least April 15, by which time he had made his feeler to Nin. Most likely he was in Barcelona even a little earlier. This would have been well before Dos Passos's arrival in Barcelona on April 27 or (just possibly) a day later.

Chapter 13

1. The durability of Martha Gellhorn's loyalty to the Popular Front line on the Spanish Civil War is illustrated by her review of Ken Loach's film, *Land*

and Freedom, which appeared in the London *Evening Standard*, October 5, 1995, three years before her death. It is a stinging attack, dismissing the POUM as a "cult, irrelevant to the great drama of the war." Gellhorn likewise dismisses as "outrageous rubbish" claims that were even then increasingly well documented, that the Republican Army, the International Brigades, and the government of Negrin were under Soviet control. Gellhorn wrote this review as if Orwell had never written. In fact, Gellhorn dismissed Orwell and his arguments all her life. Needless to add, her review entirely ignored research that not only confirmed Orwell's observations about Soviet influence but revealed that influence to have been far more profound than even Orwell suspected. I rely on Arkadi Vaksberg's *Hotel Lux* for my account of Koltsov's recall to the USSR in the late spring of 1937. Koltsov confided the details of his interview with Stalin to his brother, immediately after the event took place. *Hotel Lux* is essential for an understanding of the purge trials of "antifascists" Stalin planned to stage once his alliance with Hitler was joined. That Koltsov was to join Litvinov as a prime defendant to be "liquidated" indicates not only the key role Koltsov had played in Popular Front propaganda in Europe but also the importance Stalin attributed to that propaganda. The absorbing and complex tale of Koltsov's relation to the regime is discussed at length in Vaksberg, Chapter 5. There are several sources for my account of Hemingway's confrontation with Dos Passos at the boat train on May 11, 1937. Both Ludington and Spencer Carr describe it, Spencer Carr relying on Dos Passos's account in *Century's Ebb* and Dos Passos's notes for the novel, while Ludington adds an interview with William L. White, who was, I gather, a friend of Dos Passos's to whom he'd told the story.

2. Orwell, *Homage to Catalonia*, 131. Orwell's famous description of the "Days of May" appears in Chapters X and XI.

3. Ibid., 130–131.

4. Moorehead, *Gellhorn*, 125–127.

5. Vaksberg, *Hotel Lux*, 153–154.

6. Ibid. The bizarre story of Koltsov and his relation to the regime is told in Chapter 5.

7. In *Century's Ebb*, Dos Passos says that he and Katy spent early May with the Murphys at their "Villa America" in Antibes. This is doubtful: the couple's biography indicates that the Murphys were in New York in May 1937. Their famous house was probably closed. See Vaill, *Everybody Was So Young*, Chapter 21.

8. See Ludington, *John Dos Passos*, 374; Carr, *John Dos Passos*, 372; and *Century's Ebb*, 99. Ludington and Carr rely partly on Dos Passos's unpublished notes for *Century's Ebb*.

9. Payne, *The Spanish Civil War, The Soviet Union, and Communism,* Chapter 10, 221.

10. The best account of the machinations leading to Negrin's government, and his policies immediately upon taking office, can be found in ibid., Chapters 9 and 10.

Chapter 14

1. Pauline's state of mind at this juncture, along with her improvements to the Key West property, are sketched in every biography in varying degrees of detail, though most fully and with the benefit of Patrick's reflections in Kert, *The Hemingway Women.* Passages from Pauline's letters to Hemingway are cited in Baker and elsewhere, and many originals can be found in both the Princeton and Kennedy Library archives. Beyond the standard biographies, the best published account of Ivens's role at the Carnegie Hall Congress is found in Schoots, who naturally follows Ivens's account in *The Camera and I* (New York: International Publishers, 1976) and elsewhere. It is Schoots's research that shows that Ivens went to Bimini while Hemingway was writing the speech and accompanied him to New York to deliver it. An excellent scholarly study of the League of American Writers, incidentally, can be found in the Yale University Library: it is the doctoral dissertation of none other than the novelist and writer Tom Wolfe! Hemingway's anxiety and reluctance over making his speech are sketched in Baker and other biographies, including the biography of Archibald MacLeish. My discussion of his performance on stage is a composite of the recollections of several witnesses. The details of the NKVD murder of Andrés Nin are taken mainly from the account found in John Costello and Oleg Tsarev, *Deadly Illusions: The KGB Orlov Dossier Reveals Stalin's Master Spy* (New York: Crown, 1993) with crucial further details summarized by Stanley Payne in his notes on the murder in *The Spanish Civil War, The Soviet Union, and Communism,* 362–363. The passage showing Hemingway's acceptance of the Stalinist version of Nin's disappearance appears in Chapter 18 of *For Whom the Bell Tolls,* with Robert Jordan in conversation with Karkov, the character modeled on Koltsov. Constancia de la Mora's once influential memoir was translated in English as *In a Place of Splendor.* The derogatory description of the White House dinner for the screening of *The Spanish Earth,* which appears in most Hemingway biographies, is based on Hemingway's letter to Mrs. Paul Pfeiffer, August 2, 1937 (*Letters,* 459). Less often cited is Ivens's more polite and more politically sophisticated account in *The Camera and I,* on which I rely here. Otto Katz's role arranging the West Coast screenings of *The Spanish Earth* is

established in his FOIA FBI dossier, 65-9266, Section 2, letter of Fritz Lang to Otto and Ilsa Katz, July 2[?], 1937. The story of Hemingway's relation to *Ken* is told in Baker, with occasional refinements in later biographies. Back files of this publication are now almost unfindable. Both his biographers and many critics have explored Dos Passos's modernism and its various influences, including that of the Soviet avant-garde. An especially interesting insight into how Dos Passos learned from his friendship with Léger can be found in *The Best Times*.

2. Patrick's speculations are found in Kert, *The Hemingway Women*, 302. Schoots's excellent account of the Hollywood screenings cites at length the fine speech Ivens gave at the Fredric March screening.

3. The "fingerwoman" remark is in an undated July letter to EH. "I hate like hell," letter from MG to EH, July 24, 1937.

4. Martha Gellhorn, undated letter to EH from the summer of 1937, Firestone Library Special Collections.

5. Letter from Dawn Powell to Dos Passos, undated (University of Virginia Dos Passos Archive), cited in Ludington, *John Dos Passos,* 376–377.

6. Hemingway, *Letters,* 460.

7. John Dos Passos, introduction to *Panama, or the Adventures of My Seven Uncles,* poems by Blaise Cendrars, translated by John Dos Passos (New York and London: Harper and Brothers, 1931), cited in John Dos Passos, *The Fourteenth Chronicle: Letters and Diaries of John Dos Passos,* edited by Townsend Ludington (Boston: Gambit, 1973), 378.

Chapter 15

1. I base my account of the totalitarian drift of the Spanish Republic at this time on Burnett Bolloten, *The Spanish Civil War,* especially chapter 54, and Payne, *The Spanish Civil War,* especially chapters 10 and 11. The general tenor of Hemingway's second sojourn in Madrid is described in most biographies, including Kert, although some of the emerging troubles between Hemingway and Martha Gellhorn, including their quarrel over her lecture tour, have become known or clear only with Caroline Moorehead's biography. Moorehead is my source for quotations from Martha's "Spanish Diary," and the letter of April 7, 1950, to Dr. David Gurewitsch, in which she speaks of her sexual difficulties with Hemingway. Interested readers will find reasonably reliable, if romanticized, portraits of Hemingway in the memoirs of both Herbert Matthews and Sefton Delmer. (Note that both memoirists, acting out of discretion, neglect to mention Martha Gellhorn's presence at many of the events they describe.) The man who brought Hemingway the news of Pauline's inten-

tion to join him in Madrid was the journalist Jay Allen, who with his wife was a confidant to both the Hemingways as a couple and whose interview with Carlos Baker about this period is an important source for most biographers, including Kert, 312. Preparations for the Aragón assault and the Republic's preemptive offensive at Teruel are well-known events in the history of the war. Hemingway's account of his own experiences in Teruel appears in his dispatch to NANA of December 23, 1937, "The Fall of Teruel," in *By-Line: Ernest Hemingway: Selected Articles and Dispatches of Four Decades,* edited by William White (New York: Simon and Schuster, Touchstone Books, 1998.) Information on the execution of Vladimir Gorev comes from many sources. I rely here on Bolloten, *Spanish Civil War,* 311, who cites Alexander Orlov's *Secret History of Stalin's Crimes* (New York: Random House, 1953). It was Orlov who pointed out that the general was arrested only two days after being decorated in the Kremlin by Soviet President Kalinin for "his outstanding services in the Spanish Civil War." A discussion of Gorev's "fate" can be found in the memoirs of Ilya Ehrenburg, *Eve of War* (London: MacGibbon and Kee, 1963). A very revealing account of Gorev's return can be found in Godfrey Blunden's little-known but thoroughly remarkable novel, *A Room on the Route* (New York: Lippincott, 1946), 66.

2. Hemingway rarely named his later heroes very felicitously: there's something a little stilted and fake in names like "Philip Rawlings" and "Robert Jordan." Yet his choice of such names was rarely arbitrary. To make a wild guess about the resonance of the name "Rawlings," Hemingway was at this time having a correspondence with Marjorie Kinnan Rawlings, author of *The Yearling* and a fellow Max Perkins writer. Mrs. Rawlings was hardly the first to notice the disparity between Hemingway the great artist and Hemingway the brawling bully. Like many, she had no trouble spotting the bookish, hypersensitive man behind the posturing he-man. Yet she was one of the few with whatever tact it took to broach the issue with him directly and get a polite, coherent response. Mrs. Rawlings had dared point out to Hemingway that he saw and felt too much, and was too gifted, to run his life in the raucous way he did. His ethos of bravery, she pointed out, edged too easily into bravado, and this very falseness posed a grave risk to his gift. Hemingway's reply was a defense of his behavior, but it shows that, at least in his better moments, Hemingway could listen to well-intended criticism. Yet his decision to name the hero of *The Fifth Column* Rawlings might also be read as a very angry reply to it. It is hard to think of any Hemingway hero more fatally invested with the ugly, sadistic, bullying side of Hemingway's personality than Philip Rawlings. Mrs. Rawlings may have had to swallow hard when she saw her own name appropriated in his.

3. The moral history of the phrase "the necessary murder" grew harsh when George Orwell seized upon it and used it to attack Auden in *Inside the Whale* (Harmondsworth, England: Penguin, 1969). An impressive, and notably scrupulous, discussion of this entire controversy, along with the larger nexus of issues raised for Auden's art by his experiences in the Spanish War, can be found in *Early Auden,* by Edward Mendelson (New York: Viking, 1981), chapters IX ("The Great Divide") and XIV ("History to the Defeated").

4. Hemingway, "The Fall of Teruel," *By-Line: Ernest Hemingway,* 277.

Chapter 16

1. The story of the Hemingways' rocky time in Paris is based on an interview given by the editor of William Bird to Carlos Baker, and it is used in most biographies. Gregory Hemingway's remark about his Aunt Jinny's loathing for his father appears in his memoir *Papa: A Personal Memoir* (Boston: Houghton Mifflin, 1976). Virginia Pfeiffer's counsel to Pauline is described best in Kert. Some of Hemingway's pieces for *Ken* are collected in *By-Line: Ernest Hemingway.* Others, mercifully forgotten, are difficult to track down even in major research libraries. Ivens's letter to Hemingway of January 28, 1938, is on deposit in the Hemingway Collection of the John F. Kennedy Library, Boston, and is cited at length in Schoots. I am reasonably, though not absolutely, certain that the Murphys' party (which took place in their penthouse at the New Weston apartment building on East 50th Street in New York) was given on or about March 18, 1938. MacLeish's dating of the event, in a letter to Carlos Baker, is offhand, done from memory, and obviously wrong. (His memory of the general tenor of the evening's events seems better.) So far as I can determine, there were only two occasions in 1938 when Dos Passos, Hemingway, and the Murphys were all in New York at the same time. The March 18 date seems most probable for the party, especially in view of Hemingway's behavior immediately afterward on the *Île de France* and the date of the relevant article in *Redbook.* My account of the party itself combines the memoirs of MacLeish and Gerald Murphy. Dos Passos's piece "The Fiesta at the Fifteenth Brigade" appeared simultaneously in *Redbook* and *Journeys Between Wars,* and can now be read in *John Dos Passos: Travel Books and Other Writings.* In his letter, Hemingway says that he has "just" seen the piece in *Redbook,* which suggests that he had not yet bought or read the book. Since Dos Passos's view that Nin was dead was published elsewhere, and is not mentioned in the *Redbook* piece, it is possible that Hemingway learned about it during their exchange on the Murphys' terrace. For Stalin's policy on using foreign-born officers in Spain, see Radosh, *Spain Betrayed.* For Hitler's exploitation of Franco's delay in taking Barcelona and for Stalin's parallel but far from identical reasons for prolonging the war, see Bol-

loten, *Spanish Civil War,* chapter 54. My account of Hemingway's response to the scenes in the Ebro Valley relies on Baker's sensitive reading of Hemingway's letters during this period. I am indebted to Mr. Jesse Rossa, assistant librarian in the special Collection of the University of Delaware Library, in Newark, Delaware, for supplying me with a copy of the extremely rare clipping of "Treachery in Aragon" in the University's Hemingway Collection. It should perhaps be mentioned that neither Hemingway nor his estate ever reprinted this piece in any forum. I am not aware of any historical basis for Hemingway's claim that the Aragon offensive was the work of traitors in the Republican government collaborating with the Gestapo. Nonetheless, there was much speculation of this sort at the time. Bolloten, for example, examines without endorsing claims that Communists close to Negrin were prepared to see Teruel retaken as a means of discrediting their last important adversary in the government, the defense minister, Indalecio Prieto. In any case, there is no decisive evidence supporting any of these claims. The account of Hemingway's violent behavior on the *Anita* and on the night of Pauline's 1938 masquerade party is taken from McClendon, *Papa,* 185–187.

2. Moorehead, *Gellhorn,* 141.

3. Baker, *Ernest Hemingway,* 324.

4. Hemingway, *Letters,* 462–463.

5. Joris Ivens, letter to Ernest Hemingway, January 28, 1938. Ernest Hemingway Collection, John F. Kennedy Library, Boston. Cited in Schoots, *Living Dangerously,* 136, 137, 139.

6. Hemingway, *Letters,* 463.

7. Radosh, *Spain Betrayed,* 104.

8. Herbert Matthews, *Education of a Correspondent* (New York: Harcourt Brace, 1946), 131–132.

9. Bolloten, *Spanish Civil War,* 571.

10. Hemingway, *Complete Short Stories,* 58.

Chapter 17

1. For the change in Nazi and Soviet policy in 1938, I rely on many historians, but particularly Robert Tucker, *Stalin in Power: The Revolution from Above, 1928–1941* (New York: W. W. Norton, 1990, [1992]), especially Chapter 18. Edmund Wilson's remark about Stalin's change of attitude appears in his letter to Malcolm Cowley, October 20, 1938. Wilson, *Letters on Literature and Politics,* 309–310. Hemingway's reiteration of the phrase, "the only thing to do with a war is to win it" appears in many of his letters, dispatches, and pieces for *Ken* at this time. Dos Passos noted the date and hour of completing *Adventures of a Young Man* on the manuscript of the final draft, now in his archives. I rely on

Baker, Herbert Matthews's memoirs, Moorehead, and other Hemingway biographies for my account of Hemingway and Martha during the battle of the
Ebro, though I renew my caveat that both Matthews and Baker felt obliged to
obscure the fact that Martha was present with him throughout, in deference to
her objections. The story of Pauline's surge of hope in the fall of 1938 is in all the
biographies, and in Kert. It is not clear exactly what Hemingway meant when he
spoke of two chapters of a novel in his letters to Gingrich of October 22, 1938,
and Perkins, October 28, 1938, both in Baker, *Letters*. They may have been
sketches for *For Whom the Bell Tolls*, though Hemingway later insisted he began
the novel later, in March 1939. In any case, the manuscripts appear to be lost. My
account of the writing of "Under the Ridge," and its role in Hemingway's re-
covery of confidence at this time, relies on Baker, who is especially insightful on
this matter. Cowley's review of *The Adventures of a Young Man* appeared in
The New Republic, June 14, 1939, and Dos Passos's letter to the editors appeared
in July, during which Dos Passos also had his correspondence with Dwight Macdonald. Edmund Wilson's attack on Cowley appeared in his letter to Cowley, October 20, 1939 (Wilson, *Letters on Literature and Politics*). I am grateful to Mr.
Robert Hoskins, of Laramie, Wyoming, for information about the "bottomless
lake" near the Nordquist Ranch in Wyoming, which Hemingway uses as the
place where Robert Jordan sinks the revolver his father used in his suicide. It
should be mentioned that while the account of the father's suicide is one of the
most unabashedly autobiographical passages in *For Whom the Bell Tolls*, I do
not know that Hemingway in fact disposed of the real revolver the way Jordan
does in the book. For a trenchant critical contemporary view of *For Whom the
Bell Tolls*, with special attention to how Hemingway misread certain Spanish
mores, see Arturo Barea's "Not Spain but Hemingway," reprinted in *The Literary Reputation of Ernest Hemingway in Europe*, edited by Roger Asselineau,
with an introduction by Heinrich Straumann (New York: New York University
Press, 1965.) Pauline's final visit to the Nordquist Ranch is described in most biographies, and in Kert. Patrick Hemingway's phrase for their exchange at that
time—the "knockout punch"—is taken from his interview with Kert.

2. Baker, *Ernest Hemingway*, 335.

3. Letter to Arnold Gingrich, Paris, October 22, 1938, Hemingway, *Letters*,
472.

4. Though I have not found this anecdote confirmed in Barea's wonderful
autobiography, *The Forging of a Rebel*, he does speak there of his warm admiration of Dos Passos and all that he did in Spain. Barea was, however, confronted
by the NKVD as the war ended, and after being condemned as politically unre-
liable, obliged to leave Spain in grave danger of his life.